New Public Management in Europe

New Public Management in Europe

Adaptation and Alternatives

Edited by

Christopher Pollitt,

Sandra van Thiel

and

Vincent Homburg

First published in 2007 by
PALGRAVE MACMILLAN
Houndmills, Basingstoke, Hampshire RG21 6XS and
175 Fifth Avenue, New York, N.Y. 10010
Companies and representatives throughout the world.

PALGRAVE MACMILLAN is the global academic imprint of the Palgrave Macmillan division of St. Martin's Press, LLC and of Palgrave Macmillan Ltd. Macmillan® is a registered trademark in the United States, United Kingdom and other countries. Palgrave is a registered trademark in the European Union and other countries.

ISBN-13: 978–0–230–00693–5 hardback
ISBN-10: 0–230–00693–0 hardback

This book is printed on paper suitable for recycling and made from fully managed and sustained forest sources. Logging, pulping and manufacturing processes are expected to conform to the environmental regulations of the country of origin.

A catalogue record for this book is available from the British Library.

Library of Congress Cataloging-in-Publication Data

New public management in Europe : adaptation and alternatives / edited by Christopher Pollitt, Sandra van Thiel, and Vincent Homburg.
    p. cm.
    Includes bibliographical references and index.
    ISBN-13: 978–0–230–00693–5 (cloth)
    ISBN-10: 0–230–00693–0 (cloth)
    1. Public administration – Europe. I. Pollitt, Christopher. II. Thiel, Sandra van. III. Homburg, Vincent.

JN32.N475 2007
351.4—dc22   2006050327

10 9 8 7 6 5 4 3 2 1
16 15 14 13 12 11 10 09 08 07

Printed and bound in Great Britain by
CPI Antony Rowe, Chippenham and Eastbourne

Contents

List of Figures and Boxes

Figures

Boxes

List of Tables

Acknowledgements

This book is a joint effort by the members of the Centre for Public Management at the Department of Public Administration, Erasmus University Rotterdam. Even those researchers who did not author a chapter have participated in our discussions about the book and hence contributed to its genesis.

We would like to thank the management of CPM and the Department of Public Administration for their support, financial and otherwise, without which most of the research reported in this book and, indeed, the book itself, would not have come about.

Finally, we owe a great debt of gratitude to Vicky Balsem and Rosemarijn Smeets who took on the hard job of reading, editing and improving our texts. All remaining errors are of course ours, and only ours.

Christopher Pollitt
Sandra van Thiel
Vincent Homburg

Notes on the Contributors

Drs **Marine Allix** was a PhD student at the Department of Public Administration at Erasmus University Rotterdam between 2002 and 2005. Her research focused on the relationship between quasi-autonomous organizations and their parent departments in France and Italy. Publications on this topic have appeared in the *International Journal of Public Management*. Marine Allix lives in France and works for the municipality of Grenoble.

Drs **Arwin van Buuren** is a PhD candidate at Erasmus University Rotterdam. His thesis is about managing knowledge and expertise in controversial policy processes in the field of water management (to appear in 2006). With others he has published in several Dutch and international scientific journals such as *Evaluation Review, Science and Public Policy, International Review of Administrative Sciences* and *Emergence*.

Dr **Jurian Edelenbos** is assistant professor in Public Administration at Erasmus University Rotterdam. His main research interests concern interactive policy-making, public–private partnership, process and programme management, trust, democratic anchorage, and co-evolution. He published on these themes in journals such as *Governance, Public Administration, Public Management Review, Evaluation, Evaluation Review* and *Emergence*.

Dr **Jan Hakvoort** is associate professor in Social Science Research Methods and Techniques in Public Administration at Erasmus University Rotterdam. In 1980 he received his PhD with a dissertation entitled 'Territorial Decentralisation'. Other topics of research in recent years are: organizational culture and cultural change, New Public Management, and the use of management techniques in non-profit organizations.

Dr **Vincent Homburg** is assistant professor in Public Administration at Erasmus University Rotterdam. He received his PhD in 1999 on a dissertation entitled 'The Political Economy of Information Management'. His research interests concern e-government and the uses and effects of ICTs on public sector organizations. In 2005, he edited *The Information Ecology of E-Government* (together with Victor Bekkers). Other publications have appeared in *Knowledge, Technology and Policy, Artificial Intelligence* and *Law and Information Polity*.

Dr **Michael Hughes** is associate professor at the School of Public Policy at the University of Birmingham. He is Director of the Institute of Local Government Studies and general editor of *Knights Guide to Best Value and Public Procurement*. His research and teaching interests focus on public service performance and the role of markets and contracts in public management. He is currently lead researcher on a four-year project to evaluate local government procurement in England.

Prof. Dr **Walter Kickert** is professor of Public Management at the Department of Public Administration at Erasmus University Rotterdam. He is deputy-editor of the *European Forum* of the international journal *Public Administration*. His research interests are in international comparative public management and administrative reform. He is the successor of Christopher Pollitt as scientific director of the Dutch national research school in political and administrative sciences (Netherlands Institute of Government, NIG).

Dr **Henk Klaassen** is associate professor in Economics at the Department of Public Administration at Erasmus University Rotterdam. In 1995 he received his PhD on a dissertation entitled 'Decision Making in Mutual Dependency: the Role of a Process Architect in Public Projects'. His research focuses on policy analysis, New Public Management, output steering, and accountability in local governments.

Dr **Erik-Hans Klijn** is associate professor in Public Administration at Erasmus University Rotterdam and visiting professor at the School of Public Policy at the University of Birmingham (UK). His research and teaching activities focus on complex decision-making and management in networks, institutional design and Public–Private Partnerships. He has published widely in international journals like *JPART*, *Administration and Society*, *Public Administration*, *PAR* and *PMR*. Recently he published *Managing Uncertainties in Networks* (together with Joop Koppenjan, 2004, Routledge).

Dr **Frans-Bauke van der Meer** is associate professor of Public Administration at Erasmus University Rotterdam. His main research interests are the dynamics of administrative and organizational arrangements, and the organization, dynamics and impact of policy evaluation in multi-actor domains. He is also director of the post-experience masters programme in Public Administration at Erasmus University.

Prof. Dr **Christopher Pollitt** is professor of Public Management at Erasmus University Rotterdam. His main research interests lie in comparative public management reform, public service quality improvement and programme evaluation. Author of many texts (including *The Essential Public Manager* and *Public Management Reform: a Comparative Analysis*), he has also undertaken consultancy for many international governmental organizations and national governments. He edits the *International Review of Administrative Sciences* and is past President of the European Evaluation Society.

Prof. **Ignace Snellen** is a professor (em.) of Public Administration at Erasmus University Rotterdam. His dissertation on *Approaches to Strategy Formulation* (1975) was based on studies and experiences in the world of multinational enterprises. Over the past twenty years he has worked at different universities (Nijmagen, Tilburg, Rotterdam and Leiden) where he specialized in the foundations of public administration as a discipline, and informatization. He has authored more than 250 publications, including *Public Administration in an Information Age: a Handbook* (edited with W. van de Donk, 1998) and *Conciliation of Rationalities: the Essence of Public Administration* (2000, Administrative Theory & Praxis).

Prof. Dr **Bram Steijn** is professor of HRM in the Public Sector at the Department of Public Administration at Erasmus University Rotterdam. His main research interests concern HRM-related issues like job satisfaction, leadership, and public sector motivation. He has also published on the relationship between ICT, organization and labour. In recent years he has published in *Work, Employment and Society, New Technology, Work and Employment, Review of Public Personnel Administration* and the *International Review of Administrative Sciences*.

Prof. Dr Ing **Geert Teisman** is professor in Public Administration at Erasmus University Rotterdam. He achieved degrees in transport and sociology. His PhD thesis about complex decision-making was first published in 1992 and followed by a second and third edition in 1995 and 1998. He is specialized in management of complex decision-making processes. On a regular basis he gives advice to governments and private organizations on complex decision-making, strategic planning, public–private partnerships, process management, intergovernmental co-operation in metropolitan areas and policy evaluation. His publications have appeared in *Public Administration, Public Administration Review* and *Public Policy and Money*.

Dr **Sandra van Thiel** is associate professor in Public Administration at Erasmus University Rotterdam. Her main research interests concern quasiautonomous organizations, at different levels of government and in different countries. She published *Quangos: Trends, Causes and Consequences* (2001, Ashgate). Other publications have appeared in journals such as *Governance, International Journal of Public Management,* and *Journal of Public Policy*. Sandra van Thiel is executive director of the Netherlands Institute of Government (NIG).

1

Introduction

Vincent Homburg, Christopher Pollitt and Sandra van Thiel

The emergence of public management reforms

For more than a century, Western public bureaucracies have been inspired and constructed according to what is usually known as the 'classic public administration paradigm'. In Europe, this paradigm was heavily influenced by Weberian ideas of bureaucracy and, in the United States, by Woodrow Wilson's battle with late nineteenth-century American political patronage: '... poisonous atmosphere of [city] government, the crooked secrets of state administration, the confusion, sinecurism and corruption ever again discovered in the bureaux at Washington' (Wilson, 1887: 206). Classic public administration models developed over more than two centuries. Especially the German and French models are often mentioned as examples of administrations that have persisted throughout times of instability and turbulence (König and Beck, 1997; Kickert, 1997).

The 'classic' public administration paradigm remained relatively undisturbed until the late 1970s (Behn, 1998; Gruening, 2001; Pollitt and Bouckaert, 2004). Subsequently, as a reaction to financial crises, turmoil over inflexible procedures and waning public acceptance of old style public administration, an 'unending wave of reforms' (Pollitt, 2002) has emerged. These changes occurred in rhetoric and the actual practice of public administration.

Rhetorical changes emerged from a rise in popularity of so called 'managerialism' in the public sector (Pollitt, 1990). This made a number of management gurus (like Osborne and Gaebler, 1992) rather influential, setting the agenda for administrative reforms throughout the world. With managerialism, concepts like *efficiency, results orientation, customer orientation and value for money* were placed on the agenda of administrative reform (cf. Hood, 1994).

This has not been mere talk and rhetoric. Managerial reforms have actually taken place in the practice of public administration throughout the world, and notably in the United States, the Anglo-Saxon countries and continental Europe (see *inter alia* Kickert, 1997; Feigenbaum, Henig and Hamnett, 1999; OECD, 2002b; Christensen and Laegreid, 2003; Pollitt and Bouckaert, 2004).

For example, in the United Kingdom, the Next Steps programme has had an enormous impact on the structure and functioning of public administration (Pollitt and Talbot, 2004; Pollitt, Talbot, Caulfield and Smullen, 2004). In the Netherlands, as well as in many Western states, the preference for policy implementation by monolithic bureaucracies has changed in favour of alternative arrangements such as privatization, or the creation of quasi-autonomous organizations or public–private partnerships (van Thiel, 2001; Rosenau, 2000). Throughout the world, governments have begun to experiment with and actually implement benchmarking, performance-related budgeting, accruals accounting, contracting-out, public–private partnerships and so on (see for example Minogue, Polidano and Hulme, 1998, on developing countries).

It may be tempting to assume that, because of the similarity of antecedents of reforms (budget deficits, public distrust of public administration and so on), the actual implementation and manifestations of reforms are similar in various countries. Indeed, the label that has been given to these reforms – New Public Management or NPM – suggests commonality and uniformity. However, more detailed analyses show that underlying ideas and their implementation fluctuate enormously (cf. Pollitt and Bouckaert, 2004). Studies into this diversity are still scarce and often favour an Anglo-American perspective on NPM (Barzelay, 2001: 168). In this book we aim (i) to show the range of diversity in the actual implementation of NPM in a number of (continental) European countries, and (ii) to offer an explanation for these differences, in particular why reforms in continental European countries may differ from the predominantly Anglo-American types of reform described and known as NPM. The central research question of this book can thus be stated as follows:

How have the predominantly Anglo-American ideas of the NPM been translated and implemented in the states of continental Europe? What trade-offs and adaptations can be identified in specific types of context and how can we begin to explain these?

At least two useful perspectives come to mind. A first perspective is related to the heterogeneous nature of the concept of NPM itself (Lynn, 1998). If one takes a closer look at the NPM literature, it would appear that what is called NPM is a rather heterogeneous set of management techniques and approaches (Gruening, 2001; Lynn, 1998), from which it is difficult to derive generalized statements about impact, manifestations or consequences. Moreover, NPM suffers from inherent contradictions. For example, important goals of the administrative reform are an increase of efficiency (reduction of costs) and equity (tailor-made products or services) at the same time. From this point of view, therefore, variation might be explained as 'selective shopping' from a varied and somewhat contradictory shop (the NPM). This perspective is elaborated more fully below.

A second and probably more intriguing perspective is to look at the variety of institutional settings in which new public management ideas and practices

~~are~~ implemented, in terms of starting points, path dependencies and implementation competencies (cf. Hood, 2000). Too many analyses of NPM reforms disregard or oversimplify the heterogeneity of institutional contexts in which reforms are applied. Although basic mechanisms and principles are comparable, the structure, functioning and implementation of principles and mechanisms of public administration differ considerably between Anglo-American traditions and continental European traditions, and even between various continental traditions (Pollitt and Bouckaert, 2004; Proeller and Schedler, 2005). It is our contention that these differences offer powerful explanations for the differences in administrative reforms between countries.

Therefore, the focus in this book is not on (descriptions of) generalized, superficially convergent patterns of administrative reforms. Rather, the analysis focuses on ways in which *specific* NPM ideas and instruments are shaped, implemented and crafted in continental Europe, as opposed to the dominant global (or perhaps predominant Anglo-American) clamour for reforms (see Kettl, 2005).

Before we describe the outline of this book, some more groundwork is done to establish a common conceptual framework. First, NPM is discussed and contrasted with the classic public administration paradigm. Next, we will define the core concepts used in this book. Finally, the outline of the book is sketched.

The New Public Management and the classic public administration paradigm: a confrontation of principles

There are many different views on NPM; what it is, where it came from and whether it actually (still) exists. However, there is one common denominator: NPM is a departure from the classic public administration paradigm (cf. Hood, 1994). Especially the notion of decentralization, either within or between governments, conflicts with the classic public management paradigm's notion of (strict) hierarchy and rules, and centralization by integration.

In the classic public administration paradigm, the organization of the public sector is generally assumed to be based on six principles (cf. Peters, 1996; Groth, 1999):

(1) An apolitical public service.
(2) Hierarchy and rules.
(3) Permanence and stability.
(4) An institutionalized civil service.
(5) Internal regulation.
(6) Equality.

As mentioned before, the classical paradigm came under criticism in the late 1970s and early 1980s, especially but certainly not exclusively by thinkers of the 'New Right' (cf. Clarke and Newman, 1997: 14). They pointed to under-performance in the public sector and increasing fiscal deficits, blaming it on the classical model of public administration. Furthermore, with the expansion of the scope of markets, citizens – in their role as users of public services – increasingly began to think more like customers (or at least some politicians said they did). For example, citizens displayed a decline in traditional forms of deference towards civil servants and politicians.

The growing importance of politicians and commentators who empha-sized market-like mechanisms as a way to control deficits, and the increasing resentment of citizens with quality of public services (which is not the same as thinking like a customer) coincided with the development in the acade-mic realm of theories like neo-institutional economics and public choice theory (Gruening, 2001), and gradually NPM as a doctrine emerged.

The literature lists a wealth of reforms under the heading of NPM. In general, one finds the following (Gruening, 2001; Pollitt, 2003; Pollitt and Bouckaert, 2004):

- Lean and highly decentralized structures, like semi-autonomous organiza-tions, rather than large, multi-purpose, hierarchical ministries or depart-ments. Thus, for example, the UK, the Netherlands, Norway and Italy all had programmes for separating out certain functions or activities and plac-ing them in 'arm's length' executive agencies (cf. Pollitt et al., 2004).
- The use of divisional structures in public service resulting in breaking down former unitary bureaucracies, as well as in inter-organizational relations with organizations in private and voluntary sectors (public–private part-nerships, PPP), resulting in blurred and broadened frontiers between the public sector, the market sector and the voluntary sector (Hacque, 2001).
- A widespread emphasis on contracts (or contract-like relationships) instead of formal, hierarchical relationships. Throughout Western Europe, for example, local authorities, which had previously collected refuge or cleaned the streets using staff from their own works depart-ments, contracted these functions out. Even if the existing unit continued to carry out the work, it now had to do so under a set of carefully speci-fied contractual conditions or in competition with private companies.
- A much wider than hitherto deployment of markets (or market-type) mechanisms (MTMs) for the delivery of public services. For example, during the 1980s UK local authorities were obliged by central government not only to use contracts but to do so through a process of mandatory competitive tendering (Ascher, 1987). Other examples are found in the privatization of, for example, social housing and the introduction of more competition in health care or education (cf. Le Grand and Bartlett, 1993).

- More attention for the management of organizations and management skills of public servants – as opposed to policy advice and legal skills which were dominant in the classic public administration paradigm. Additionally, changes in attitudes were aimed for, for example the introduction of a customer (rather than citizen) orientation, or in other words a focus on providing high quality services that serve narrower (less universal, more individualistic) interests of citizens. Finally, there was the introduction of performance-related systems for recruiting, promoting and paying staff and in general increased flexibility in hiring and firing staff (cf. Farnham, Horton, Barlow and Hondeghem, 1996).
- A shift in the focus of management systems and efforts from inputs like staff or buildings, and processes (for example teaching, inspecting) towards outputs (test results, inspection reports) and outcomes (safety, health, standards of literacy in the community). This performance orientation is combined with an increased emphasis on accountability for performance by decentralized or even privatized units to principals and other stakeholders, but also horizontally, that is in comparison with peer organizations through benchmarking (Hood, James, Peters and Scott, 2004).
- A shift towards more measurement and quantification, especially in the form of systems of performance indicators and/or explicit standards. Instead of just 'trusting the doctor', measures are developed that show how often the doctor prescribes drugs, how often patients develop postoperative complications, the length of waiting lists and the degree of compliance with the best practice protocols, and so on.

Browsing through the list, one notices that NPM is a rather chameleon-like and paradoxical creature – something that springs up for different reasons in different places. Consequently, it is hard to demarcate NPM. For example, Vigoda and Golembiewski (2001) consider participative policy and decision-making forms also as a part of NPM. Gruening, on the contrary, emphasizes that NPM seems to emphasize the citizens' power of exit as opposed to the power of voice, and argues that notions of participation are not profoundly anchored in NPM (Gruening, 2001). Box (1998) even claims that NPM takes an unfavourable approach to participation. As mentioned before, in this book we will discuss NPM reforms that serve narrower (less universal, less resilient, more individualistic) interests of citizens, and therefore we will exclude participation from our analysis.

The New Public Management and institutional contexts

Analysis of institutional context
The thrust of this book is that the reforms that constitute NPM are crafted, shaped, implemented and interpreted in specific institutional contexts.

Although this line of argumentation is rather susceptible to oversimplification, it is at the same time attractive in the sense that it explains changes of scope, focus and speed of specific reforms in terms of the institutional context in which the reforms are implemented. For example, Pollitt and Bouckaert (2004) observe variety in the adoption of reforms between countries attempting to 'lighten' existing bureaucracy (Germany during the 1980s), modernizers (Belgium, Finland, France, Italy, the Netherlands and Sweden), marketizers (the UK, New Zealand, the USA), and countries striving for a minimal or 'nightwatchman' state (notably the late Thatcher period in the UK). Furthermore, they identify 'core' NPM reforms and a distinct reform model called the neo-Weberian state (NWS). In the latter model, classic Weberian principles are mixed with elements like citizen orientation, consultation, result orientation and professionalization of the public service.

The starting point of an analysis of how institutional context affects or interferes with reforms is an examination of the institutional origins. Continental European and Anglo-Saxon traditions differ considerably in the degree to which public administration and political thought is rooted in a Roman Law tradition, emphasizing the state as entity (see Chapter 3 for a more extensive argument). In continental European political thought, the state is a separate entity that acts through organs (parliament, agencies) and whose competencies are demarcated by a constitution (Proeller and Schedler, 2005). In an Anglo-Saxon or Anglophone tradition on the other hand the focus is on institutions (Johnson, 2000) rather than on an abstract state that is conceptually and legally distinct from society and the economy. Moreover, in an Anglo-Saxon tradition government is seen as instrumental or even ancillary to the needs of society and economy (Proeller and Schedler, 2005). In a continental European tradition, the emphasis on rule-bound acts has over time resulted in a large body of special administrative law, with specialized courts. Proeller and Schedler explain the differences in scale, pace and speed of adoption of private sector-style management techniques between the United Kingdom on the one hand and Germany and France as representatives of a continental European tradition on the other hand, primarily in terms of the existence of vast amounts of administrative law in the latter countries.

Within a continental European tradition, it is furthermore possible to differentiate between three structural aspects of the legalistic administrative culture.

First, there is a difference between centralism (most notable in the French administrative system, where most of the political and administrative control is concentrated in one centre, namely Paris) and federalism (in, for example, Germany, where responsibilities and rights are distributed among different levels of the state).

Second, there is the existence of rather strict, unequivocal hierarchies (again, most notable in France where formal hierarchies are sometimes mapped geographically) versus the existence of coexisting, partly overlapping and smaller hierarchies. In general, traditional unequivocal hierarchies tend to be more stable and resistant to reforms.

Third, there is a difference in employment in bureaucracies, and therefore in management of human resources in bureaucracies. The difference entails the degree to which public employees are part of a specially trained, professional public service and are therefore given special deference and respect (or at least have the impression themselves that they are given deference and respect). In the French *grand corps* system, careers are to be managed impersonally, emphasizing seniority over performance (Stevens, 1988). Rouban argues 'that the very idea of management ... has never seduced higher civil servants ... and that they would help more to renew political control over public administration than to rationalize day-to-day administrative action' (Rouban, 1997: 142). In Italy, on the other hand, the majority of public sector employees are not given special deference and respect. It can be expected that the degree to which civil servants are considered to be a part of a professional group with specific human resource management practices, does not preclude adoption of more or less radical NPM practices (see, for example, James, 2003).

Possible trade-offs

In addressing the central research question of this book, we do not only address the translation, shaping and interpretation of ideas of the NPM in various institutional contexts, but also the identification of specific trade-offs in specific types of context. With trade-offs, we refer to qualities of both the classic public administration paradigm and the NPM that cannot be achieved simultaneously. Pollitt and Bouckaert (2004) have identified ten such (seemingly) incompatible statements about public administration and management:

- Increase (political) control of bureaucracy versus free managers to manage versus empower citizens (all three gain at the same time?).
- Promote flexibility and innovation versus increase citizen trust and therefore governmental legitimacy.
- Make savings versus improve performance.
- Make government more responsible for tasks versus reduce government's tasks.
- Motivate staff versus weaken tenure.
- Reduce the intra-governmental administrative burden versus clamour for accountability.
- Create more single-purpose agencies versus 'joined up government'.
- Decentralization versus co-ordination.
- Increase effectiveness versus sharpen managerial accountability.
- Improve quality versus cut costs.

At a very general level it is probably not possible to give definitive answers to these possible trade-offs – too much depends on the specific contexts. Therefore, in this book, our aim is to link particular trade-offs to particular types of context, in order to develop a more differentiated feel for the consequences of specific reform programmes in specific situations. This is a complex piece of analysis, which has begun in different ways in a number of the main chapters, and then returned to for an attempted synthesis in the final chapter.

Theory development

The analysis of the links between contexts and trade-offs referred to above represents a significant stage in theory-construction. More generally, in order to reflect on the translation and implementation of NPM ideas and elements in continental European states, both the notion of NPM itself, as well as the institutional context in which ideas are crafted, shaped and interpreted, are further analysed. This approach enables us more thoroughly to understand the convergence (or divergence) of specific constituting elements of NPM between Anglo-Saxon and continental European traditions, as well as within the various continental traditions. Thus we can reflect more deeply on issues of change and continuity within the classic public administration paradigm and the New Public Management. From a point of view of theory development, it is therefore of interest to explain how and why radical reforms sometimes succeed, whereas in other institutional contexts incremental change is more likely.

Outline of the book

There are twelve chapters. After this introduction, two chapters will discuss the spread of NPM ideas and practices in Western European countries. First, Christopher Pollitt discusses the notions of convergence and divergence of NPM concepts using examples from a variety of countries. He develops a model of change which may fit large parts of Western Europe better than 'the NPM story' (Chapter 2). In Chapter 3 Walter Kickert analyses and compares actual patterns of public management reforms in Spain, France and Italy; three countries with particular, Napoleonic state traditions. Apparently, the historical-institutional context of a particular state and administration affects not only the form and content of the administrative 'public management' reforms, but also the scientific study of public management in that country.

Then we turn to a number of chapters that deal with specific instruments or elements from the NPM toolkit, mostly following the list outlined above. In Chapter 4, Sandra van Thiel and Christopher Pollitt discuss and compare the management and control of executive agencies in the Netherlands and the United Kingdom. In Chapter 5, Erik-Hans Klijn, Jurian Edelenbos and Michael Hughes focus on the variety of contractual arrangements in the partnerships between the public and private sector, in the UK and the Netherlands. Chapter 6 (by Sandra van Thiel, Bram Steijn and Marine Allix) describes the introduction and effects of the personnel reforms that are part of the NPM. Examples are taken from a variety of countries including France, Italy, Denmark, the Netherlands, Germany and the UK. Next, Jan Hakvoort and Henk Klaassen report on a number of New Management tools, especially benchmarking and new financial instruments (Chapter 7). In Chapter 8, Vincent Homburg and Ig Snellen report on the relationship between the increased use of information and communication technologies (ICTs) and administrative reform in the UK, the Netherlands and Denmark. Finally, Christopher Pollitt addresses the use of performance indicators in Dutch and English hospitals in Chapter 9.

In the third part of this book we offer three reflections. First, Frans-Bauke van der Meer addresses the issue of evaluation in the context of the NPM (Chapter 10). He discusses both the use of evaluation in the context of New Public Management, as well as the methodology of evaluating administrative reform itself. Next, Geert Teisman and Arwin van Buuren reflect on the New Public Management paradigm using a competing perspective, namely complexity theory (Chapter 11). By doing so, they offer alternative explanations for the differences in the implementation of NPM reforms. Their analysis leads to a new research agenda for those interested in public management research. The final chapter then looks back over all the earlier contributions and tries to regain the 'big picture'.

2
Convergence or Divergence: What has been Happening in Europe?

Christopher Pollitt

Introduction

Many people – including a number of prominent experts – believe that there is a considerable degree of convergence between public management reforms all over the world. If this were true it would represent a remarkable example of 'globalization' in a field of activity (national public administrations) which, a generation ago, was usually seen as distinctively different ('French centralism/ statism', the 'British way', 'German juridicism', and so on). But is it true that national reform trajectories are converging and, if so, what are they converging on, and why? In this chapter we will examine these questions, with particular reference to Europe.

Aims of the chapter

More specifically, this chapter aims:

(1) To set up and explore the concept of 'convergence' in public management, noting that a number of prominent academics have stated or assumed that extensive global convergence towards NPM is or has already taken place.
(2) To review the reasons why we might expect convergence.
(3) To review the evidence for convergence.
(4) To reinterpret and reframe the convergence/divergence debate.

The believers

First, a British minister:

> All around the world governments are recognizing the opportunity to improve the quality and effectiveness of the public sector. Privatization,

market testing and private finance are being used in almost every developed country. It's not so difficult to see why. (Dorrell, 1993)

Second, two American consultants, who played central roles in the 'reinventing government' movement, which included the US National Performance Review (NPR) of 1992–9. Referring to what they called 'the rise of entrepreneurial government' they claimed that 'a similar process is underway throughout the developed world' and that it was 'inevitable' (Osborne and Gaebler, 1992: 328 and 325).

Third, a highly respected American professor of public administration:

> The movement has been so striking because of the number of nations that have taken up the reform agenda in such a short time and because of how similar their basic strategies have been. (Kettl, 2005: 1)

Fourth, an Australian professor, author of a widely sold textbook on public administration:

> A new model of public management has effectively supplanted the traditional model of public administration and the public sector in future will inevitably be managerial, in both theory and practice. (Hughes, 2003: 45)

> There are various ideas of what is involved in public management reforms. However, as the process has continued there has been convergence as to what is involved in the reforms. (Hughes, 2003: 51)

And, finally, a recent OECD overview document:

> In the past twenty years governments have made major changes in the way they manage the public sector. Most OECD public administrations have become more efficient, more transparent and customer oriented, more flexible and more focused on performance. (OECD, 2005: 10)

What is the nature of the perceived convergence?

Believers in convergence do not all have exactly the same thing in mind, but they seem to share a general orientation. That orientation is towards NPM-type reforms, the chief elements of which were summarized in Chapter 1. Thus Dorrell mentions privatization and market testing, while Hughes describes a focus on results, improved financial management, more flexibility in staffing and organization, a shift to competition and to contracts and a stress on private sector styles of management (Hughes, 2003: 54–8). The OECD refers to a performance focus, a customer orientation and an emphasis on efficiency. One might therefore say that the claimed convergence was towards a *smaller and less distinctive public sector*. The 'new public sector' henceforth would include both more private sector *practices* (for example performance-related pay, internal markets, customer surveys) and more private sector *participation* (as consultants, contractors, partners, and in the case of many privatizations and public–private partnerships, owners). Thus the public sector would be less different from the for-profit market sector than previously. Some commentators have dubbed this the 'supermarket state' model (Christensen and Lægreid, 2003) and others have described the popularity of strategies of 'marketization' (introducing competition to the public sector) and 'minimization' – making the state smaller through privatization and contracting-out – (Pollitt and Bouckaert, 2004).

Critics of the convergence model

All this sounds fairly conclusive – clearly there is a substantial body of expert opinion in support of the idea of global convergence. Yet there is also an equally expert parade of disbelievers – individuals who question the proclaimed convergence in various ways. For example:

> Reform ideas engendered on a global level, through the dominance of certain countries or international organizations, are transformed when they spread, meaning that reform ideas with similar labels may acquire different content. (Christensen and Lægreid, 2003: 301)

Or, in a study of executive agencies in four European states:

> Some of [the] variety is remarkably stable: the Swedish agency system is still there, after more than two centuries, as is the centralized British system of two warring parties (after more than a century) and the strong Dutch system of quiet, consensual negotiation and consultation. These embedded structures and cultural norms shape and constrain most reforms and reorganizations, and, further, they colour daily life for senior managers in many state agencies. (Pollitt et al., 2004: 265)

This theme is forcefully taken up in the next chapter of this book, where Walter Kickert reviews the administrative histories of France, Spain and Italy, and argues that 'Anglo-Saxon' New Public Management types of reform have simply not been the main item on the agenda for these Mediterranean countries over the past twenty years – and in some cases have been tried, but with disappointing results.

Academics investigating the use of quality improvement techniques in European public sectors have recently made an interesting distinction between reform rhetoric and underlying changes in actual practice.

They say:

> The globalization of public sector management consultancies and the enlargement of the EU have both played a significant role in spreading the quality 'rhetoric' throughout public sectors all over Europe. However, this 'discursive convergence' should not be misinterpreted as a convergence of political concepts or administrative cultures, both of which are subject to distinctly separate drivers from those influencing the rhetoric.
>
> We get a completely different picture when we look into decision-making on quality programmes in the public sector. There are not only big differences between CEE countries, but also within Western Europe as far as the role of the central government in quality improvement programmes for public services is concerned. (Löffler and Vintar, 2004: 5–6)

Rather earlier, a leading Swedish professor published a paper criticizing the way the OECD had presented public management reforms as though there were some general convergence towards an NPM model (Premfors, 1998). He compared the picture of general trends drawn in the OECD documents of the mid-1990s with what had actually happened in Sweden, and found that they did not match well at all. More generally, he saw that:

> In the international discourse concerning recent administrative reform developments there is a dominant overall interpretation propagated by a dominant storyteller: the public management programme (PUMA) of the OECD. This article takes issue with this story, arguing that instead of a singular pattern of adaptation there have been and there are several different reform trajectories in Western-style democracies, largely predicated on historically-determined patterns of state–society relations and significant variations in political cultures. (Premfors, 1998: 141)

Later in this chapter we will find that the OECD has changed its 'story' somewhat, so that, in its 2005 publication it gives more space to contextual variations than it did in the publications of the mid-1990s which Premfors was writing about.

The French experience, apparently, also diverged significantly from the NPM model. Guyomarch (1999: 171) put it like this:

> In France, the importance of administrative law, the successful experience of nationalized, monopoly, public service providers in the post war period, and the idea of a 'general interest', represented at local level by the prefect, explain many of the distinctive features of the hybrid modernization reforms.

A number of German scholars have also written to stress German distinctiveness, and to point out how German reforms have not at all closely approximated to the Anglo-Saxon model of NPM (for example Derlien, 1998). Instead a picture is drawn of 'disjointed incrementalist' change, with different types of reform taking place at different levels and locations in a highly decentralized system (Wollmann, 2003). Certainly at the federal level the evidence for implementation of the NPM model has been sparse.

And, finally, no less a person than the Chancellor of Germany who in his 2005 retirement speech attacked the 'Anglo-Saxon model' and delivered the following declaration of divergence:

> I say to my British friend that people in Germany, in Europe, don't want complete denationalization, they don't want the privatization of long term risks ... They want a state that is not in front of their nose but at their side. (Schröder, translation of farewell speech, reported by Dempsey, 2005 – notice that Chancellor Schröder, like quite a few citizens of the UK, does not appear to realize that Britain is *in* Europe, both geographically and constitutionally.)

Unpacking the concept

A first step in unravelling the mystery of the divergent views of the experts is to unpack the concept of convergence itself. We will show that it has several different aspects or meanings, and this can itself account for some of the disagreements – the different experts are actually talking about different things.

Two basic questions are 'what is converging?' and 'what does convergence mean?' The answer to the first question immediately reveals the scope for divergent interpretations of the evidence. For example, it could be reform talk that is converging – *discursive convergence*, in which everybody has the same vocabulary and the same apparent agenda. Ideas like 'a customer orientation' or 'results-based budgeting' could feature in all the government reports and ministerial speeches and conferences. Or it could be that actual decisions were converging – that many countries were adopting Total Quality Management (TQM) or Regulatory Impact Analysis (RIA). This can be termed *decisional convergence*, and it can be traced in the public record – legislation, white papers, government announcements and so on. A third possibility is that actual operational practices were converging. Such *operational convergence* would represent a further step down the road, because it would mean that hundreds or thousands of public servants had changed their day-to-day behaviours, and were converging on a single set of new routines. To establish whether operational convergence was taking place one would normally have to carry out fieldwork in a number of different countries – something which for most academics is quite hard to organize. Finally – most ambitiously – there could be a convergence of the achievements of public administration, the results or outcomes of operational activities. Thus, for example, a particular management technique might lead to the time taken to issue a passport falling in every state that adopted that technique. Or a new way of managing waste collection could mean that different states converged towards a new, lower level of costs per tonne of waste disposed. We could call this *results convergence*. To detect it would require some type of comparative evaluation – a difficult exercise methodologically and organizationally, and one that, in practice, is rarely undertaken.

The first point to be made about this kind of differentiation of the concept of convergence is that it opens up a strong likelihood that different experts, when they make their judgements about the extent of convergence, may be looking at different things (Pollitt, 2002). Since there may be yawning gaps at each stage in the process (from discursive convergence to decisional convergence to operational convergence to results convergence), the extent of convergence will probably appear very different depending on which level of evidence one is looking at. Discursive convergence is highly likely to be more extensive than operational convergence, for example (as the Löffler and Vintar quotation above indicated was the case for quality improvement schemes). Fashions in talk and terminology can build up and fade away quite quickly, but changing the daily routines of the public servants who deliver education, or driving licences, or the regulation of firms is much harder to achieve. So it is not surprising that the believers in convergence often tend to cite government pronouncements and decisions, whereas some of their more sceptical critics point to empirical studies of what goes on inside operational organizations to show that big differences continue to exist (for example, Pollitt, 2005).

A second point is that, from the perspective of scientific knowledge creation, some kinds of convergence are much less difficult to research than others, and this too, may influence the academic literature. Basically it is far easier to research discursive and decisional convergence than either operational or results convergence. This is because the former two types are visible in public domain texts – indeed, nowadays the academic scarcely has to leave his or her office to be able to conduct this type of investigation. By contrast operational and results convergence – the very stages at which less convergence might be expected – require fieldwork and the gathering of the kind of internal organizational data that hitherto have usually not been freely available over the net. Thus we might expect a bias in the academic literature as a whole in favour of the first two types of convergence. Indeed, it is noticeable that many of the believers in convergence are writing at a high level of generalization, focusing mainly on talk and decisions, while quite a few of their critics are pointing to the findings of more detailed studies of actual operations.

A third point concerns the nature of the relationship between discursive convergence and operational convergence. When three or four countries are all discussing agencies, for example Total Quality Management (TQM) *and* we are able to show that they have all created agencies and installed TQM projects, then surely can we speak of real operational convergence? The answer is, only partly. The reason is that the same technique, with the same name, may be 'translated' quite differently within one national or local context as compared with another (Sahlin-Andersson, 2001; Smullen, 2004; Zbaracki, 1998). So there is some convergence in titles and labels, but rather less in practices and, especially, in the relationship of those new practices to the other practices and routines of the organizations concerned. 'Translations' are perhaps particularly likely when terms travel across language barriers, which they almost always do when 'Anglo-Saxon' NPM ideas arrive in continental Europe. To give just two examples, first, not every European language even has a term that directly translates into 'management', and second, there are a multitude of differences of interpretation around the term 'efficiency' and its Dutch and French 'equivalents'!

In short, part of the disagreement between experts about the extent of convergence is because they are looking at different stages of convergence. In addition, some of the belief in convergence may arise from the superficial application of labels and terms which turn out to embody both different meanings and different practices when examined more closely. Or, to put the matter more crudely, Anglophone Anglo-Saxons are perhaps particularly likely to overestimate the extent of convergence towards the NPM model.

There is a further – and rather important – methodological reason for differences of opinion between experts. It concerns the breadth of the frame in which research is conducted. If one takes a narrow frame, and simply looks for evidence of the presence of NPM features (contracting-out, for example, or performance-related pay) then one is only looking for *particular* elements, not at the *general* picture of administrative activity and reform within whatever jurisdictions are under examination. This is the *de facto* approach adopted in some academic writing. With this approach, therefore, one is likely to exaggerate the overall effects of NPM, because one is not looking at anything else. It is rather like checking to see whether there is any rainfall in each member of a set of countries and, finding that there is, declaring that there is a convergence towards wetness, even though rainfall in one country may be only 50mm per annum, and in another 5000mm per annum. In the first country rainfall is rare, in the second a daily event. In exactly the same way, one may find the occasional public agency using advanced quality improvement techniques or performance indicators in Lithuania, or Tanzania, but to suppose that this makes them similar to the UK or Sweden (where most public agencies use such techniques as a matter of routine) is fallacious. By contrast, a broad framed approach may lead the investigator to the conclusion that, yes, there are certainly elements of the NPM in a particular public sector, but that, taken together, these do not (or do not yet) represent the main line of activity or even the principal component of reform. It is very doubtful whether this state of affairs could be described as 'convergence' on the NPM model. In essence this is the kind of conclusion we will see that Walter Kickert reaches concerning Italy, Spain and France in Chapter 3.

These reflections on 'convergence' help to explain some of the differences of interpretation, but they probably do not explain all of it. We also need to try to look at the evidence itself – what has been going on in the continental European countries, and how does this compare with the 'core NPM states' of Australia, New Zealand, the UK and the USA?

Reform trajectories

Having unpacked the concept of convergence, we can now turn to the evidence of what has actually been going on in continental Europe. Here we will draw on two main sources, a recent academic comparison of reform trajectories in twelve countries (Pollitt and Bouckaert, 2004) and the latest overview by the OECD – *Modernising Government: the Way Forward* (OECD, 2005). Neither work makes a clear distinction between the four stages of convergence, but both do try to focus mainly on decisions and on operational changes rather than just on reform rhetoric. We will now briefly characterize these two publications in respect of the light they cast upon the convergence/divergence debate.

Pollitt and Bouckaert describe and analyse the main central government management reforms since 1980 in twelve countries, and in the European Commission. They identify significant differences in the reform trajectories of different groups of countries, with Australia, New Zealand, the UK and the USA as 'core NPM' states which have pursued the strategies of marketizing and privatizing faster and further than the other states. The analysis attempts to relate these differences to certain broader features of the different countries concerned. Thus radical NPM trajectories seem to have been associated with countries that have majoritarian political systems (Australia, NZ, UK, USA), centralized administrative systems (NZ, UK) and a prevailing ideology which combines a public interest view of government with an individualist and pro-business set of cultural norms (Australia, NZ, UK, USA). Conversely, countries which lack all or most of these features have not been enthusiastic about the NPM recipe. Think back to Chancellor Schröder's remarks quoted earlier – Germany is not a majoritarian political system, does not have a centralized administration and, although pro-business, has long displayed a strongly *rechtsstaat* view of the role of the state. The connecting explanations are as follows. First, majoritarian political systems permit a single party to push through its ideas (in this case NPM ideas) without having to make so many concessions and compromises to other parties, as one does in a coalition system. Second, centralized administrative systems (such as those in the UK and New Zealand, in both of which local government is dominated by central government and has very little autonomy) permit governments to spread their chosen reforms more rapidly across many departments and agencies. Third, a *rechtsstaat* system usually means that every change has to be embodied in law, and that most senior civil servants are jurists, with a legal mentality, and that these factors tend to slow down management change. The core NPM countries are all 'non-*rechtsstaat*'. For example, during the late 1980s and 1990s the UK government was able to create more than 120 executive agencies which employed more than 70 per cent of the civil service without introducing any new legislation at all – a situation which would have been unimaginable in Germany, Sweden or France. Finally countries with an individualist culture and pro-business attitudes are more likely to warm to NPM ideas than are countries with either a collectivist culture and/or a less admiring attitude towards private sector businesses. The best known attempts to measure cultural features in different countries show that the core NPM countries tend to rank higher on individualism than most of the continental states (Hofstede, 2001: 500, and see the discussion in Pollitt and Bouckaert, 2004: 52–7).

The 2005 OECD publication *Modernising Government* is a review of modernization initiatives in most of the thirty OECD member states over the preceding twenty years. It suggests that, although there were widely shared objectives – to make public sectors more responsive, transparent and efficient – there were a variety of 'different policy paths' (p. 3). It goes on to identify certain trends which it considers have been very widespread, in particular:

- Greater openness in government (with a great deal of new hard and 'soft' law across many countries).
- An enhanced focus on performance.
- A shift from *ex ante* to *ex post* accountability and control (which chimes with the increased focus on measuring performance).
- A proliferation of semi-autonomous public bodies at arm's length from central ministries and departments.

In respect of these very general characteristics, therefore, one might say that the OECD are believers in some mild convergence. However, the review also identifies other important reforms where there have been large differences between different groups of countries. The use of market-type mechanisms is one of these, and reform of the employment arrangements of civil servants is another. They find, for example, that there are wide variations in the degree to which performance-related pay is actually applied. Significantly, the OECD concludes that:

Modernization is dependent on context. While all governments are being affected by global trends, there are no public management cure-alls.

History, culture and the stage of development give governments different characteristics and priorities. Adaptation can be assisted by learning from other governments but, unless countries are very similar indeed, learning will work better at the level of system dynamics than at the level of instruments and specific practices. (OECD, 2005: 13)

They go on to acknowledge that 'the same reform instruments perform differently and produce very diverse results in different country contexts' (p. 22), which sounds at odds with any strong model of convergence – certainly at the level of specific tools and practices where some true believers in the NPM are very enthusiastic. Furthermore, they stress the need to understand 'the nature and dynamics of the public administration system as a whole' (p. 22) – in other words to take the broad view which was mentioned before, not a narrow 'plug in the new mechanism' approach.

Other European models: the neo-Weberian state?

We can now return to the general issue of the impact of NPM reforms on Europe. We have already seen that there are many informed voices speaking against the idea of 'strong' convergence, that is that all countries are heading fast towards the pure NPM model of marketization and privatization. We have also seen that various distinguished commentators are keen to stress the distinctiveness of the reforms in Germany, or France or Sweden. Yet at the same time it is plain that certain elements of the NPM package – contracting-out, for example, or quality improvement schemes – have been widely adopted in many countries, including those of continental Europe. Evidently the pattern is complex, and resists simple characterization. But is there no 'big picture' at all, or can some useful categories be perceived through the cloud of local details?

Pollitt and Bouckaert argue that among the twelve countries they examine there are two substantial groupings, and then some 'hybrid' or 'hard-to-classify' cases. The first, and best-known grouping is that of the New Public Management 'marketizers' – Australia, New Zealand, the UK and, in words if not always in deeds, the USA. This is the *core NPM group* – they all see a large role for private sector forms and techniques in the process of restructuring the public sector. They are all – as noted above – majoritarian political systems, and the two most radical (NZ and the UK) are also administratively highly centralized. They are all highly individualist cultures, with much less understanding of or patience for collectivist and consensual practices than most continental European countries. All think in terms of 'the government' rather than 'the state'.

The second grouping are the continental European 'modernizers' – Belgium, Finland, France, the Netherlands, Italy and Sweden (and Germany, particularly if one goes below the federal level). They continue to place greater emphasis on the state as *the* irreplaceable integrative force in society, with a legal personality and operative value system that cannot be reduced to the private sector discourse of efficiency, competitiveness and consumer satisfaction (see, vividly, Dempsey, 2005). They thus continue, in modern form, their nineteenth- and twentieth-century traditions of strong statehood and high status for the top civil servants. The speed and precise mixture of change has differed between members of this modernizing group – this is not a tidy, neat package that everyone buys at the same moment. Reform has arrived later for the 'central Europeans' – Belgium, Germany and Italy – than for the 'northern Europeans' – Finland, the Netherlands and Sweden. France has matched the faster pace of the northern group, but has been more resistant to marketizing ideas, and to much of the Anglophone rhetoric around NPM. In addition, the northern countries have imparted their modernization efforts with a stronger citizen-oriented, participatory flavour than have the central Europeans. Decision-making in Italy has inevitably been affected by the political turbulence which that country has experienced, in contrast, say, to the much more measured, consensual process of reform in Finland or the Netherlands, and Italy is probably the least good 'fit' for this classification. Nevertheless, when compared with the core NPM group, we can say that the continental Europeans as a whole have shared a more optimistic attitude towards the future role of the state, a more constructive/less 'blaming' approach to the reform of the public services, and a less panoptic enthusiasm towards the potential private sector role within the public domain. In these respects the continentals have converged, but not on the NPM model.

The NPM core states are well represented in the Anglophone literature (Boston et al., 2004; Christensen and Lægreid, 2003; Hood, 1996; Kettl, 2005; Lane, 2000). The continental European groups are much less so, and are sometimes portrayed simply as rather backward administrations, who have been slow to climb aboard the NPM bandwagon. We argue that this is a somewhat Anglo-centric interpretation, and suggest that there is a far more positive – if divergent – interpretation, which better fits the known facts. This would be that what is visible in the recent trajectories of continental European states is a distinctive reform model, one which Bouckaert and Pollitt (2004) term the *neo-Weberian state (NWS)*. In comparison with NPM marketization, the NWS has the following emphases:

'Weberian' elements

- Reaffirmation of the role of the state as the main facilitator of solutions to the new problems of globalization, technological change, shifting demographics and environmental threat.
- Reaffirmation of the role of representative democracy (central, regional and local) as the legitimating element within the state apparatus.

- Reaffirmation of the role of administrative law – suitably modernized – in preserving the basic principles pertaining to the citizen–state relationship, including equality before the law, legal security and the availability of specialized legal scrutiny of state actions.
- Preservation of the idea of a public service with a distinctive status, culture and terms and conditions.

'Neo' elements

- Shift from an internal orientation towards bureaucratic rules to an external orientation towards meeting citizens' needs and wishes. The primary route to achieving this is not the employment of market mechanisms (although they may be selectively and occasionally useful) but the creation of a professional culture of quality and service.
- Supplementation (not replacement) of the role of representative democracy by a range of devices for consultation with and the direct representation of citizens' views (this aspect being more visible in the northern European states and Germany at the local level than in Belgium, France or Italy).
- In the management of resources within government, a modernization of the relevant laws to encourage a greater orientation on the achievement of results rather than merely the correct following of procedure. This is expressed partly in a shift in the balance from ex ante to ex post controls, but not a complete abandonment of the former.
- A professionalization of the public service, so that the 'bureaucrat' becomes not simply an expert in the law relevant to his or her sphere of activity, but also a professional manager, oriented to meeting the needs of his/her citizens/users (Pollitt and Bouckaert, 2004: 99–100).

Viewed from inside, there are, of course, many significant differences between the members of this group of continental states. But looked at from a distance, what is striking in comparison with the core NPM states is how far the underlying assumptions of a positive state, a distinctive public service and a particular legal order survive as the foundations beneath the various packages of modernizing reforms. The story has been one of a *modernization* of the Weberian tradition, not its outright rejection in favour of the market model. The process has been one of addition, not demolition (even if some of the additions fitted on the foundations rather awkwardly).

Finally, the marketizers and anti-state minimizers who were quite common in the UK, New Zealand and the USA never commanded the same degree of political voice in either the central European states or even the northern group. The prophets of the core NPM states envisaged an entrepreneurial, market-oriented society, with a light icing of government on top. The northern variant of the NWS foresaw a citizens' state, with extensive participation facilitated by a modernized system of public law that would guarantee rights and duties. Proponents of the central European variant of the NWS favoured a professional state – modern, efficient and flexible, yet still uniquely identified with the 'higher purposes' of the general interest.

However, the precision of the NWS model – or the NPM model for that matter – must not be exaggerated. The pattern is very rough and approximate, for both political and organizational reasons. Politically, governments change and may hold different visions of the future, so that, following elections, certain types of reform are de-emphasized and other types given greater salience. The arrival of Mr Blair's Labour government in power in the UK in 1997 did not by any means completely alter the trajectory of UK reforms, but it did shift the emphasis. The automatic preference for private sector solutions was replaced with talk of partnerships. Some MTMs were partially dismantled (for example, in the NHS), though others were retained. Greater emphasis was laid on horizontal co-ordination or 'joined-up' government. In general it might be said that the change of administration shifted the UK from the radical end of the 'marketizing' group towards the 'marketizing'/'modernizing' borderline. Similarly, in the US the arrival in power of the Clinton Democrats resulted in an end to the neglect and sometimes scorn which the federal civil service had suffered between 1980 and 1992. In rhetorical terms it shifted reform away from a mixture of minimalism (especially under Reagan) and marketization and towards modernization as the dominant motif. The election of President George W. Bush at first seemed likely to mark a swing back to marketizing and, indeed, plans for further large-scale contracting-out were announced. However, 9/11 introduced a new dimension, and the subsequent proposal for a new Department of Homeland Security at first sight strikes a somewhat inconsistent, centralizing and interventionist note. The devil is in the detail, however, and the 2002 Homeland Security Act also contains provisions that, in true NPM style, weaken (federal) employee protection and strengthen management flexibility.

A second set of political reasons for variations is to be found among the pressures represented by external socio-economic forces and by political demands. Even if the plans and intentions of governments embrace a degree of convergence, these plans can be blown off course in a particular country by such contingencies. Consider, for example, the balance between three basic types of reform objective. First, there is the objective of reducing public expenditure, or at least restraining its rate of growth. Second, there is the laudable desire to design better performing public services, higher quality, greater efficiency and so on. Third, there is the aim of sharpening accountability and therefore, hopefully, enhancing the legitimacy of the administration in the eyes of the public. These three widely held objectives exist in some tension with each other. Trouble for governments may blow up on any of these three fronts at quite short notice. An economic downturn may heighten the need for economies and cuts – even for a NWS government that wants to strengthen the state. Revelations of low standards in, for example, nursing homes or airline safety or animal welfare, may lead to strident and popular calls for something to be done – even in radical NPM states where the governments would rather not interfere in the private sector. The discovery of cases of corruption or gross waste or concealment of important decisions may fuel calls for greater transparency and stricter accountability procedures (as happened with the European Commission crisis in 1999). When one or more such events occur, political leaders and their senior officials have to alter course, at least for the time being. Progress along a particular reform trajectory wobbles or halts. A small-scale example might be when the needs of the national economy seem to require a budget cut, and the impact on particular public service organizations is that they abandon their plans for service improvement, which can no longer be afforded. Alternatively, attempts to decentralize authority and increase managerial discretion and flexibility may be halted if a particular 'decentralized' manager is discovered to have acted corruptly, so that calls for tighter centralized control cannot be resisted.

Organizational factors also intrude to spoil the possibility of any truly neat pattern. There are frequently implementation difficulties, and these can persuade governments to change instruments, or to 'soft pedal' on types of reform about which they were previously very enthusiastic. Mr Major's UK Conservative government soon retreated from the rhetoric of vigorous competition with respect to the NHS provider market, and took steps to see that it was closely managed, in an effort to avoid volatility (Pollitt, Birchall and Putman, 1998). Following criticism, the Dutch government of the mid-1990s became more cautious about creating highly autonomous ZBOs and tended to favour more controllable executive agencies instead. In the 1990s M. Jospin's government in France retreated from some of its public service reform proposals when faced with large-scale strikes by resistant trade unions.

Overall, therefore, our interpretation is that, whilst there has undoubtedly been great diversity, and while many trajectories turn out to be partial or interrupted, there is a rough but discernible longer-term pattern beneath the welter of detail. Whilst this pattern certainly does not mean that each individual reform instrument (performance budgets, contracting-out, and so on) can be ascribed exclusively to one single trajectory (still less to one group of countries and not to others) it *does* suggest that there are some usually continuing broad differences between different groups of countries (that is convergence within these groups rather than continent-wide or global). The trajectories and rhetoric of reform were significantly different as between, first, the Anglo-Australasian-American core NPM enthusiasts; second, the early and participatory modernizers in Northern Europe (NWS, first variant); and, third, the somewhat later, more managerially oriented modernizers in central Europe and the EU Commission (NWS, second variant). It also seems likely that these differences are indeed related to the types of politico-administrative regimes. In terms of trajectories or strategies, not every country is converging on the NPM model.

Concluding reflections

This chapter has explored the convergence/divergence debate and eventually come down in favour of a mixed position. The key elements of this position are as follows:

- The 'strong' version of convergence on the NPM model simply does not fit with the evidence. There is too much diversity and difference (and even outright rejection and conscious opposition). Some commentators may have overemphasized the degree of convergence because they were looking mainly at Anglophone discourse, and/or because they were *only* looking for NPM-type developments and not noticing what *other* reforms were taking place in continental European countries.
- Nevertheless there *is* evidence that, although the whole NPM package has not been 'bought' by many continental European countries, these countries have made selective and limited use of certain of its elements or instruments (for example contracting-out, performance-related pay, privatization). But this did not mean that the respective administrative systems were converging as totalities.
- Even the evidence of widespread use of specific instruments and techniques has to be interpreted cautiously, because there is a good deal of research to indicate that such elements are frequently extensively adapted or 'translated' when they are imported into new contexts. Techniques such as TQM, benchmarking, Regulatory Impact Analysis, performance budgeting and performance-related pay are very far from being standardized, 'plug-in' mechanisms.
- The story of reform in continental Europe should not be read only in relation to NPM. Hitherto, the Anglophone literature has tended to overlook the possibility that there are alternative models which are being implemented (perhaps because these models have lacked the title and the publicity which the NPM has received). One way of characterizing these alternatives – in the case of continental Europe – is as some kind of neo-Weberian state (NWS).
- The NWS appears to have at least two principal variants. The first stresses citizen participation and legitimation as a crucial aspect of modernization, and this emphasis has been most clearly visible in the Nordic countries and the Netherlands. The second places more emphasis on professionalization, modern, more flexible systems of budgeting and operational management,

and the modernization of administrative law. This variant has been more evident in France, Germany, Spain and Portugal.

Again, it should be stressed that this is an untidy and incomplete picture. There are certainly anomalies. Switzerland, for example, is a central European state and has engaged in a very substantial modernization effort – but one shaped and conditioned by the fact that this country already had a unique system of intense citizen participation in public affairs including referenda and citizen proposals. Italy is particularly hard to categorize. On the one hand it has seen huge administrative and political changes since the political crisis of the early 1990s, but on the other, levels of corruption and patronage remain very high by Northern European standards (see Chapter 3 and Transparency International, 2005).

Finally, one might speculate on *why* so many voices have been drawn to the NPM-convergence model. Partly, as explained above, this interpretation may well be an artefact of the concepts and methods adopted to conduct research. Partly, also, there may be a linguistic barrier: the British and Americans are hardly famous for their language skills, and it may be that some have simply never read accounts of developments in continental Europe, other than the few which are published in English. (Dutch, French and German public administration scholars, by contrast, are almost invariably able to read English.) Additionally, however, we should not neglect to note that significant material interests hang upon the debate we have been conducting in this chapter. So long as the NPM model is seen as 'the future', and so long as there is 'no other show in town', then British and American and Australasian consultants and public servants are seen as the leading authorities on modernization. They are the high priests of the future and, as such, reap many of the benefits of the now huge international trade in public management consultancy and advice (Saint-Martin, 2000). They are the ones with key positions in the OECD and the World Bank, and in international consultancy firms. They are the ones sent to Eastern Europe and the developing world to give advice. They are the keynote speakers at international conferences. It is easy to see how the myth of convergence has been created and sustained. Continental Europe, by comparison, has been a dark continent.

3
Public Management Reforms in Countries with a Napoleonic State Model: France, Italy and Spain

Walter Kickert

Introduction

This chapter addresses a main theme of this book: the influence of various institutional settings of states and administrations on the way public management ideas and practices are implemented. Different historical-institutional backgrounds of European states and administration do affect the form and content of their administrative reform. Western states and administrations do differ considerably in many relevant respects. That influences the path of their administrative 'public management' reforms (Kickert, 1997, 2000; Pollitt and Bouckaert, 2004). This chapter will concentrate on the administrative reforms in three European countries that significantly differ from the Anglo-Saxon state model, that is, on the three European countries – France, Italy and Spain – that have a Napoleonic state tradition. In comparison to the relative success of New Public Management (NPM) reforms in Anglo-Saxon countries, France shows more modest examples of that type of reform and Italy and Spain are relative 'failures' in terms of NPM reforms. One of the explanations for this difference is that Anglo-Saxon state models differ from continental European legal state traditions, such as reflected in the Napoleonic model (Wunder, 1995). France forms its origin and Italy and Spain have adopted the Napoleonic model. As stated in the introductory chapter of this book the French Napoleonic state model differs from the Anglo-Saxon model in the sense that it is highly centralized, hierarchical and uniform, and that officials are part of a highly trained, professional 'corps' system. Furthermore, the Napoleonic state is highly legalistic. Administrative law strongly governs the acts of administration and administrators in the 'état de droit' (*Rechtsstaat*). This chapter will therefore begin with a closer examination of the Napoleonic state model.

The chapter will then proceed with a 'thick description' of the administrative reforms in the three countries. Southern European countries are notably underrepresented in comparative studies of government and administration (Sotiropoulos, 2004). Quite understandably Spain, Portugal and Greece during their dictatorships only played a marginal role in democratic Western Europe. After the authoritative dictatorships disappeared (military revolution in Portugal in April 1974, coup against the colonels in Greece in July 1974, death of Franco in Spain in November 1975) and the transition to democracy, the interest in the international political and administrative science community has grown, but mainly in special topics like the transition to democracy, the integration into the European Union, and special policy areas. International dissemination of general knowledge about state, government and administration of southern countries like Greece, Italy, Spain and Portugal remains restricted, even in the field of comparative politics and government, let alone in the scientific community interested in public management reforms. That is why this chapter, before proceeding to a comparative analysis of administrative reforms in the three countries, first presents a general historical-institutional 'tour d'horizon' on the three countries' state, government and administration. Although similar in some respects, the three countries are quite distinct in their historical-institutional developments and in their current form of government, politics and administration. Their approaches to administrative reforms also differ.

Napoleonic state tradition

The Mediterranean countries Italy and Spain have founded their states on the French model, that is the Napoleonic model (Wright, 1990; Wunder, 1995). The nation-state is united and the state serves the general interest. The administration is centralized, hierarchical, uniform, accountable and controlled. The administration consists of highly trained and qualified civil servants, who are organized in professional 'corps'.

This Napoleonic model has its roots in the centuries-long history of state formation in France, especially in the abolishment of the absolutist Bourbon monarchy by the French Revolution, and the subsequent establishment of a liberal constitutional *Rechtsstaat*. The establishment of the liberal constitutional democratic *Rechtsstaat* not only became a fundamental turning point in the French development of state and administration, but also in many other continental European countries (Finer, 1954; Heper, 1987; Page, 1992).

For the sake of clarity this brief sketch will simply presume a common European path towards a liberal constitutional democratic *Rechtsstaat*. In historical reality that path differed amongst different European countries. The French path from absolute monarchy to a constitutional parliamentary democracy was indirect. The revolutionary abolishment of the Bourbon monarchy was a decade later followed by the Napoleonic Empire, after which the monarchy was restored, albeit only constitutionally. Only a few revolutions and empires later was a parliamentary democratic constitution established in France. State formation of other European countries also varied a good deal. The German state formation was not based on a revolution of the bourgeoisie, but on the hegemony of the Prussian elite, in particular the 'iron chancellor' Bismarck. The nineteenth-century German idea of the *Rechtsstaat* meant that the sovereign was to be bound by laws and rules (Benz, 2001). The rules were to be equally and fairly applied to all state subjects, and judges and administrators were to be neutral. Contrary to the French 'principe de légalité' in which the law is the expression of the 'volonté général' of the people (Ziller, 2003), in Prussia and Habsburg Austria the emperors remained in absolute power. Parliamentary democracy was only established in Germany after the First World War. As we will see later on, Italy and Spain also followed their own paths.

The liberal constitution introduced the legalistic *Rechtsstaat* thinking about state and administration. Parliament became the highest sovereign authority in the state. Legislation became the fundament of state and administration. Administration should be based on the primacy of the law. Constitution, laws and regulations became the exclusive source of administrative action. The key tasks of state and administration were narrowed down to the legislation and execution of laws and regulations. Administration was restricted to merely executing legislation, and administering rules and regulations based on the law. In the liberal *Rechtsstaat* every free citizen possessed legal security and equality before the law. Therefore, the law gained the monopoly of the only relevant expertise for the effective functioning of the state. This led to the *Juristenmonopol* (monopoly of lawyers) within continental European administrations. State officials were predominantly lawyers.

The establishment of liberal constitutional democracies also marked the beginning of modern professional bureaucracy. In an absolute monarchy state officials were the personal servants of the king. With the coming of the liberal constitutional democracy the king was no longer in personal control of the state and administration. Parliament became the highest authority in the state. Ministers became responsible and accountable to parliament. State officials transformed from personal servants of the king into servants of the impersonal state. State officials became properly educated and trained professionals with the proper expertise.

The nineteenth century witnessed the beginning of professional bureaucracies, like the transformation of the British civil service into a meritocracy after the Northcote-Trevelyan reform of 1853. Serving the British state was no longer the prerogative of the gentry. A qualified, non-political, administrative class educated in liberal universities replaced the aristocracy (Drewry and Butcher, 1988). In France the transformation into a highly qualified professional bureaucracy happened under the regime of Napoleon (Thuiller and Tulard, 1984). In Prussia the mighty and professional state bureaucracy had been created by the Hohenzollern rulers already in the seventeenth and eighteenth centuries (Hartung, 1950).

Another of its characteristics was that officials henceforth fulfilled an official, formally described task in the state administration, a formal and protected position that was accompanied by a formal and lifelong appointment. Officials received a regular salary and pension. In order to further minimize any personal influence of political rulers on the functioning of state officials, their career path in the administration's hierarchy was henceforth determined by seniority only. Their career did no longer depend on the judgement and appreciation by a king or any other political rulers. Their career was guaranteed, certain and predictable.

This historical description of modern bureaucracy coincides with the characteristics of the ideal type model of 'bureaucracy' that the sociologist Weber (1972) constructed early in the twentieth century. Weber described bureaucracy as a form of legal-rational authority which was precise, stable, disciplined and reliable, and superior in efficiency. Legality and legitimacy were the main traits of bureaucracy. Its characteristics were rules and regulations, hierarchy and accountability, and official documents. Weber described the positions of officials in a bureaucracy exactly as the previous historical sketch: professional training and expertise, impersonal formal position, formal tenured appointment, regular salary and pension, and a career in hierarchy (see for example Stillman, 1992).

Administration and reform in France

State and administration in France

During the *ancien régime* of the Bourbon monarchy, public offices could be bought from or gifted by the crown and were even hereditary. Public offices became saleable and hereditary property and due to their considerable purchase prices had to yield major sources of private income. Offices were sold to the highest bidder, not necessarily to the best qualified. State officials and public administration were distrusted and despised by the French population.

The origin of the highly qualified and esteemed French administration lies in the period of Napoleon Bonaparte's reign, first as consul, soon afterwards as emperor. The administration of Imperial France under Napoleon was transformed into a highly qualified bureaucracy (Thuillier and Tulard, 1984). Public offices required formal entrance examinations, and high qualifications were needed to acquire the function. Public officials were qualified, effective, and furthermore cost-efficient and hard working. Officials were organized in a multitude of professional corps, a small number of which are the so-called 'grand corps' incorporating the administrative elite. These professional corps were self-regulating as to recruitment, appointment, promotion and payment. Since Napoleon the 'haute fonction publique' gained high popular esteem. In view of the tradition of strong central state steering ('étatism') France gradually became an 'administrative state' run by an elite of high officials, organized in the 'grand corps'.

Another characteristic of French administration is the rather fluid osmosis between politics and administration. There is no strict separation between politics and administration. Members of the 'grand corps' can acquire a political function and afterwards return into the administrative functions of the corps. As a matter of fact many ministers, premiers and presidents are former 'haute fonctionnaire public', member of a 'grand corps' and 'ancien élève' of the Ecole Nationale d'Administration (ENA). Besides the frequent political nominations of top officials and the 'cabinets ministériels' illustrate the close links between politics and administration.

Another argument adding to the 'administrative state' is the custom that top officials near the end of their career acquire (well paid) top positions in private business, that is, are appointed by the government as 'président-directeur-général' of one of the many large nationalized state companies – the so called 'pantouflage' (Rouban, 1998). A small elite of ENA-trained top officials run both the public administration and the private business sector. In France the administrative elite governs the whole state, economy and society. Hence the allegation that France is an 'état administrative'.

Administrative reforms in France

The French state and administration typically reflects the Napoleonic model (Wright, 1990). The nation is united and the state serves the general interest. The administration is powerful, centralized, hierarchical, uniform, accountable and controlled. The administration is trained and qualified and is organized in professional 'grand corps'. The traditional French form of public governance ('gestion publique') is strongly juridical, based on principles of equality and the general interest ('intérêt général'), highly centralized and uniform in the whole of France. It possesses 'tutelage' over other instances. Public personnel have a legal 'statut de fonctionnaires'. There is strict financial accountability (Gibert and Thoenig, 1993; Guillaume et al., 2002).

The power of the state was strengthened under the Fifth Republic, established by General Charles de Gaulle in 1958 (Wright, 1989). National plans gave directives and indications for the economic and social developments. National government planning ('Commissariat Général du Plan') reached its heyday in the 1960s and 1970s (Bezes, 2002a). These were the times of rationalization of government activities, the creation of economic models, the use of economic forecasting models, the development of sociological studies of administration (notably by Michel Crozier). In 1968 the 'Rationalization de Choix Budgétaires' (RCB) was established, more or less resembling the North-American Planning Programming and Budgeting System. In the 1970s the issue of administrative reform reached the French political agenda (Bezes, 2002b). Attacking the huge, slow, inflexible state bureaucracy became a political issue. Laws were made to protect the citizens against the administration. Decentralization of the state and administration became a priority and politicians wanted to restore the political control of the state's machinery (Bezes, 2002b).

The nationalization of industry in the beginning of the 1980s increased the public sector. National banks got a firm monetary grip. Government further expanded the role of administration. The civil service permeated all levels of social and economic decision-making, both public and private. The Fifth Republic had, however, also ensured the democratic control and political subordination of administration. The power of administration was also weakened by its internal divisions. The administration is not a coherent unity, but complex, diverse and fragmented. The alleged and potential power of administration may be huge, its effective power is less so (Wright, 1989).

Besides the strong central state steering, other characteristics of the 'specific French model of administration' (Muller, 1992) are its strong sectoral corporatism and compartmentalization, and the typical 'territorial administration' of regions, 'départements' and municipalities. The professional corps, especially the 'grand corps', together with the trade unions have an enormous influence on the personnel management of the French state in terms of entrance examinations, recruitment, promotion and payment. The corps and unions effectively defend their legal privileges. The French civil service is based on a strong legal statute, which is carefully safeguarded and can only be reformed at very high cost. A typical 'territorial' specificity of French administration is the traditional intertwining of local and national politics. Many local politicians and mayors are also active in national politics, often as member of the senate, and therefore have a substantial influence on national government, while the strong central administration has a large network of executive units at the regional and local level.

The traditional Napoleonic model has undergone great pressure (Wright, 1990). Some characteristics have remained unchanged, like the strong role of administration, uniformity, the expertise and 'grand corps', but the administration has also had to adapt to the external pressures. First to the political and social pressures on its fragmentation and juridification. However, due to the economic recession and budgetary crisis, above all to the pressures on efficiency and productivity, privatization, contracting-out and deregulation were also carried out in France. The fiscal crisis and budget retrenchments forced French administration to introduce a more businesslike, managerial style of governance.

In his survey of administrative modernization in France, Rouban (1997) also emphasized the specificity of French administration. The classical

French notion of 'service public' (a crucial notion in the French public sector denoting the core tasks of the state, the tasks that are of 'intérêt général' and carried out by 'l'administration') was still alive and prevented the government from outright neo-liberal 'management' reforms. The prominent role that higher civil servants play in French administration implied the preservation of a social balance within their ranks. Their purchasing power had dropped. They increasingly quit the public service for better paid jobs in the private sector. Their ranks were submitted to a growing politicization. Their career perspectives had deteriorated.

Rouban (1997) distinguished four periods of modernization. First, the period 1984–86 when the economic crisis ended the illusions of the socialist government. The growth of the civil service was severely reduced. Modernization initiatives were taken. A policy of better quality and lower costs was introduced in the public service.

Second, the period of 1986–88 when the right came to power and explicitly developed a neo-liberal reform programme. The civil service was severely criticized for its excessive costs and archaic culture, and hence developed a defensive response that prevented major reforms from actual realization.

The third period 1988–92, when the Socialists returned to power and Rocard became prime minister, formed a breakthrough in modernization. A major mile stone in the reforms has been the 'Renouveau du Service Public' launched by the 'circulaire' of Prime Minister Rocard in February, 1989. This reform consisted of the following cluster of micro-reforms: 'cercles de qualité' (similar to total quality management), 'projets de service' (increase of managerial autonomy for executive agencies), and 'centres de responsabilité' (management contracts between ministry and agency, plus client orientation). The management knowledge and insights were at first mainly to be found with external experts, advisers and consultants, but gradually disseminated into the administration (Bezes, 2002b). According to Rouban (1997) this modernization was a compromise between the progressive introduction of public management and the preservation of the traditional public legal and financial framework.

In the following fourth period the attention shifted from administrative to state reform ('réforme de l'État'). The aforementioned 1994 report on state reforms, the 1995 commissariat for state reform, and the tri-annual plan on state reform in 1996, confirmed this shift. The subject gained an increasing importance within the administration, and was increasingly institutionalized (Bezes, 2002b). It became a political hot issue. Several prime ministers put 'réforme de l'Etat' on their own political agenda (Bezes, 2001). The reforms were not only of the public management type, such as result-oriented budgeting, customer orientation, management contracts, human resource management, and more. The attention also shifted towards more fundamental state reform. Deconcentration and decentralization of central state functions were addressed (for example the 1992 Act on Territorial

Administration). The 1994 report on state reforms addressed questions about the future global role of the state, and a commissariat for state reform was created in 1995, which published a tri-annual plan on state reform in 1996. After the Juppé government in 1995 added the more fundamental issue of 'state reform' to the 'public service reform', the Jospin government in 1997 opted for a 'state reform' based on two main missions: proximity of the state (deconcentration and decentralization), and a more effective state. The Raffarin government continued along these lines, and announced in 2002 its three main reform objectives: a better effectiveness based on the diffusion of a managerial culture in administration, an improvement of human resources management, and an improvement in customer satisfaction by the simplification of regulations. The Raffarin state reform consists of three core themes: effectiveness, proximity and simplicity.

According to Chevallier (2004) the 'réforme de l'Etat' has gained strong political commitment (the Raffarin government has a 'ministre de la Fonction Publique, de la Réforme de l'Etat et de l'Aménagement du Territoire', assisted by a vice-minister for state reform) and has increasingly been institutionalized in the administration, in which the three 'trans-sectorial' ministries (Finance, Public Function, and Home Affairs) have played an important role (Bezes, 2002b). Chevallier (2004) characterized the state reforms by three essential aspects. First, a reconsideration of the missions of the state. The role of the state in economy, social security and more, has become more modest. The 'regulating' state can devolve its operational executive tasks to independent bodies. Second, the principle of proximity. The traditional centrally con-trolled territorial administration has been enforced by deconcentration and decentralization. Third, the need for effectiveness, such as the three E's of public management, value for money, service quality, customer satisfaction, and result-oriented budgeting.

According to Chevallier (2004) and Rouban (2003) French state reforms were not cosmetic and superficial, but quite fundamental. However, the strongly institutionalized counter-forces against reform, such as the legal civil service statute, the mighty corps and trade unions, and the close links between the political and administrative elite, remain intact in France.

Administration and reform in Italy

State formation in Italy

In Italy a united nation-state was only established in the second half of the nineteenth century (Clark, 1990; Smith, 1997). A nationalistic movement led to a revolt, the 'Risorgimento' (1848–70), led by Mazzini and Garibaldi. National unification was taken over by the Piedmonte Kingdom (northern area around Torino), which ultimately succeeded in occupying the entire peninsula, after military assistance from France and Prussia. So the 'Risorgimento' in 1870 led to the Kingdom of Italy, a constitutional liberal democracy, supported by the northern towns. The rest of Italy considered the nation formation as a military occupation by the northern Piedmonte, with foreign military help. Real unification and nation-state formation was a long process, in which education in the national language and military conscription have played a major role. The division between the prosperous industrial northern Italy and the poor rural south, with the administrative centre, Rome, in between, still exists today.

The parliamentary democracy after the First World War led to such unrest and chaos that the call for rest and order culminated in a dictatorship. With the help of industrialists and large landowners, and not hindered by police, army and government, the fascist terror movement in 1922 led a march of the black-shirt militias on Rome. The government resigned and the king appointed Mussolini as prime minister. The seizure of power by Mussolini soon led to a fascist dictatorship which was only ended in 1943 when the Allied troops fought their way north after their landing in Sicily. The king fired Mussolini as premier and Italy quickly reached an armistice in the idle hope of post-war benevolence of the Allied victors. The Nazis promptly reacted with an occupation. A bloody partisan war of armed resistance groups followed.

The trauma of fascist dictatorship further enhanced the traditional distrust and dislike of the state by the Italians. Italians of old have a strongly individualistic 'civic culture', in which the family stands central, and a very low 'collectivistic' attitude (Putnam et al., 1993). Rules and regulations are made to be violated. The trauma of fascism and Mussolini has of course pressed its mark on post-war politics. The king, who had not offered resistance to Mussolini, was sent away and a Republic was announced. Parliamentary democracy was henceforth considered a valuable commodity.

Post-war politics in Italy

After the end of fascism and the Second World War, Italian politics became dominated by three large parties, the Christian-Democrats, the Socialists, and the Communists. Although the first post-war cabinet was a co-operative grand coalition aimed at the common restoration and renewal, the Communists were soon excluded from government power. Political parties in Italy are not only advocates of a political ideology, but above all machines that provide jobs, pensions, payments, seeds, insurances and the more. Clientelism and patronage are major features of politics in Italy, and so by implication is corruption. Italian parties are certainly not homogeneous, but strongly divided into factions that compete for power and resources. The internal party divisions usually are much stronger than the rivalry between parties. The divisiveness of politics is furthermore enhanced by the parliamentary division into sectoral commissions, which rather autonomously carry out their own relevant legislation (Clark, 1990; Ginsbourg, 1990).

Popular dissatisfaction with the Italian political system has resulted in a rather revolutionary reaction in the 1970s with many protests and riots. This was also accompanied by violent terrorism. The popular dissatisfaction again resulted in the 1990s in a massive protest, this time against the widespread corruption, the so-called 'tangentopoli', investigated in operation 'clean hands' by the Milanese magistrate Di Pietro (Morlino and Tarchi, 1996). The electoral punishment of the Christian-Democrats because of this resulted in the political outsider and entrepreneurial private businessman Berlusconi coming to political power (Smith, 1997).

The political system changed in the 1990s (Ferrera and Gualmini, 2003). In 1993 the electoral system changed from proportional representation to majority, leading to a political bipolarism with two dominant party coalitions, resulting in a more stable parliament and government (Bartolini et al., 2004; Cassese, 2002). The traditional five parties evaporated in the 1994 elections. The traditional political establishment more or less vanished. New parties (for example Lega Nord and Forza Italia) emerged. Governments became stronger. The 'technical' cabinets of Amato, Ciampi and Dini were less influenced by party politics. The first 1994 Berlusconi government was unstable, but his 'house of freedom' coalition won the elections in 2001 with an overwhelming majority. Prime Minister Berlusconi exercised strong personal leadership, which was unique in Italy (Ferrera and Gualmini, 2003).

Administration in Italy

After the Second World War the ruling Christian-Democrats had inherited an old-fashioned, slow, legalistic, overstaffed civil service, which was commonly considered to sabotage rather than support modernizations (Cassese, 1984; Clark, 1990). The answer of Christian-Democrat politics and government was to circumvent the official administration ('sottogoverno'). Political control over a ministerial department was strengthened by the creation of ministerial cabinets, which assisted the minister, and guided and controlled the department. Furthermore, most departmental top officials were political appointees. Nevertheless civil service and the regular administration were still considered incapable of doing anything more than simple executive routine works. Politicians have therefore created a 'parallel administration' to carry out the really important post-war social, economic and welfare planning and policy-making. A huge and complex apparatus of public bodies, agencies, para-statal entities, public enterprises and more was established, thereby by-passing the regular civil service. No need to say that all senior positions in these organizations were political. Agencies, positions and jobs were divided between the political parties (and internal party factions) so that everyone acquired 'a piece of the cake'. The lack of effective democratic and especially financial control over this multitude of agencies, allowed the politicians to generate substantial political funds. Political control over local government, health care, public transport and the like, implied the control over an enormous number of jobs, which could be given to political supporters and clients (Cassese, 1984; Clark, 1990). The Italian civil service has a number of characteristics (Cassese, 1984, 1993; Clark, 1990). First, it has a huge size, the more so in the south. In Italy the civil service includes teachers, nurses, railwaymen and postmen. Even allowing for this, its size is still enormous compared to other Western European countries.

Second, the civil service consists predominantly of southerners. Civil servants usually come from southern, conservative, low-class backgrounds. Due to the high unemployment in the south, civil service positions often were the only guarantee for job and career security. Northerners could get better paid jobs in trade and industry. Party patronage provided the jobs for loyal followers. Although entrance into the civil service is officially regulated via formal examinations, in the south the majority of new civil servants did not pass that formal route, but a political one. A civil servant is ill-paid and has low status. As a consequence civil servants are frequently not interested in good work performance. Side jobs are not unusual. The poor service quality and cost-inefficiency of the civil service are notorious.

Thirdly senior civil servants are mainly recruited from lawyers. Italian universities have exceptionally high numbers of law students. Lawyers consequently suffer from high unemployment. Acquiring a job in the civil service often is the only employment possible. The legalistic attitude of lawyers combined with their low-class, backward southern origins, makes the civil service conservative, slow, inefficient, and opposed to reforms.

In his analysis of the higher civil service, the public law professor and minister of the civil service from 1993 to 1994 in the Ciampi government, Cassese (1999), called it an 'ossified world'. The higher civil service is not part of the political leadership unlike the top officials in France and Britain. The failure of the Scuola Superiore della Pubblica Amministrazione, to meet its original objectives as a training and selection school for top officials, illustrates the difference with the ENA in France (Della Cannanea, 1998). There is a strict division between politics and administration. Officials have a safe job and career guarantee, but have hardly any power or status. Top officials had an absolutely secure career perspective. Periodical promotions were based on seniority only, and not on performance evaluations that could be politically endangered. As a consequence top officials were old before acquiring senior ranks, and therefore only remained shortly in top positions (Cassese, 1984). Everything in the civil service was formally, legally regulated in order to ensure absolute security and political non-interference. The majority of top officials were southern recruited lawyers.

Politicians had no influence on this rigid, inflexible, non-adaptive, reform-opposed system. Politicians exercised influence by political appointments or dismissals of top officials, and by creating their own ministerial cabinets. Most importantly politicians had circumvented the rigid civil service by setting up a parallel administration of public bodies and agencies. Top officials were well aware of this deadlock. Distrust of politicians, sabotage, and extremely legalistic behaviour were the result. In return for absolute job and career security top officials have lost all power and influence. Policy-making is not carried out by officials. Preparation of legislation is done in the ministerial cabinets. Officials only perform executive routine work, yet even that can be sabotaged. Many laws and acts are not implemented and executed by the administration.

In order to realize its political plans and policies the government mainly uses the instrument of legislation. The number of laws, decrees and regulations passed in the Italian parliament is relatively huge. This, however, mainly enhances the influence of parliament over administration, and even further diminishes the government's influence (Cassese, 1984).

Administrative reforms in Italy

The 1990s were the era of state and administrative reform in Italy. The political turmoil and social uproar against political corruption ('tangentopoli') formed a fertile ground for reforms. Successive civil service ministers carried out a number of far-reaching state reforms. As mentioned before the electoral system was modified from a proportional into a majority system, resulting in a more stable parliament and government (Ferrera and Gualmini, 2003). Fundamental state reforms were the strengthening of local and regional government by decentralization, for example in the 'Bassanini laws' of 1997 (Bassanini, 2002). The national executive was also restructured. The power of the prime minister was enhanced and the number of ministries was reduced.

An important administrative reform was the distinction made in 1993 between government steering and policy-making on the one hand, and executive management and administration on the other (Battini, 1998; Cassese, 2002). The latter became the exclusive responsibility of officials. Their labour conditions were privatized. Their job was no longer based on the 'public function statute' but on a contract. In 1998 the executive management tasks and responsibilities of the 'dirigenza' (higher civil service) were further specified.

Another important reform for the functioning of the higher civil service was the legalization in 1998 and 2002 of political nominations of top officials (Cassese, 2002). Officials had an absolutely secure career perspective, promotions were exclusively based on seniority, so top officials were old and could only be replaced upon retirement. With the 1998 law the 55 highest officials (secretary-generals and heads of departments) could be appointed by a new government within 90 days of its installment. Directors were to be nominated for a duration of two to seven years. And 5 per cent of the 'dirigenza' could consist of external appointments. The 2002 law went even further. Division heads could also be appointed within 90 days of a new government's installment, and the maximum duration for director-generals was reduced to three years, for directors to five years. Now 10 per cent of the 'dirigenza' was to be externally appointed. According to Cassese (2002) the main reason for this reform was that the newly created political parties wanted influence, jobs and power. The effect was that top officials became highly dependent on their minister and consequentially had to be absolutely loyal. A side-effect was that a function had now to be paid for twice, both for the predecessor who was sent on study-leave, and his successor. According to Cassese (2002) this reform broke the traditional deadlock of a civil service with career security but without power. Officials have gained the power over executive management and their salaries have been doubled.

In his analysis of the reforms in the 1990s Capano (2003) distinguished four main parts in the reform measures.

First, the decentralization of the state to regions and municipalities. The imbalance between strong central state power – most tax collections are central – and decentral government – where most public expenditures take place – was redressed. This decentralization of authority was accompanied by a management reform of local government. Emphasis was put on new city managers, better accounting and control, and performance-related payment was introduced.

Second, central state administration was reformed. The notorious fragmentation and lack of co-ordination, was countered by a reduction of the number of ministries, and by eliminating duplications and segmentation. Businesslike management was introduced in executive agencies.

Third, the civil service was reformed. A clear separation between politics and administration was made. And a privatization of the working relationships and labour conditions was introduced.

Fourth, a simplification of regulation and administration was carried out by a reduction of the number of laws and regulations, and by deregulation.

Capano (2003) showed that the usual list of public management principles, such as result-orientedness, value for money, citizen-customer orientedness, customer satisfaction, service quality, performance control, performance-related payment, and temporary contract, all played an important role in these reforms. However, he reached the conclusion that in actual fact nothing much really changed, that the hegemony of the legalistic paradigm was not broken. Public management reforms have not become a new administrative paradigm in Italy, and have not replaced the traditional juridical paradigm. The reforms have been adapted and incorporated in the legalistic paradigm. Reform in Italy, as any other government activity, exclusively takes place by legislation, regulation and decree. This observation is shared by others (Panozzo, 2000), who stipulates that the introduction of businesslike management techniques like accounting ('controllo di gestione') is based on an economical frame of reference that is completely different from the juridical way of thinking. Accountability based on economical effectiveness and efficiency is contradictory to legal accountability. The accountability reform has, however, been translated by the lawyers into their juridical language, as the reform had to be framed in legislation. Economic management discourse was translated into legal discourse. The reformers did not want that to happen. The reform was meant to break down the legalistic monopoly. Apparently, that has failed.

Administration and reform in Spain

State formation in Spain

Although under the dictatorship of General Franco (1939–75) Spain played a marginal role in democratic Europe, one should realize that Spain is one of the oldest states in Europe and has a proud history of imperial grandeur. Under the Habsburg monarchy in the sixteenth and seventeenth centuries Spain had been a mighty empire in Europe as well as overseas. America had been discovered by the great voyage of Columbus. Like Portugal, which became independent of Spain in 1640, Spain profited from the huge wealth that was shipped in from its colonies. The Habsburg Empire, however, had gradually lost its grandeur in the eighteenth century and further faded away in the nineteenth century after the defeat by Napoleon, a series of revolts, and the loss of the American colonies (Carr, 1980; Heywood, 1995; Magone, 2004).

Politics in nineteenth-century Spain consisted mainly of the fight between progressive Liberals and conservative Catholics. The Carlists attempted in two civil wars to destroy liberalism and its institutions and to restore a traditional Catholic society. Periods of reactionary conservatism were alternated by periods of moderate liberal dominance in politics and government. Changes in power in Spain traditionally came in the form of a military coup d'état by revolting military officers ('pronunciamento') and a revolutionary uprising with street barricades manned by middle-class progressives and working-class labourers. Both the conservative Carlists and the progressive Liberals had no choice but to rely on the support of sympathetic generals. Instead of elections, the 'pronunciamento' was the instrument of political change. The choice of government was in the hands of the army.

Spanish governments were a continuous alternation of power between the conservative and liberal parties, in fact maintaining the power balance unaltered, disguised in a façade of parliamentary democracy.

The political power division in the capital Madrid was enforced at the local level through electoral manipulation by local party bosses ('caciquismo'). The local party bosses ('caciques'), by means of patronage, clientelism (Hopkin, 2001) and corruption (the party boss was in control of the local administration and judiciary, and could thus provide his clientele with a variety of jobs, or grant licences, tax reductions, arrange favourable court judgements, and so on), ensured that the local elections yielded the outcome that had been predetermined by the government in Madrid. The opposition party was granted a decent number of seats to keep the balance. Parliamentary democracy was a farce, the party negotiations had determined the results before the elections.

Protests and revolts were frequent. The late nineteenth-century rise of a socialist working-class movement did not leave Spain unaffected. Moreover, Spain also knew an active anarchist labour movement. And above all, Spain had strong separatist movements in the form of the regional nationalism of particularly Catalonia (capital Barcelona) and the Basque country (capital Bilbao). By the turn of the century Spain was fiercely divided between mutually hostile groups, mounting to an escalation of violence after the First World War. The escalation of strikes, insurrections, military suppression, revolution and street warfare, in 1923 led to the fall of the parliamentary system and the dictatorship of General Primo de Rivera. He too proved unable to construct a stable political system and had to resign in 1930. The Second Republic, proclaimed in 1931, was a progressive and brave experiment to try to convert Spain into a genuine democracy. The many deep mutual hostilities between bitter fighting groups, however, rendered the attempt in vain (Carr, 1980).

Franco dictatorship

General Franco's military uprising in 1936 started the savage Civil War – symbolized in Pablo Picasso's famous artistic condemnation of the atrocities in Guernica – which resulted in the complete annihilation of all progressive forces and ultimate restoration of the reactionary conservative Spanish political forces. The times of political balance between Progressives and Conservatives were over. General Franco, the victor of the Civil War, ruled Spain as 'Caudillo' by the grace of God. The dictator installed an authoritarian conservative regime without any room for progressive reforms. State, government and administration were strongly centralized and the bureaucracy became deeply politicized. Only trustworthy Falangists were admitted to occupy political and administrative positions.

Franco's economic policy to restore the war-devastated Spanish economy had been to install a state-centred corporatism. The strong state regulation of the Spanish economy had led to a protective insulation from the economic world market. That autarkic economic policy reached its limitations with the industrialization of the 1950s. The technocrats associated with the Catholic lay order 'Opus Dei' became the architects of a new open economic policy. Spain became a normal market economy with free competition and non-regulated prices, and the non-protected national economy opened up to the Western world market. The economic development plans led to an immense economic growth rate in the 1960s. Although Franco claimed the success, the 'economic miracle' probably was the inevitable spurt that industrialization brings to a backward economy (Carr, 1980). The economic prosperity of Spain in the 1970s led to rising expectations for more political freedom. The unchanged authoritarian political ideology of the Franco regime contrasted with the open modern economics of free capitalism.

Regional separatism has been a central issue in Spanish politics since the nineteenth century (Carr, 1980; Heywood, 1995). As a reaction to the development of a single united Spanish national identity, regions became increasingly aware of their own cultural traditions and culture. The industrialized and economically prosperous regions of Catalonia (textile industry) and Basque country (steel industry and ship building) became sufficiently powerful to make regional demands to the central capital Madrid (Castile). The reaction of the political power centre Madrid to regional demands varied over time. In periods of progressive republics some regional diversity was permitted, but the conservatives usually reacted with rigid centralism. Under General Franco state centralism was extreme and rigid. That repressive regime led to the escalation of the regional demands of the Basque country into violent protests and hard-line armed separatism, the ETA terrorist actions. When the Franco repression ended and democracy began, it was hoped that Basque separatism would no longer have to rely on violence and terrorism, the more so as the new democratic constitution of 1978 granted considerable autonomy to the regions. That hope was, however, dashed.

Government and politics in democratic Spain

After the death of Franco in 1975 a transition to constitutional democracy was inevitable, but the Spanish tradition of violent uprisings and revolutions and the horrible memory of the savage Civil War was a frightening perspective (Heywood, 1995; Gibbons, 1999; Magone, 2004). The problem was that, for a peaceful transition, the vested rulers of the Franco regime had to voluntarily hand over their powers to the democratic newcomers. Prime Minister Suarez, himself a former secretary-general of the Falange party and therefore trusted by the Francoists, managed to dismantle the regime. He legalized the formerly clandestine Socialist and Communist parties, called free general elections, and drew up a democratic constitution in consensus with all the political parties in parliament (including Communists and Socialists), which was approved by parliament in 1978. It made Spain a pluralist liberal democracy, and linked up Spain to the other Western European democracies. Membership of the European Community and the NATO became high political priorities.

King Juan Carlos, the legal successor of General Franco, played an active role in the transition to democracy, and later in saving the new democracy after the military occupation of the parliament (Cortes) by Lieutenant-Colonel Tejero in 1981. It made the formal but mainly symbolic head of the state immensely popular.

The constitutional balance of powers between the executive and the legislature emphasizes the stability and strength of government. Spain has tried to avoid the political instability and weakness of post-war French and Italian governments. Within government the prime minister is not merely a 'primus inter pares' but the leader of the Council of Ministers. The prime minister is free to appoint or dismiss members of the government. Prime Minister Gonzalez has indeed become a very dominant political leader during his long period in office (1982–96). His Socialist Party (PSOE) possessed an absolute parliamentary majority between 1982 and 1993. The Centrum Democrat Party (UCD) disintegrated during the 1980s, thus enabling the Socialist government to rule virtually without opposition. Only in the early 1990s did the centre-right Popular Party (PP), under the leadership of Aznar, gain sufficient support to act as serious opposition (and won the elections in 1996). The role of parliament was rather marginalized during the period of Socialist hegemony. Political decisions were usually made without involvement of parliamentary politics.

The legitimacy of political parties was challenged by a series of corruption scandals in the early 1990s involving leading political figures. In 1990 the brother of the deputy prime minister (Guerra) was accused of having used socialist party funds for private business purposes. As in Italy, judges and magistrates played a central role in the revelation and prosecution of these political corruption scandals. The Spanish judiciary, which in public opinion was blamed as highly inefficient, due to lack of staff and resources, and as highly politicized, due to Socialist Party appointments, could well use the positive mass media coverage (Heywood, 1995).

Administration in Spain

Modern Spanish bureaucracy was founded in the early nineteenth century along the lines of the French Napoleonic model, that is, a unitary state serving the general interest, with a centralized, hierarchical, uniform administration. The other characteristic of the Napoleonic model, that is, a professional 'corps' of trained and qualified experts, was also introduced. In 1833 the traditional practice that professional posts in the bureaucracy were hereditary, was abolished. Entrance into the administration was only possible after extensive training and examination, which led to the creation of professional special corps ('cuerpos') for different administrative tasks (engineers, tax inspectors, diplomats, and so on). Political parties reacted with the introduction of a spoils system, whereby officials were replaced after elections. The spoils system was abolished by the 1918 'Maura statute', an attempt to modernize, rationalize and professionalize the administration, and to fight corruption. Political patronage, nepotism and corruption, however, continued after the Maura reform (Alba, 1998; Heywood, 1995; Subirats, 1990).

The Spanish bureaucracy was notoriously inefficient. Real political power during the turbulent period of uprisings and revolutions, in fact was in the hands of the military. They had much more influence on state affairs than the civilian administration. After General Franco's victory in 1939 the civil administration was completely 'purged' of all republican sympathizers and became strongly politicized. All civil servants had to declare political loyalty to the regime. It is only after the Franco regime consolidated and became highly centralized and bureaucratized, that the professional administrative elite (the special corps) became influential (Alba, 1998; Heywood, 1995; Subirats, 1990). After the initial phase of the Franco regime, when administrative positions were given to loyal followers and as reward for heroic performances in the Civil War, a process of professionalization of the administration started. After the Second World War Spain was obliged to provide its population with some degree of social benefits and services. Political loyalty and ideological management was not sufficient to run a welfare administration, professional expertise and skills were indispensable to fulfil such a complex task. This led to a sort of reform in the late 1950s and 1960s, which Subirats (1990) typified as 'juridification'. Administrative structures and authorities were formalized. The civil service system was rationalized and professionalized. The reforms were juridical and procedural in nature. The reforms were an attempt to create a Western European sort of *Rechtsstaat*, a more rational and professional administration, while leaving the political authoritarianism intact. The Opus Dei technocrats passed a number of administrative reforms, particularly the 1964 law on civil state officials, creating a central personnel body, unifying the general corps, and restructuring the payment system. The reform only had marginal effects, but did lay the legal basis for the later merit-based system of selection of top officials, which was later adapted by the socialist reforms.

Administrative reforms in democratic Spain

The first decade after the transition to democracy Spanish administration remained relatively unaffected by reforms (Alba, 1995, 1998; Heywood, 1995; Subirats, 1990, 1999; Zapico-Goni, 1993). The administration was not 'purged', on the contrary, former leading politicians from the Falangist party played an important role in the transition and former high-ranking, politicized career-professionals maintained tied positions in the civil service. Spain had more serious and urgent problems. Establishing pluralist democracy, creating a new democratic constitution, defining constitutional institutions like parliament, government and the judiciary, developing the legal framework of a *Rechtsstaat*, were given higher priority than the 'technical' reform of 'the machinery of government'.

Moreover, the constitutional creation of regional autonomy by establishing seventeen autonomous 'communities' constituted a major reform of the state and administration.

Politicians did realize that administrative reforms were desirable and necessary. The bad reputation of Spanish bureaucratic backwardness, and the lack of a modern and efficient public administration were considered major obstacles for Spain's competitive prospects by economists. When the Socialist party won the elections in 1982, administrative reform was recognized as an important issue. The Socialists made up a political programme for the modernization of bureaucracy, but the effects were only marginal. When the Socialists in 1986 again won an absolute majority, a more vigorous attempt was made (Alba, 1998; Subirats, 1990). A ministry of Public Administration was established. The new minister began with a thorough two-year study resulting in a 1989 report 'Reflections on Modernizing the Administration' that was to serve as the basis for reform proposals. The 1992 plan for modernization formed a departure from the traditional legalistic approach of administration. It openly embarked on a managerial course, emphasizing result-orientation, effectiveness, efficiency and customers.

Public management reforms

In the 1980s, when most West European states were carrying out managerial reforms and downsizing their public budget, Spain was just beginning to build up its hitherto relatively small public sector. The post-war expansion of the Western welfare state in Spain only occurred after Franco's death. In Spain the population demanded an expansion of public services and welfare goods (Heywood, 1995; Torres and Pina 2004; Gallego, 2003). It is only in the 1990s, with the EU treaty of Maastricht functioning as an external pressure for budget restriction, that budgetary retrenchment became a real priority in Spanish politics.

The reforms in Spain in the 1990s were similar to the worldwide New Public Management reforms (Torres and Pina, 2004).

Privatization under the socialist government was not so much based on a neo-liberal ideology, but rather on neutral rational efficiency arguments (Gibbons, 1999; Heywood, 1995). However, privatization did not mean that the Spanish state was no longer in control. The Socialists maintained a major controlling share in most privatized companies.

In Spain the municipal provision of public utilities like water and electricity, was carried out in public–private partnerships, long before this became a modern management technique. The Spanish public sector used to be so small that services could simply not be provided by local government and were therefore left in the hands of the private sector (Torres and Pina, 2004).

Separation between policy and execution and increasing the autonomy of executive agencies, has also taken place. Spain has its own traditional sort of 'quangos', together with numerous public bodies, agencies, corporations and foundations (Gibbons, 1999). Their existence is, however, historical and hardly related to managerial arguments.

Neither has the introduction of new budgetary techniques such as accrual accounting, resulted in a widespread change of the financial management system of Spanish central, regional and local administration.

Torres and Pina (2004) reached the conclusion that in Spain managerial reforms have only been introduced piecemeal as a set of isolated initiatives, without an encompassing reform plan, and without real political backing. Gallego (2003) explained the failure of the reforms in terms of political controversies between ministries, and shifting political priorities. The legalistic bureaucratic attitude still prevails in administration. Torres and Pina (2004) concluded that the major challenge for reform is to transform the traditional conservative corporatist organization of Spanish administration.

Resistance to change: the special corps

Let us finally pay some attention to the factor that seems most to hinder administrative reforms in Spain, the administrative elite organized in the special corps ('cuerpos'). The reforms had to be carried out by the despised bureaucracy itself, and not surprisingly Spanish civil servants were rather sceptical of the proposed changes. The preservation of privileges was the concern of civil service trade unions, but above all of the elite corps (Alba, 1995, 1998; Alvarez de Cienfuegos, 1999; Heywood, 1995; Subirats, 1990).

The historical origin of the corps was to counter-balance the politicization of administration. Within every ministry specialized groups of officials (special corps) existed with a specific university degree, selected by examination, who could not be removed. The special corps were self-regulating in terms of recruitment, promotion, appointments and payment. The members of these corps had a monopoly over the top positions in the ministries and were relatively better paid. During the Franco regime the special corps came to dominate virtually all decision-making in every department. Although the 1964 reform measures by the Opus Dei technocrats introduced a generalist corps to counter-balance the fragmentation and compartmentalization caused by the special corps, their power remained intact. During the first years of the democracy many former senior civil servants were part of the centre-right Suarez government, which had no intention of confronting the higher bureaucracy. When the Socialists won the elections in 1982 they attempted to reduce the power of the corps by opening up top positions for non-career employees. The main effect was a massive politicization of the bureaucratic elite by a wave of political appointments in administrative top positions.

The corps members still occupy the majority of administrative top positions, even the posts of politically appointed director-generals. At the ministries of Foreign Affairs, and Economy and Finance, they constitute virtually all top positions. Some ministries are monopolized by a single elite corps (for example diplomats in Foreign Affairs, labour inspectors in Labour). Elsewhere different special corps compete for top positions within the same ministry. The ministry of Public Administration is dominated by members of the generalist corps of state civil administrators (Alvarez de Cienfuegos, 1999).

Political party patronage has further increased in the 1980s with the opening up of top positions for externals, and the creation of 'ministerial cabinets' (technical and political advisers who are personally selected by the minister) in all ministries. The victory of the centre-right Popular Party (PP) in 1996 and advent of the Aznar government, did not change the political patronage system. Within a year almost all top officials appointed by the Socialists had been replaced and thousands of lower ranking civil servants also replaced. Notice though that both the Socialist and the Popular Party's political appointments were often filled by highly qualified senior officials. The Spanish political and administrative elite is strongly intertwined. Senior bureaucrats occupy posts in political parties, government and parliament, as well as in industry (Alvarez de Cienfuegos, 1999; Baena, 2002).

Conclusions and discussion: reforms in the south

Although the introduction might have made the misleading impression that France, Italy and Spain share the same Napoleonic state tradition and would therefore be similar in their current forms of state, administration and reform, the differences are profound. The three even differ as to the very characteristics of the Napoleonic model: contemporary Spain and Italy do not have a strong central unitary state, but a regionally decentralized state. The legalistic *Rechtsstaat* was restored in Italy only after the war, and only recently introduced in Spain. Italy does not have a powerful central administration, neither does it have an elite of professional top officials.

More than managerial reforms

The form and content of the public management reforms differed, although in all three countries the predominant legalistic thinking of state and administration represented an important feature. Apparently the failure to break through the monopoly of legalism was indeed a main obstacle in Italy. In France that factor also played an important role in the debate on public management reforms. In Spain, however, that can hardly be a main obstacle as the juridification of the administration only dates from recent times. Here the main obstacle rather seemed to be that other more fundamental reforms were more urgent. The transition to democracy, the creation of a constitution and democratic institutions, and the establishment of a democratic *Rechtsstaat* were more urgent than effectiveness and efficiency. Only after the consolidation of democracy and the expansion of the public welfare sector, did Spain turn to the 'technical-financial' problem of public management. Moreover, Spain and Italy have carried out administrative reforms that were politically more important than managerial efficiency, that is, the decentralization and regionalization of the state. In France too, that type of 'réforme de l'État' was considered more important than mere administrative reforms, let alone managerial ones.

Three sorts of administrative reform

Roughly speaking three sorts of administrative reforms can be discerned in the southern countries Italy and Spain (as well as in Greece and Portugal) (Sotiropoulos, 2004; Spanou, 1996).

First 'rationalization and professionalization' in the Weberian bureaucratic sense, that is, introduction of *Rechtsstaat* type of rules and procedures. The juridification resulted in legalism and formalism. In Spain this 'juridification' type of reform was first introduced in the 1950s and 1960s (Subirats, 1990) when the Opus Dei technocrats were allowed to modernize the economy and administration. In Italy juridification of the administration also was a reaction to the strong post-war politicization, to protect the administration from political interference, to ensure job and career security of civil servants. Another explanation for the strong degree of formalism and juridification is that in Southern Europe most civil servants were and still are administrative lawyers.

Second, 'democratization' of the civil service in the sense of getting rid of the old regime's reactionary forces in administration. The supporters of the former dictatorships were replaced by supporters of the new democracy. This purging of the civil service actually hardly happened. After the transition to democracy in Spain and Portugal the old administrative elite remained in place and in charge. The so called 'democratization of the civil service' mainly was an excuse for the party that won the election to replace the former officials by its own followers. The arrival into power of the Socialist Party (PSOE) in Spain in 1982 was a massive example of the spoils system. That practice was repeated by the Popular Party in 1996 when Aznar won the elections. In Greece the alternation between Socialist Party (PASOK) and the New Democracy (ND) has time and again led to removals and replacements of officials (Spanou, 1996). And that is also the case in Portugal (Sotiropoulos, 2004; Sousa, 2001).

Third, 'modernization' in the public management sense. Typically that has included budget deficits, cutbacks, need for efficiency increases, in short, New Public Management. In Southern Europe that budgetary recognition was mainly due to external pressure, that is, the EU (Maastricht) treaty on maximum debt and deficit, and started only in the early 1990s. Spain (as well as Greece and Portugal) only started to expand their welfare sectors after their transition to democracy (military revolution in Portugal in April 1974, end of the colonels' regime in Greece in July 1974), so the 1980s were a period of enormous growth of the public sector, contrary to the retrenchments and retreat of the welfare states in Western Europe at that time. Moreover, public management reforms were often abused by politicians. Privatization, contracting-out and public–private partnerships were abused to generate personal and party incomes (corruption). Human resource management reforms were often abused to increase political interference and political appointments. Public management reforms turned out to have small or even adverse effects.

Failure of reforms in the south

In southern countries like Spain and Italy (as well as Portugal and Greece) a main problem of reforms is that, more or less irrespective of their form and content, they never seem to have had significant effects (Alba, 1995, 1998; Cassese, 1984, 1993, 1999; Heywood, 1995; Subirats, 1990; Zapico-Goni, 1993). The failure of administrative reforms has a long tradition, and is not restricted to recent public management reforms. According to Sotiropoulos (2004), besides the legalism and formalism in southern administrations, a main reason for reform failure was the politicization of the administrations. In Southern Europe the civil service is not about providing high quality, low cost public services, but a reservoir of jobs and favours to be distributed by political parties to their supporters. Top officials of the party previously in office are always replaced by loyal followers of the new incoming government. In other words, political clientelism at the bottom of the civil service and at the top. A side-effect is widespread corruption (Williams et al., 2000). Bureaucracies in southern countries were and still are notorious for their rigidity, inefficiency, bad service delivery and lack of client orientation.

Socio-economical and cultural context

Before proceeding with an analysis of the typical southern characteristics of state and administration, let us first have a look at contextual factors.

As to the socio-economical context, Sotiropouolos (2004) noted that Southern European states have traditionally 'assisted' the development of capitalism for a longer time and to a greater extent than north-western European states. The Italian and Spanish state already in the nineteenth century actively interfered in the economy through patronage of certain industrial sectors (Clark, 1990; Carr, 1980). Public ownership of industries in sectors like textile, steel, shipbuilding and railways was common. So were protectionism, subsidies and control of economic sectors. The principal personal benefactors of this state assistance were elite families of large landowners, industrialists, bankers and ship-owners. Active state control of industry and economy existed in Italy and Spain before Mussolini and Franco created their own forms of 'state corporatism'. Neither should it be confused with the postwar economic planning by, for example, the French government.

Another economic similarity is that both in Italy and Spain economical development took place unevenly, concentrated in northern Italy, respectively in Catalonia and the Basque country. In both countries that formed the material ground for regional separatist movements. Notice furthermore that both countries experienced an enormous economic boom in the 1960s. That transferred Italy from an underdeveloped economy into the top ten of economic world powers. Although not that successful in Spain, the economic prosperity certainly contributed to its transition to democracy and was the precondition for the post-Franco expansion of the public welfare sector.

As to the socio-cultural context, the individualistic 'civic culture' in Italy is notorious. Italians despise the state, have hardly any collectivist beliefs, norms and values, and the only thing they attach value to is their own individual family. Spanish civic culture is also individualistic in European comparison. The French do highly esteem the state, although they certainly do not have such strong authoritarian state traditions (*Obrigkeitsstaat*) and collective beliefs and values as the Germans.

A marked difference is their national identity and culture. Whereas France is a centuries-old nation-state with a united national identity, the nineteenth-century development of a national identity and culture in Spain reinforced the regional consciousness of their own separate cultures. In Italy the formation in 1870 of the united nation-state was considered as a military occupation by the northern Piedmonte in the rest of the country.

Government, politics and administration

Notwithstanding its state reform of decentralization, France remains a unitary centralized state. Spain and Italy are decentralized regional states. The decentralization measures in the 1997 'Bassanini reforms' following the public uproar of the early 1990s, were considered more important than managerial reforms. The violent regional separatism, which Spain inherited from the Franco repression, forced it to grant the regions substantial autonomy in the democratic constitution of 1978, leaving little time and energy for other reforms.

According to Pollitt and Bouckaert (2004) differences in political significance of the government and its leader, can explain the extent and degree of reforms. In France the Fifth Republic guaranteed a strong government and president. And administrative reforms did become a high agenda priority of politicians, ministers, premiers and presidents. However, apart from the 'circulaire' that premier Rocard attached his name to, French politicians seemed more interested in state reforms than in managerial ones.

The 1978 Spanish constitution also guaranteed a strong government and a strong prime minister. Moreover, the Socialists twice won an absolute majority in parliament, so that Gonzalez was able to personally govern the country without much parliamentary interference. Administrative reforms stood high on the political agenda. Nevertheless administrative reforms were hardly effective in Spain.

After the post-war restoration of democracy in Italy, parliamentary politics came to dominate, governments were weak and unstable, and prime ministers were almost powerless mediators between a multitude of conflicting political factions. The 1993 change in the electoral system gradually moved the multi-party consensus system to political bipolarism with two dominant party coalitions, leading to stronger and more stable governments, and to stronger personal leadership of the prime minister. The fact that many reforms took place during the 1990s, however, seems more related to the widespread popular dissatisfaction of the early 1990s than to the government's leadership.

Although all three countries formally have a Napoleonic model of administration, factually the administrations strongly differ. The French public administration consists of highly trained and qualified civil servants, and enjoys a high public esteem. In contrast, Italian and Spanish public administration are despised for their notorious inefficiency and rigidity. Although the French model of competitive entrance examinations and professional qualifications for jobs in the civil service also exists in Italy and Spain, actual practice is that jobs are predominantly provided by political party patronage. Civil servants in Italy and Spain are badly paid and have a low status, are not interested in work performance and customers. Absenteeism, side jobs, and corruption are usual. Bad service quality and inefficiency are notorious.

The situation at the top of the civil service also differs. Italian administration has no powerful elite of top officials. Italian top officials have a high job and career security, but hardly any power or status. The Spanish administration does have powerful top officials, organized in professional 'special corps'. Like in France the members of the Spanish professional 'special corps' do belong to the politico-administrative elite. Unlike the French members of the 'grand corps', the Spanish members of the 'special corps' strongly resisted the administrative reforms.

Politicization of administration

In contrast to France, where trained and qualified professionals run a rational and professional administration, in Italian and Spanish administration the factor of overriding importance is politicization. Political control of administration, relations between politicians and bureaucrats, political nominations of officials, party patronage and clientelism in Southern European countries like Italy and Spain fundamentally differ from the political practice that is usual in Western Europe (Hopkin, 2001; Sotiropoulos, 2004).

First one should realize that political parties in Italy and Spain differ from Western European ones. Political parties in Southern Europe are not only advocates of policy and ideology, but organizations that provide jobs, pensions, payments, subsidies, insurances and more, to party members. Political clientelism (selective distribution of state resources by political parties to win clients' electoral support) and patronage (unequal, hierarchical, personalized exchange of favours between patron and client) are basic characteristics of southern politics, and so is corruption (abuse of public power for private personal or party gain) (Eisenstadt and Lemarchand, 1981; Heidenheimer et al., 1989; Heywood, 1997; Williams, 2000).

Political parties in Italy and Spain offer their voters jobs in the public sector. That has been the case of old in Italy and Spain ('caciquismo'), and after abolishing dictatorship became widespread in post-war Italy, and was reinstated in Spain by the Socialists after 1982. Although officially public jobs can only be obtained after professional training and competitive entrance examination, many Italian and Spanish civil servants bypassed that path with a political shortcut (Alba, 1998; Cassese, 1993). The higher the public jobs, the more important party affiliation becomes.

Although the practice of political appointments of higher ranking officials formally exists in the United States (spoils system) and Germany ('politische Beamten'), and informally exists in other countries like Belgium and France, the extent of party politicization of career top officials in Southern Europe is much higher. In Spain the advent in 1982 of the Socialists in government led to a huge wave of replacements of top officials. That practice was repeated by the Popular Party in 1996 when Aznar won the elections. In Italy party politicization of top officials used to be much less because of the safe job and career guarantee they enjoyed, but the recent 1998 and 2002 laws on political nominations of top officials seem to reverse that.

The profound politicization of Italian and Spanish public administration is not a momentary aberration of contemporary politicians, but an almost two centuries-long tradition. Such a historical-institutional fact is not simply abolished by administrative modernization. Which makes public management reforms somehow look like swimming against the tide.

4
The Management and Control of Executive Agencies: an Anglo-Dutch Comparison

Sandra van Thiel and Christopher Pollitt[1]

In Chapter 3 Walter Kickert explored recent developments in three continental countries where New Public Management (NPM) reforms have been attempted, but in various ways have been absorbed, adapted or resisted so as not to fundamentally disturb the basic bureaucratic traditions and culture of the countries concerned. Later, in Chapter 9, we will look at a situation where the UK introduced performance indicators early and on a large scale, whereas the Netherlands only moved twenty years later, and very cautiously even then. In both those chapters, therefore, we find diversity between countries and continuity of national traditions, and only marginal convergence by continental states towards Anglo-American-style NPM. The subject of this chapter may at first sight seem a much more promising example of international convergence, as we are going to examine the creation, management and control of central government executive agencies in the UK and the Netherlands.

Semi-autonomous executive agencies have been a particularly common and widespread part of NPM reforms in many countries (OECD, 2002; Pollitt, Talbot, Caulfield and Smullen, 2004). More particularly, programmes for the creation of agencies were launched in the UK in 1988 and in the Netherlands in 1991. The first report promoting executive agencies even referred to the UK programme (usually called the 'Next Steps') as a precedent or model for the Dutch initiative (Ministry of Finance, 1991). In both countries, these entities were supposed to receive managerial autonomy to carry out executive tasks, but to remain under ministerial direction. In both countries, 'agencification' was to be accompanied by a more managerial style, with new systems of costing, budgeting and target-setting. Agencies were supposed to gain enhanced operational freedoms, by paying the price of sharper accountability for their performance (Pollitt et al., 2004: ch. 2). Surely, this is an example of convergence towards the NPM prescription of smaller, 'flatter', single-purpose organizations with a results-orientation and enough autonomy to enable professional managers to work their magic? Or not?

The main aim of this chapter is to compare the management and control of executive agencies in the Netherlands and the UK, with a view to identifying and explaining both similarities and differences. To do this we will also need to glance back briefly at the creation of these organizations.

The outline of this chapter is as follows. There are two country sections in which we will first briefly describe the introduction of executive agencies in the two countries. Then we turn our attention to the management and control issues that evolved after their establishment (see for example James, 2003; Office for Public Service Reform, 2002; Kraak and Van Oosteroom, 2002) and to the instruments that were developed to deal with these issues. We will conclude this chapter with a comparative section, explaining the differences and similarities in the management and control of UK and Dutch executive agencies.

Executive agencies in the Netherlands

Despite the reference to the UK Next Steps programme in the report that introduced executive agencies to Dutch central government (Ministry of Finance, 1991), the Dutch government has never chosen a top-down model in which departmental divisions or bureaus were forcedly transformed into agencies. Instead, the initiative to become an executive agency (in Dutch: *agentschap*) has always been with the ministerial divisions themselves (Kraak and Van Oosteroom, 2002). In fact, to become an executive agency, departmental units nowadays have to meet an extensive range of demanding requirements (see below). Consequently, it takes most organizations several years before they can become an *agentschap* (cf. Van Thiel, 2004). Agency status is therefore considered desirable, not mandatory.[2] The Dutch agency reform can probably be described best as an incremental learning process (trial and error) that led to numerous changes in the original design – if there ever was an original design. We will present a quick overview.

Overview of agency development

The idea of executive agencies was introduced in the Netherlands in the early 1990s as part of a programme to reform the financial management of the central government. Under the new financial act of 1994 (*Comptabiliteitswet*), executive agencies were allowed – unlike ministries – to use an accrual accounting system. However, to do so they needed to be disaggregated from the parent ministry. Executive agencies thus became semi-autonomous, although they have no legal personality and still fall under full ministerial accountability. The latter was an important consideration at that time because of the political controversy on ZBOs; statutory bodies carrying out public tasks, but at arm's length of central government

(Pollitt et al., 2004: ch. 4). ZBOs' autonomy had led to great concern among politicians because of the limited competencies of ministers to control and steer them (cf. Algemene Rekenkamer, 1995; Van Thiel, 2001). Executive agencies were presented as a good alternative because, although they were semi-autonomous as well, they would still have to adhere to (hierarchical) ministerial interventions.

These novel developments took place within a politico-administrative system famous for its consensual, multi-party nature. Negotiated, consensual solutions are very much the norm in the Netherlands, and the multi-party political system with coalition governments 'fits' with and institutionalizes this habit (Lijphart, 1984, 1999). Culturally, the Dutch are fairly egalitarian and individualist, so strong hierarchical actions are unusual – everyone is expected to get round the table and agree, not just accept orders (Hofstede, 2001: 500). Administratively central government is quite large (almost three-quarters of Dutch public employment) but also fairly fragmented. Each ministry commands considerable autonomy (more than would be the case in the UK) and there is no central authority comparable in power to the British Treasury and the Cabinet Office (Pollitt et al., 2004: chs 4 and 6). The implications of this institutional and cultural backdrop for agencies was fairly significant. On the one hand it meant that the process through which agencies emerged was a longer drawn-out, more negotiated one. It also meant that the central 'template' for steering agencies was probably not so detailed and tight as in the centralized UK – there was perhaps more room for variation by individual ministries. On the other hand agencies were sup-posed to some extent to represent 'the new' – a way of working that was sharper and more businesslike than traditional consensual practices.

The first agencies (three) were established in 1994, others would soon follow. Nowadays (late 2005) there are over 30 executive agencies and some 20 more in the process of becoming agencies. Most agencies are charged with the payment of benefits or subsidies, or the collection of taxes or fees (28 per cent in 2004), and the management and maintenance of databases and buildings (about 22 per cent).[3] Among the units wanting to become an agency, we find a large number of inspectorates. By the end of 2007, there will be over 50 *agentschappen*, which will employ almost 80 per cent of the national civil service (Van Oosteroom and Van Thiel, 2004). The Ministry of Finance has been the driving force behind the rise of executive agencies in the Netherlands; all official documents have been written or commissioned by them, including evaluations (Smullen, forthcoming). Also, a special unit from this ministry has been in charge of offering practical guidance and assistance to ministerial divisions wanting to become an agency. Finally, this ministry has to co-approve the decision to establish executive agencies, and it is in control of agencies' capital reserves.

The experiences with earlier agencies and two official evaluations led to several additions to the establishment requirements and procedures (Smullen,

Box 4.1: Criteria for the establishment of executive agencies in the Netherlands, 2005

---

1. There has to be an analysis of the environment, and all relations with relevant stakeholders.
2. All products and/or services have to be described and made measurable.
3. All business processes have to be described.
4. Products and/or services are expressed in cost prices, in a transparent way to allow ex ante and ex post cost calculations.
5. A clear indication is given of the expected efficiency gains, before the agency is established.
6. The planning and control cycle is result-oriented, and fits with departmental management cycles.
7. Risks have to be described, as well as ways to neutralize them and who is responsible for them.
8. There is a plan for the first year's accruals account, agreed upon by the financial units of the parent ministry.
9. There is a plan for the transition from a cash based system to an accrual accounting one.
10. The one-year trial period for the results-oriented planning and control cycle is well prepared.
11. The one-year trial period for the accrual accounting system is well prepared.
12. An external accountant has approved the annual budget of the past year(s).

(for more information, see www.minfin.nl, this is our short translation)

Pollitt and Van Thiel, 2001: 194). Nowadays, there are twelve requirements (see Box 4.1). When an organization has met all these requirements there is a one-year trial period, after which the final decision to establish the agency is taken by the parent department, the Ministry of Finances, the cabinet and parliament.

Management and control

Parent departments' interest in the management and control of executive agencies started growing only after their establishment (Homburg and Van Thiel, 2001). Because of the focus on efficiency gains, the potential *political* consequences of the creation of independent agencies were initially overlooked. Two consecutive evaluations (Ministry of Finance, 1998; Berenschot, 2002) and reports from the national audit office on quasi-autonomous organizations called attention to the lack of control and steering by ministries. In response to these criticisms, the requirements for the establishment of executive agencies were tightened (cf. Box 4.1).

Also, based on experiences with the first agencies, ministries started to develop models for the steering and control of agencies. One of these models, of the Ministry of Economic Affairs to be precise, was adopted by the Ministry of Finance and has now become more or less the standard (Kraak and Van Oosteroom, 2002). This model stresses that there are multiple relationships between ministries and executive agencies. Ministries are the principal, owner and supervisor of agencies. Each role has its own characteristics and interests, leading to different needs – and instruments – for the management and control of independent agencies. The *principal* charges agencies with tasks, in exchange for a budget. In economic theory, this is known as the principal–agent relation (Pratt and Zeckhauser, 1991). Final agreements are determined in negotiations between the two, and laid down in a contract. It is in the interest of the principal to achieve the most efficient agreement, that is the highest production at the lowest cost. This is where a possible role-conflict lies for ministries, because the *owner* is concerned with the continuity of the agency. A reduction in size of the agency, for example due to a loss of tasks, may threaten the survival of the agency. When agency employees are still civil servants (as is the case with Dutch executive agencies), the costs of reorganizations and dismissal will have to be borne by the parent department.

The *supervisor* has to make sure that agencies' performance is in line with the contractual agreements and the law more generally. The role of supervisor is important to the two other roles; the principal wants to know whether agencies have met the terms of the contract and the owner wants to know whether a contract will be renewed, cancelled or altered. Parent ministries need performance information from agencies also for political purposes though, in particular because a minister has to publicly account for the expenditures of public means and/or the achievement of political objectives, or lack thereof, to parliament and voters. Sometimes the principal and/or owner can fulfil the role of supervisor as well.

To organize the steering of executive agencies, parent departments can decide to separate the three roles or combine them. Most ministries have preferred to separate the different roles. For example, the Ministry of Economics has assigned the role of principal to policy divisions, the ownership role is carried out by the central financial unit and supervision is carried out by among others audit units. In other cases, liaison officers have been appointed, either within a policy or financial division, or in the staff office of the secretary general. There is little uniformity in these arrangements as even within one ministry the steering model in use can be different for different agencies.

In 2005, the ownership role for 22 executive agencies was formally charged to the secretary-general or his deputy, and in ten cases to a director-general.[4] In practice, a financial or policy unit of the department provides secretarial support. That is why most contacts between executive agencies and ministries go primarily through policy divisions (41 per cent) and financial units (20 per cent, Van Thiel et al., 2004a).

There are, however, also examples of combinations of the three roles. A so-called interface division is then put in charge of the co-ordination of all contacts between the ministry and the agency. An interface imposes high requirements on civil servants ('account managers'). They have to have knowledge of the content of relevant policies, financial aspects, audit techniques, political developments, and so on. Moreover, they need to have good diplomatic skills as well (cf. Van Thiel et al., 2004b). In the Netherlands, at least two ministries have (had) such interface units: the Ministry of Education had a division called RZO and the financial directorate of the Ministry of Housing has a special subdivision called TOPZO.

So far, experiences with interface organizations have been reasonably positive, but they do not always live up to their promises (Van Twist and Plug, 1998). Interfaces often assume an intermediary position, rather than steering agencies. This is probably partly due to the high complexity of the work processes; operational contacts often occur without the interface's involvement. Interfaces have, however, also suffered from the bureaupolitics within ministries, between policy and financial divisions – which caused for example the downfall of the interface RZO in the educational ministry (cf. Van Thiel, 2004).

Instruments for the management of executive agencies

The roles of principal, owner and supervisor are not new to the public domain, but the separation of policy and administration brings two important changes. Firstly, relations between parent departments and independent agencies are more business-like and at arm's length (less informal). There are fewer opportunities for (direct) intervention by the parent ministry in agency operations. Changes in tasks and budgets need to be negotiated and cannot be dictated. Secondly, independent agencies can work for multiple principals and even for private market parties. As a result, parent departments have to share the attention and devotion of their executive agencies. Hierarchical relations are thus replaced by mutual dependency (or in economic terms: a bilateral monopoly) and shared interests in good policy-making and implementation. These new relationships call for new steering instruments (Kickert, 2001), or for adjustments of existing instruments.

There are several instruments to steer executive agencies (Van Thiel, 2003). Not all of these are used, however, by all ministries, and some will be used for particular roles only, while others can be used for more than one role (see Box 4.2 for an overview). There is little research into the actual use of instruments, but we will offer data where possible.

Instruments for the principal

Agencies' tasks are laid down in the agency statutes (that is the written decision to establish the agency) and the laws/policy that are carried out by the agency. These tasks are operationalized in a (quasi-)contract between a ministry and agency. About 75 per cent of the agencies in 2004 had such a contract, often referred to as the management contract (36 per cent) or annual plan (8 per cent, Van Thiel et al., 2004a). Management contracts

Box 4.2: Roles and instruments of Dutch ministries to steer executive agencies

```
┌─────────────────────────────────────────────────────────────────┐
│              ┌──────────────────────────────┐                      │
│              │          SUPERVISOR          │                      │
│              │            Audit             │                      │
│              │         Inspectorate         │                      │
│              │     Independent regulator    │                      │
│              │            Board             │                      │
│              └──────────────────────────────┘                      │
│                                                                    │
│   ┌──────────────────────────┐   ┌──────────────────────────────┐│
│   │        PRINCIPAL         │   │            OWNER             ││
│   │                          │   │                              ││
│   │   General legislation    │   │           Budget             ││
│   │        Statute           │   │       Annual account         ││
│   │   Management contract    │   │   Tariffs, fees, cost prices ││
│   │     Feasibility test     │   │    Performance indicators    ││
│   │                          │   │      Information protocol     ││
│   └──────────────────────────┘   └──────────────────────────────┘│
└─────────────────────────────────────────────────────────────────┘
```

contain all the agreements on the expected agency performance and appropriate budgets. Contracts will specify results, not through which operational processes agencies achieve those results. They are a form of result-oriented steering by parent departments. Unfortunately, these contracts are not made public. We can only infer what has been agreed upon by investigating annual reports and accounts in which agencies have to report about their performance afterwards (output, finances).

No matter how detailed statutes and contracts are, the parent department remains dependent on the agency for the quality of policy implementation, as well as for the development of new policy. After all, executive agencies are the sole source of executive (street-level) knowledge. Hence, there are frequent contacts on policy issues, for example, when agencies have doubts about the interpretation of certain policy regulations or run into practical problems that require a change in the policy rules ('loopholes').

In the case of the development of new policies, agencies can be involved, for example, through the deployment of the so-called feasibility test. To perform such a test, an agency will investigate whether a new policy measure proposed by the parent department is feasible, at what cost, on which terms and with which consequences or effects (Kickert, 2001). The results can lead to changes in or even withdrawal of a proposal. Parent ministries can not only grant agencies the use of this instrument, but can also decide on the conditions under which such tests are carried out. For example, whether ministries have to pay for these tests, and who will have access to the results (are they a matter of public record?).

Instruments for the owner

The management and control of agencies by the parent ministry in its role as owner focuses particularly on the budget. The ministry's reach is somewhat limited, however, by the managerial autonomy of the executive agency. For example, decisions about small investments or hiring temporary staff can often be taken without consultation with the ministry – as long as the agency stays within the agreed budget. In theory, the parent ministry cannot interfere with such aspects.

Most agencies receive their budget from the ministry or state budget; in 2001 only four out of 22 agencies received the majority of their revenues from other sources (like premiums, tariffs and fees; Smullen et al., 2001: 196). Within an agency budget we can distinguish running and programme costs (Kickert, 2001). Running costs are all company costs that are necessary for implementing policies, such as salary, housing, information technology, and so on. Programme costs are the cost of policy programmes, such as the total sum of benefits or subsidies. Some agencies generate programme revenues as well like collecting taxes or charging fees. The height of fees and tariffs can be an instrument for parent ministries to steer agencies, if the minister has to approve or set them.

Agency budgets are determined annually and laid down in the management contract. The agency then translates the budget plan into activities, for the coming year and for the long-term. Afterwards, the agency has to account for its performance and expenditures (annual report and account).

Apart from the budget, the management contract also includes agreements on the expected performance, usually expressed by means of performance indicators. The use of performance indicators has become quite popular in the public sector, as Chapters 7 (NPM tools) and 9 (hospital indicators) show. The use of performance indicators to manage or control independent agencies is not limited to the role of owner; the principal also uses them.

Finally, to determine which information has to be provided by the agency to the parent department, in any role, and vice versa, a so-called information protocol or charter can be drawn up. This specifies which and when information is exchanged between the parent department and the agency. This could include monthly or quarterly reports, budget information, terms for feasibility tests, annual reports, and the agreements on, for instance, dealing with the media (press releases, spokesperson) and parliament.

Instruments for supervision

Ministries can organize the supervision of executive agencies in various ways (cf. Hood et al., 2005). For example, policy or financial divisions can be put in charge of supervision, but more often an audit or inspection division will be. An interesting development in this respect is that an increasing number of inspectorates have applied to become executive agencies themselves.

Ministries can also appoint independent regulators to oversee agencies. Most of these external regulators operate, however, in markets, such as the telecommunications (OPTA) and financial markets (AFM). They make sure that companies keep to the market rules. This is especially important in the case of privatized government companies, because of their monopoly. In the Netherlands, public sector organizations are allowed to undertake commercial activities but only under strict conditions, to prevent unfair competition. For example, market activities should not use knowledge or assets that have been paid from public means (cross-subsidizing). Regulators are in charge of keeping public sector organizations in check.

Parent ministries have, however, more options to install supervisors. For example, they can establish a board of supervisors within an agency. The parent ministry can even appoint members of such boards. Boards can take different roles, however, ranging from attending to the ministries' interests, to representing clients, supervising the director and/or serving the best interests of the agency (cf. Cornforth, 2003). So, there is no guarantee that boards will exclusively focus on the interests of the parent ministry. That is also true for the range of external bodies that are legally entitled to investigate independent agencies, such as the National Audit Office and the Ombudsman. Their reports can, however, provide information to ministries on executive agencies.

Executive agencies in the United Kingdom

Overview of agency development

When addressing international audiences British academics are frequently asked 'can you point us to the legislation on which the creation of Executive Agencies is based please?' The questioners are usually shocked by the (accurate) reply that there isn't any. The prime minister and other ministers are able to exercise the powers of 'the Crown in Parliament' or what is known as 'Crown Prerogative'. They are accountable to Parliament in one sense, but they also exercise enormous Crown powers (for example British prime ministers can declare war or sign treaties without seeking Parliament's approval).

As a consequence of these arrangements, ministries, agencies and departments have no independent standing in law and the prime minister, and in some cases ministers, can often change the structure and functions of government bodies without recourse to legislation or Parliament (Pollitt, 1984).

The informality of constitutional arrangements is part of the wider and distinctive institutional and cultural background to the reforms. The UK has a strongly adversarial, majoritarian political system, in which most of the time only two parties really matter and only one is in government and can control the House of Commons (Lijphart, 1984). So, unlike the situation in the Netherlands, a single-party government can just decide what it wants and (usually) be confident of getting it through the legislature. A powerful prime minister (and Mrs Thatcher was certainly in a powerful position when the Next Steps agencies were launched in 1988) can act quickly and decisively without having to slog through long inter-party negotiations. Furthermore, the administrative system is rather centralized, with the Treasury and the Cabinet Office in a strong position to impose models of public service reform on not only the rest of central government but, to a considerable extent, on local authorities also (Pollitt and Bouckaert, 2004). Culturally, politics is dominated by two-party adversarialism, so that many if not most reforms are likely to become footballs kicked about quite violently between the two main parties. The civil service, however, is non-partisan, and, in this case, quietly let it be known that it was behind the agency reforms. It was therefore highly significant that, after a short initial period of criticism, the main opposition party came to a pragmatic acceptance of the Next Steps agencies programme, so that from 1990 or so onwards it received bi-partisan support. The Labour opposition was far more critical of the more strongly market-oriented reforms such as privatization and contracting-out than it was of agencies (although when Labour eventually came to power in 1997 they did little to try to reverse market-oriented reforms, and in some ways even took them further).

The overall public management reform agenda of the Conservative government during the period immediately before the launch of agencies in 1988 was certainly market-oriented. It may be summarized as follows: if possible move all or parts of public services into the private sector; if that is not possible, introduce some kind of market-type mechanisms and competition within public services; and focus on reducing costs, improving efficiency and injecting rigorous managerial practices. For the civil service this meant numerous drives to reduce costs and improve efficiency (the Rayner Scrutinies and FMI), to forcibly reduce numbers through closures, to privatize (including some executive agencies), reduce staff costs, and to contract-out services.

By 1986 Mrs Thatcher had recognized that previous reforms (the Rayner Scrutinies and the FMI) had made only limited impact on Whitehall. An internal review produced what was eventually published as the *Improving Management in Government: The Next Steps* report (Caines et al., 1988). It concluded that the previous initiatives could not succeed without larger, structural and cultural, changes to back them up. The net result, after a good deal of wrangling within Whitehall (Thain and Wright, 1996), was the 'Next Steps' programme, announced to Parliament in a short statement by Mrs Thatcher in 1988.

Over a ten-year period around 80 per cent of UK civil servants were transferred into more than 130 agencies or bodies said to be working on agency lines (for example Customs and Excise and Inland Revenue). Precise numbers have varied almost month-by-month, as new agencies are created or existing ones are merged with each other or reabsorbed into ministries or, sometimes, completely privatized.

To what degree have UK agencies been separated out from their parent ministries? The answer to this question is difficult, even in formal terms. On the one hand, agencies are formally still part of their parent ministry. The Accounting Officer of the ministry (usually the Permanent Secretary) is also responsible for all the agencies whose accounts are included in the overall ministry accounts. On the other hand, each agency produces its own annual report; holds its own budget; its Chief Executive is also an Accounting Officer for the agency (meaning each agency has two Accounting Officers); it reports its own performance; and so on.

The ambiguity of agency status is also affected by the history of each particular function. Most UK ministries were, prior to agency creation, multi-functional organizations. Some were organized internally along functional lines – for example the Home Office had separate internal structures organizing prisons, forensic science, fire service training, passports and immigration and nationality. Others, like the Department of Social Security, were organized primarily on a geographical basis, with multi-functional district organizations delivering most of the department's services to the public through a single local structure.

In fact, most agencies were pre-existing structures (Gains, 1999; Talbot, 2004) often already having a strong individual identity (for example the Meteorological Office). Many of these pre-existing entities also already had their own personnel systems. Around half of all UK civil servants worked on grades unique to their organization or functions and half on 'generalist' grades prior to Next Steps, and many personnel matters had already been devolved (Talbot, 1997).

Alongside this continuity, one notable change has been the public identification of agency Chief Executives and their willingness to speak in public about their agency's work – and sometimes even contradict government policy. Before *Next Steps* it was rare for any senior civil servant to appear in public and almost unheard of for them to say anything controversial. However, several agencies' CEs became regular speakers at conferences and even raised specific issues through the media.

The responsibility of CEs was supposed to be linked to a more contract-like relationship with the parent ministry:

> We are moving from a hierarchical system to a system in which the minister and chief executive are in a quasi-contractual position ...' (Peter Kemp – later Sir Peter Kemp – Project Manager for the Next Steps projects, answering questions from the Parliamentary Treasury and Civil Service Committee, 10 July 1990: Treasury and Civil Service Committee, 1990: 51)

In the textbook theoretical version of principal–agency contracting it is assumed that the contracting parties are legally equal and that contracts can be placed on a legal footing if necessary (although in some intra-firm cases they will not be). One fundamental difference in the case of UK agencies is that nearly all such 'contracts' have no legal standing at all. This, as we shall see, can have significant consequences for steering.

Management and control

Point-for-point direct comparison with the Dutch narrative is problematic, because in the UK the issues of management and control were discussed in a somewhat different conceptual vocabulary. The concept of 'steering', which was so prominent in the Netherlands, was much less evident in the UK. For Next Steps agencies the public and political debate was more about 'accountability' and 'performance'.

At the outset, the fact that most agencies were pre-existing organizational structures meant that new steering systems could not be written on a fresh page, but rather had to compete with existing ways of doing things (Talbot, 2004). There was therefore an inheritance, or 'carry over', of ways of doing things from the previous relationships (Gains, 1999).

Let us turn to a quite different – but rather influential – theoretical perspective. In rational choice theory, inequalities in principal–agent relationships are usually attributed to informational asymmetries. However, in practice public sector internal contracting is also characterized by power inequalities related to formal authority, public accountability and resources. These can result in 'contracts' between ministries and agencies which are very one-sided. Whilst the principals can vary the contract at will – adding new demands, changing policies and reshaping services – there is no corresponding right for the agent (agency) to demand additional resources. The issue was beautifully summed up by the Project Manager for the Next Steps project, while giving evidence to a parliamentary select committee: 'Framework agreements are meant to be durable but they can be changed at any time' (Peter Kemp, in Treasury and Civil Service Committee, 1990: 22).

On the other hand, some of the formal management techniques ('steering instruments', in the Dutch vocabulary) were genuinely new, and departed from prevailing Whitehall customs. The new system comprised framework documents, quinquennial reviews of agency status, separate budgets and business plans, annual reports, key performance indicators and, crucially, agency chief executives reporting directly to ministers (instead of reporting through permanent secretaries, as would have been the traditional practice). Overall, it was counter-cultural to the prevailing 'Yes Minister' environment of informality, collegiality and clannishness. We will look at some of these instruments more closely in a moment. Suffice it to say at this point that the shift to agency status was certainly seen as significant, whatever the formal position and history of individual functions and the ambiguity of their position. Agencies were not truly separate, but neither were they any more simply a part of their parent ministry.

Instruments for the management of executive agencies

In order to examine these instruments in more detail, we will focus on the issues of:

- Elements of agency autonomy (including spending controls and personnel controls).
- The nature of the 'contract'.
- Ministry/agency communications.

Autonomization

'Creeping autonomization' is not a bad summary of the story of Next Steps agencies. At the inception of the programme the Treasury was extremely concerned that it would lose control of the carefully crafted set of controls which it had built up to constrain ministries' spending and personnel policies (Kemp, 1993; Thain and Wright, 1996). In the opening stages of Next Steps there was therefore very limited delegation to agencies of any real power over financial or personnel issues.

During the 1980s the Treasury had, however, been developing a new approach to controlling ministries' spending. This approach involved setting very clear boundaries on what a ministry could spend overall, as well as strict controls on 'running costs': that is the non-programme overheads. This allowed the Treasury gradually to relax other controls (for example on staffing numbers and pay and grading issues) and allow ministries more freedom to choose how to spend their money within the overall spending 'envelope' (Thain and Wright, 1996). This approach proved transferable to agencies so that the Treasury (and the particular parent ministry) could set and police strong controls on how much each agency could spend on both its programmes and, most importantly from the point of view of driving up efficiency, its overheads.

These freedoms on finance issues were further enhanced by several other innovations. Firstly, some agencies were placed on slightly different funding regimes. While most remained funded directly for all their expenditure, some were moved, over a period, on to one of two new regimes. The first and largest was to become a 'net funded' agency. These were agencies that accrued income from various charges and fees (for example fees for passports or driving licences). They were allowed, under the new set of rules, to retain some of this income and offset it against their overhead costs. This created incentives for them to increase their income and enabled them to cover additional costs from the increases. The second innovation was Trading Fund Agencies, which moved onto a completely self-financing basis in which their revenues were to cover not only their running costs and the costs of the services they provided, but also provide a notional return on capital employed (that is their asset base) to the Treasury (usually set at around 5 per cent).

The third innovation consisted of changes to the accounting systems themselves, including the introduction of what is called 'end year flexibility' (allowing managers to carry over some budget from one year to the next or spend some of next year's budget this year) and of resource accounting and budgeting (accruals and capital accounting). Both of these changes allowed managers greater control over how their (strictly limited) resources were to be deployed.

Alongside these increases in financial autonomy came changes to personnel practices. During the mid-1990s the Treasury began delegating responsibility for setting pay and grading systems to agencies – first the larger ones and then all agencies. Agencies were forced, whether they wanted to or not, to conduct reviews of their pay and grading structures and to adopt new, more diverse, systems. The process of reforming these systems was closely supervised by Treasury and parent ministries, with agencies having to gain authorization at several points in the process (Talbot, 1997). Thus this was, somewhat paradoxically, a centrally imposed, devolved and dissimilar grading and pay system.

The larger agencies have been able to exercise greater autonomy, partly due to information asymmetries between themselves and the Treasury and their parent ministries. They have often had more direct access to the Treasury. On the other hand, some of these large agencies have also been highly politically sensitive and as a result ministers have been apt to intervene directly in operational as well as policy decisions – the Prison Service crisis in 1996 being the most obvious example (Learmont, 1995; Talbot, 1996; Lewis, 1997).

For smaller agencies the reality of managerial autonomy has been much more heavily circumscribed by the inequality in the power relationship between very small agencies and large ministries (Talbot, 1996, 2004). Where these smaller agencies have also been the subject of political controversy – for example in the case of the Child Support Agency – their managerial autonomy has been heavily constrained.

'Contracts'

One of the most prominent features of the Next Steps reforms was the introduction of publicly reported key performance indicators (KPIs) for every agency, specified by ministers. From 1990 onwards these KPIs were collected and published centrally in the 'Next Steps Review' with, in later editions of this central reporting, detailed comparative analysis of agencies' results and even some benchmarking against private sector firms. KPIs are formally set by ministers and were originally envisaged to form part of a quasi-contractual annual agreement covering resources, policy and performance between ministers and the agency. The reality, however, evolved somewhat differently. Firstly, the policy framework was separated out into a three-year (later five-year) framework document, which covered policy, aims, financial status and governance arrangements – more of a quasi-constitution than a quasi-contract. It said nothing about specific resources, which continued to be dealt with through normal ministry–Treasury spending processes, nor about specific performance targets, which were set separately and annually through the KPI process.

KPIs themselves were extremely variable in quantity, quality and focus. Whilst most agencies had KPIs numbering close to the average of seven to ten KPIs per agency (there was a gradual increase in numbers), there were some wide variations. The Royal Mint had only one, whilst Customs and Excise usually had nearly 40. The quality of the KPIs themselves and the data used to report them were also highly variable and the occasional external audits highlighted some major problems (National Audit Office 1995, 1998, 2000). Although KPIs were supposed to focus on outputs, this took a long time to evolve and initially there was much greater emphasis on inputs and processes. The central reporting of KPIs was highly innovative and had some impact, but this was abandoned in 1999, making comparisons across the 120 or so annual reports for individual agencies much more difficult.

KPIs were not the only form of performance accountability. One problem which emerged was that a plethora of different systems (KPIs, business plans, corporate plans, Citizen's Charter statements, market-testing plans, training plans, and so on) imposed centrally from either the Cabinet Office or the Treasury and mediated through parent ministries created a host of usually poorly aligned performance steering systems (Talbot, 1996; Hyndman and Anderson, 1998; Hyndman and Eden, 2002; Talbot, 2004).

So, could UK agencies be said to be working within a performance-contracting regime? They have certainly been required to report, sometimes extensively, on their performance, but this is not the same as performance contracting. However, the UK system has separated out performance target setting (KPIs) from the budgetary process and there has sometimes been no discernible link between the two. Furthermore, ministers have been able to impose new requirements on agencies regardless of the contents of the budget or the KPIs. There is also limited evidence of poor or good performance affecting decisions about what resources an agency gets. One could therefore argue that the reality failed to match either term in the phrase 'performance contracting'.

One test of such a system is whether KPIs are referred to during crises. There have been several examples of such crises (Prisons over escapes, Passports over delays in issuing, Child Support over failures to collect payments from absent parents). In each case, there has been an almost complete absence of discussion of formal performance – at least in public. In the case of Prisons the agency was actually succeeding against its targets for escapes set by the Home Secretary when their Director General was sacked over two high-profile escapes (Lewis, 1997).

In sum, any expectation that the presence of an elaborate performance indicator regime meant that agencies were being steered according to performance would be naive. There were at least four major reasons why this might not happen. First, in some cases the indicator set did not match the set of objectives (for example lots of indicators for some objectives, none for others). Second – for many agencies – the indicator sets themselves kept changing, year-on-year (a high 'churn' rate). Indicators were redefined or replaced with new ones. This meant that keeping track of performance changes over time was frequently difficult, or impossible. Third, the data from which indicators were formed may not have been accurate or reliable – there was usually no independent audit of the validity of the data, and, indeed, the government resisted proposals that the National Audit Office should be given the task of conducting such an audit (National Audit Office, 1995, 1998). Fourth, there was little evidence that ministers actually used PI data to steer – and where there were crises (see above) PIs were usually forgotten about in the face of media pressure.

With the advent of the new Labour government from 1997 an important new 'steering tool' appeared on the scene. This was the Public Services Agreement (PSA). This was an important control device for the Treasury, comprising a series of quasi-contractual agreements between the Treasury and each spending ministry. Each PSA specifies the main policy objectives and sets quantitative targets, usually for both outputs and outcomes. These ministry-level targets would then be cascaded and disaggregated downwards to form agency targets. PSAs were supposed to be able to reduce the problem of policy fragmentation by prescribing 'joined-up' targets for programmes that spanned more than one ministry or agency – an aspect of the PSA regime where there appears to have been some limited success (James, 2004). More generally, however:

> the system has very far from enabled the core executive to steer public services at arm's length through a tool of strategic influence. The targets do not reflect all the outcomes valued by the core executive and have changed frequently, making progress difficult to assess. (James, 2004: 415)

Ministry/agency communications

After an early review of ministry/agency relationships it was decided that a particular official – colloquially known as the 'Fraser person', after the author of the report – should be appointed to act as the channel for significant communications between the two 'sides'. Within a few years, however, a further report showed that the role of Fraser persons was a difficult one: in some cases they became *de facto* agency advocates, in others they tried to oversee agency operations, but combining the two was awkward (Treasury and Civil Service Committee, 1990). Following this, many agencies set up ministerial advisory boards (MABs), which included agency managers, ministry civil servants and sometimes non-executive members from the outside world. By 1997 about half the agencies had MABs.

There have been a series of official investigations of the relationship between ministries and agencies (see especially Efficiency Unit, 1991; Treasury and Civil Service Committee, 1990; Office for Public Service Reform and H.M. Treasury, 2002). These have charted an interesting swing in the 'official line'. The reports of the early 1990s tend to emphasize excessive interference from ministries – too many detailed requests for information and ad hoc interventions coming 'down' from the ministries to the agencies. By the time of the 2002 Review, however, concern had veered from 'oversteering' to 'understeering':

> [W]hilst agencies have been successful in achieving radical cultural change in central government to the benefit of customers, in too many cases their work has become disconnected from the increasingly well-defined aims of their ministers ... and ... the gulf between policy and delivery is considered by most to have widened. (Office of Public Services Reform, 2002: 3 and 6)

What is very hard to tell is how far this shift of emphasis reflects a real underlying change in agency behaviour, and how far it rather indicates a wish by ministers to be more interventionist and controlling.

Comparison and conclusions

The Dutch and British agency stories have much in common, and to this extent we can conclude that there is some degree of convergence on the NPM model. In both cases there was a vision of an efficient, professionally managed organization with a stronger client orientation yet still under strategic, democratic control from the minister. In both cases, this vision was operationalized by changes in financial and accounting rules, and by the creation of sets of performance targets and indicators, set within regularly revised operational plans. In both cases, the role of the Treasury/Ministry of Finance was central. In both cases, the staff of the new agencies retained their civil service status. In both cases, periodic evaluations claimed steady progress (although on the basis of very little hard evidence – especially in the Dutch case) but also pointed to aspects that required further improvement.

Alongside these similarities, there are clear and significant differences. The very starting point was different: in the UK the Next Steps programme was the answer to problems of *insufficient* managerial autonomy, which was believed to have limited previous waves of reform, while in the Netherlands agencies were the answer to *too much* autonomy, that had previously been afforded to ZBOs. Then the legal process of agency creation was very different, with a legal basis bestowed to each Dutch agency, whereas the UK agencies usually lacked any basis in statute law. Furthermore, the Dutch parliament seems to have played a somewhat more active role in Dutch agency creation, whereas the traditional executive dominance in the UK meant that the House of Commons was little more than a passive recipient of news about the government's implementation of its Next Steps programme. Then there are differences of speed and scale. The Next Steps programme raced along, shovelling three-quarters of all civil servants into well over 100 agencies, all within a decade. The Dutch programme started much more cautiously, with just over three agencies. Then it marked time for several years before starting up again from 2002, expecting an increase up to 80 per cent of the national civil service. These differences are typical of the many gaps between the 'hard core' Anglo-Saxon NPM states and the continental 'modernizers' (Pollitt and Bouckaert, 2004).

As far as the management/steering of agencies by the parent departments is concerned, we see both differences and similarities. In both countries, NPM instruments like quasi-contracts and performance indicators have been introduced to steer executive agencies and make them more accountable for their actions. The use of these instruments may in practice not be as radical as some theorists originally assumed, but they have at least served to structure the dialogues between ministries and agencies in new ways, and to require the production of new forms of performance-related information. Agencies have also been able to use new financial rules, including the right to retain surpluses (albeit up to a maximum) and to shift budgets between, for example, personnel and material costs. This autonomy has been accompanied by increased requirements to account for agency performance, in annual reports and the like. Finally, to equip themselves to handle ministry-agency quasi-contacts, parent ministries have experimented with new types of liaison mechanism – interfaces (Netherlands) and Fraser persons or Ministerial Advisory Boards (UK). The frequency with which such arrangements have been reviewed and adjusted is one important indicator that an ideal, stable balance is hard to find.

The most interesting difference between the two countries is perhaps slightly counter-intuitive. It is that the UK programme seems to have been considerably more 'open' than its Dutch counterpart. The amount of public domain information about the actual performance of the Dutch agencies has been extremely modest compared to the wealth of data available in regular UK reports (for example Chancellor of the Duchy of Lancaster, 1997; Chief Secretary to the Treasury, 2000). Furthermore, performance data do not seem to have been much used by Dutch ministries to 'discipline' agencies (cf. Kraak and Van Oosteroom, 2002), whereas the fear of punishment for missing targets was quite pronounced in the UK (Pollitt, 2006). A plausible explanation for this difference would be the 'soft' nature of the consensual Dutch culture, compared with the harder edged NPM approach in the UK. The more one-sided use of contracts and the stronger controls in the UK would not fit in the Dutch variant of the agency model. Interestingly, however, the Dutch government has – over time and based on experience and evaluations – imposed a number of stricter requirements to establish agencies, although this does not approach the *rigour* of UK practice. Perhaps the most important difference between the two countries is the hardest one to pin down. In one sense it is cultural, in another political and in yet another almost mundanely procedural. It is – to express it crudely – that the whole rhetoric and machinery of 'performance' has more 'bite' in the UK than in the Netherlands. UK agencies have more measures, more widely publicized measures and a more developed dialogue on performance with ministries. There is more 'action' in the system – more connection of results to individual appraisals, more punishment for failure and even more reward for success. Both the Treasury and Number 10 Downing Street actively monitor individual agencies and do not hesitate to query performance failures. In the Netherlands, by contrast, the whole process is enveloped within a multi-party game of compromise and consensus and a departmental game in which one ministry does not interfere in the affairs of another. This is NPM, certainly, but a variety which is conducted in a milder climate.

Notes

1. The authors would like to thank Rebecca Cooke for her help in translating some Dutch texts that were used in writing this chapter.
2. Except for so-called ZBOs that have been transformed into executive agencies; as ZBOs have more autonomy, these organizations (may) see their agency status as a degradation.
3. Data taken from a survey among 19 executive agencies (Van Thiel et al., 2004a).
4. Data taken from Harteveld (2005, Master of Public Management thesis, University of Twente).

5
Public–Private Partnership: a Two-Headed Reform. A Comparison of PPP in England and the Netherlands

Erik-Hans Klijn, Jurian Edelenbos and Michael Hughes

Introduction

Public–private partnerships (PPP) have become a popular policy instrument in many Western European countries. Governments increasingly refer to PPP as an important instrument to modernize public policy (see Chapter 1) with the assumption that involvement of private actors in the provision of services, or in the realization of policy goals, will increase quality and give better value for money. Many government policy documents stress both the added value created by PPPs and the role of *contract* in implementing this particular aspect of public management reform. The link is the assumption that contracting-out services to private actors increases efficiency and value for money and can be managed by specifying requirements and by using innovative contracting forms. On the other hand, however, there is an emphasis on *partnership* and close interaction between public and private actors to generate a responsive and flexible problem-solving capacity that can respond to 'wicked' societal problems and produce innovative results that could not have been specified in advance. The rhetoric of the policy stresses the benefits of 'tight' contracts and 'loose' partnerships, but fails to recognize the potential conflicts created.

The main goal of this chapter is to look at the PPP practices of the Netherlands and the UK from a contractual and a partnership point of view. We try to gain insight in what organizational forms are dominant in PPP practices in both countries, what the similarities and the dissimilarities are. First, we will look more closely at public–private partnership as an instrument and trace the ambiguous character of this reform. We then pay attention to the PPP discussion and practice in the Netherlands and the UK. And we finish with a comparison and some conclusions.

PPP: contractual reforms or managed partnerships?

In this section we will describe and review two forms of public–private partnerships: the *contractual* form, and the *partnership* form.

What is PPP? The nature of the reform

Public–private partnership can be described as a more or less sustainable co-operation between public and private actors in which joint products and/or services are developed and in which risks, costs and profits are shared (Klijn and Teisman, 2000: 85). Policy-makers assume that a more intensive co-operation between public and private parties will produce better and more efficient policy outcomes and policy products. Their key 'partnership' mechanism is that private parties are involved earlier and more intensively in the decision-making process, than is the case with more traditional client–supplier or principal–agent relationships.

This indicates a close fit between PPP and the New Public Management (see Chapter 1) emphasis on private sector involvement, value for money, and output performance. PPP is also aligned with the concept of separating policy formation and implementation. Policy documents on PPP emphasize the role of the private consortium in implementing the service or realizing the policy output. However, we also see some ambiguities: just as in private–private partnerships there is a tension in PPPs between *creating* added value through partnerships (which requires trust and information exchange) and *distributing* it through the contract relationship – the classic 'zero-sum game'.

Two forms of PPP: contract or partnerships?

A distinction is often made between PPP concessions or contracts and PPP as an organizational co-operation project or partnership (Teisman, 1998; Klijn and Teisman, 2000; Kenniscentrum, 2002; Sullivan and Skelcher, 2002; Hodge and Greve, 2005). In a PPP *concession* the design, building, financing and commercial operation of an infrastructure project (such as a road, or a building like a school) are integrated into a contract. The added value lies in the lower costs of co-ordination between the various components (often expressed as 'efficiency' or 'value for money' gains). Even though these efficiencies are necessary for a PPP concession, they would not be sufficient to attract private or public sector interest. Their interest arises from the opportunity to create substantive added value; for example, the Private Finance Initiative (PFI) tendering system used in the UK for road construction bundles design, build, finance, operation and contracting-out to private consortia for a period of 30 years. The consortium can use more sustainable (expensive) building materials to save on future maintenance costs (Haynes and Roden, 1999). The payment system rewards the 'availability' of roads (NAO, 2002; NAO, 2003) rather than second-guessing the costs of constructing them. The opportunity for a long-term involvement in a project provides both the potential for devising new solutions to problems and protects a risk aversion to untested approaches.

In a PPP as *organizational co-operation project*, separate activities are integrated to create added value. In this case, PPP is a *partnership*. This type of co-operation is usually found in urban reconstruction and regeneration projects where measures to strengthen transport are combined with measures aimed at improving the living environment and/or housing and measures aimed at strengthening the economy. In this method of co-operation, added value is generated by combining substantive activities and projects which then reinforce each other. This also makes it possible to achieve a financial trade-off between profitable and less profitable but socially interesting components.

In these two forms of PPP, the method of co-production is regulated in different ways. In the contract form there is limited co-production between public and private actors. This primarily consists of interaction at the start of a PPP project regarding the basic principles of the project to be contracted-out. This mode of co-operation is a variation on the classic method of contract allocation. Here, however, attempts are made to increase added value for both public and private parties through 'new forms' of contract relationship. Ideas about new contract forms crop up in a large number of countries, but are worked out in particular detail in the UK's PFI projects, with a variety of isomorphic processes leading to their adoption elsewhere (DiMaggio and Powell, 1983). The ideas of the Dutch expertise centre for PPP, for example, have been largely adopted from the English PFI model. The precondition for success for this type of approach to co-production is that the public party should be able to specify the problem (though not the solution, which would be the case in a 'traditional' contracting arrangement) and that clear rules for the tendering process exist (Klijn, 2002). The organizational co-operation constructions, or partnerships, model of PPP involves a far more intensive interaction because the various project components, which are often the domain of diverse private and public actors, have to be co-ordinated. Moreover, it is more difficult to clearly delineate in advance the content and ambitions of the co-operation.

The difference in responsibility and risk division between the two forms is crucial. In a contract relationship there is a clear delineation of responsibility and risk and both ex ante and ex post negotiations will test that delineation. The commissioning party (the public party) is responsible for the problem/project specifications. After some co-production in the early phase (pre-contract negotiations), responsibilities are very strictly divided between public and private parties. Once the tendering process has been concluded the relationship is one of regulation. The principal (the public actor) monitors the behaviour and actions of the agent (the private actors).

In a partnership the co-production is longer-term and more intensive since parties are also jointly responsible for the implementation. At the least, co-ordination is necessary because the parties' contributions have to be

Table 5.1: Co-production in PPP through contracts and partnership

Characteristics	Contract arrangements	Partnership arrangements
Type of relationship	Client (public party) and contractor (private party)	Joint decision-making (searching for linkages)
Division of responsibility	Clear division (both in developing and in implementing projects)	Shared responsibility (in development activities but often during realization)
Specification of problem and solution	Public party specifies problem and solution/product	Public and private party involved in joint process of problem and solution specification
Scope of project	Tendency to search for clear divisions; any scope expansion must fall within the delineated responsibilities	Tendency to search for scope expansion and linking of elements
Preconditions for success	Clear contract and tendering rules and clearly formulated problems/project requirements	Linking ambitions and goals, effective rules for interaction to create commitment and profitable co-operation
Organizing principles	Separation of principal and agent, strict rules for tendering, competition during tendering, rules for judging outputs	Most important rules; joint rules for decision-making, exit, conflict regulation, joint production and division of benefits
Management principles	Strongly based on principles of project management (specifying goals, organizing time planning, organizing manpower)	Based on principles of process management (searching for goals, linking and connecting actors' activities, and linking of decisions)
Information exchange	Strictly separated and used as strategic resource	Indispensable resource that needs to be shared
Pay-off rules	Actors maximize their own profit (pay-off rules separate profits of actors). Transaction costs are mainly made in monitoring agent and tendering procedure	Actors maximize joint benefit (pay-off rules tie actors to each other). Transaction costs are mainly made in organizing process and exchange of information
Type of co-production	Limited and occurring primarily prior to the tendering process; after that only monitoring; no co-production	Extensive during the whole process; at first primarily regarding nature of ambitions and searching for linkages, later on more co-production in jointly realizing ambitions

Source: Adapted from Teisman, 1998 and Klijn and Teisman, 2000.

tailored to one another, and more joint product or policy development takes place. A comparison between contract – in whatever form – and partnership is illustrated in Table 5.1. Comparison of contracting and partnership suggests two different organizational forms. The different characteristics described in Table 5.1 suggest that these two forms are not easy to 'mix' – they are institutionally quite separate. The differences between the contract and partnership forms suggest they may have different purposes, and that they might be appropriate in different circumstances. Contracting would be suitable where there is a clear product or service specification, and where complexity (in terms of number of involved actors, contested nature of the decisions, scope of the project) is not too large (Kirkpatrick, 1999; Williamson, 1985, 1996).

PPP in the Netherlands: the difference between rhetoric and reality

The first Dutch reference to PPP can be traced to the mid-1980s. Privatization of state-owned firms and outsourcing public tasks and goods became popular due both to budget cuts and discussions on the retreat of the state. It was at this time that the idea of PPP received attention. In the Netherlands, however, the concept of New Public Management gaining currency in the UK, USA, New Zealand and Australia, was not yet a dominant part of policy-makers' discourse (cf. Chapter 2). In the Netherlands, PPP emerged in official documents in 1986. In the 'government agreement' between the parties making up the coalition of 1986 one can read: 'New forms of Public–Private Cooperation will be established with local governments, the local and regional private actors and if necessary central government, that will be aimed towards increasing the investment volume, for instance, urban restructuring.'

Two road tunnel projects (Wijkertunnel and Tunnel onder de Noord) were initiated within this policy context (both by means of a DBMF (Design, Build, Maintenance and Finance) contract, paid for by shadow tolls). Interest in PPP, however, was to wane. The evaluation of the two tunnel projects showed that the projects were more expensive compared to public financing. Two further PPP projects involved Netherlands railways. These were promoted as exemplars of PPP. The high-speed railway (from Amsterdam to Paris) proved difficult to start (it is scheduled for completion in 2007) and the Betuwelijn (a new rail route from Rotterdam harbour to the German border to transport goods) did not attract financial investments from private actors up to 2006, the year it was finished. These experiences reduced the initial expectations of PPP in the Netherlands.

The discussion on PPP in the Netherlands

In the late 1990s, however, the concept of PPP was revived in political discussions. The coalition agreement of the Cabinet Kok II (the second coalition cabinet of the Social-Democrat Party and the Liberal-Conservative Party), which came into power in 1998 said that: 'The aim is a controlled enlargement of the PPP practice in the Netherlands. The required knowledge, expertise and experience will be combined in a knowledge centre according to the report "Knowledge through cooperation". This knowledge centre will draft policy conditions in close cooperation with the sector ministries for PPP and provide support with concrete PPP projects and advice for PPP projects.'

A PPP Knowledge Centre was established in the Ministry of Finance, reporting to the Ministry Council and Parliament. A review of these reports (especially the annual overviews) suggests that early optimism – with 'easy' ripe-fruit projects for the picking – was not justified. The 2001 Knowledge Centre report (pp. 41–2) concluded that tendering or contracting was proceeding slowly because:

- Different public sector actors had different views about individual projects.
- The public sector found it difficult to formulate a clear and functionally specified output.
- Project subsidies distorted the incentive structure for private sector actors.
- Private actors were excluded from key process stages.

A year later the tone had become more critical (Kenniscentrum PPS, 2002). There was disappointment about the progress of the contractual concession form of PPP, with the conclusion that whilst the concept of PPP and the mechanisms were sound, the actual results in terms of realized projects are too limited. The Knowledge Centre suggested that public actors needed to develop a new approach. They noted that many proposed PPP were relatively small – with transaction costs to both sides out of proportion to the benefits they would receive. This was a theme of subsequent reports with the message that: 'The application of PPP is still too incidental' (Kenniscentrum 2004: 2) and a plea for realism in the development of potential PPP projects: 'a precondition is that both the public and the private sectors have realistic expectations of the potential of PPP. The public sector should not try to entice the market (and other government authorities) with projects that they have not already determined to be unfeasible and the private sector must not submit proposals if their only "added value" is postponed payment' (Kenniscentrum, 2004: 2).

This report signalled that the first DBMF road project had been signed. It also reinforced the message that public actors, including central public actors, should pay a different and more active role in identifying and promoting PPP projects (see Kenniscentrum, 2004). A consistent view in these reports was that the public sector should define output specifications and should create room for private actors to search for innovative ways to implement and create products.

PPP projects in the Netherlands: an overview

Most active PPP projects in the Netherlands take place in the sectors of Transport and Housing and Urban Development. A study of 51 known PPP projects in 2002 by Ecorys revealed that they were either infrastructure projects or area development projects (cf. Table 5.2).

The Ecorys report makes a distinction between two different forms of PPP: *joined plan development* and *implementation*. The first form dominates in the area development projects involving many different actors and complex networks of interdependency. These projects show intense interaction and complex decision-making. Contracts are only part of the whole co-operation process. In the second form the relationship is closer to the classic 'principal–agent' type. The principal (public authority) chooses someone to implement a project by means of a tendering process. One important difference between the two types is that starting points and goals are often not clear at the start of the joint development project and are subject to further negotiation and decision-making. Those PPPs aimed at implementation often have a more clear and specified character. The two types of projects also encounter different types of initiation problems. In joint development projects there is a large time investment involved in identifying actors and in understanding their views, interests and perspectives. For the initiation PPP project there has to be a minimum scope/value/finance guarantee for it to be of interest to the private sector.

PPP: early stage or implementation?

In the Netherlands, PPP has become an important instrument in government policy, but the actual realization of PPP projects is less advanced. Most

Table 5.2: PPP projects divided to their character (51 projects)

Type of project	% of projects
Infrastructure projects:	54
• Roads	24
• Other transport infrastructure	22
• Other projects	8
Area development:	46
• Industrial areas	14
• Green infrastructure	12
• Urban development/restructuring	8
• Vinex (= new extensions of cities)	6
• Combination projects	6

Source: Ecorys, 2002.

projects are in a plan development phase (area development projects) or in the pre-tendering stage (infrastructure/product PPPs). Overall, however, an increasing number of proposals are getting through to realization (Kenniscentrum, 2004). A recent study of managerial behaviour in eighteen complex PPP projects (Klijn et al., 2006) suggests that private sector actors are beginning to have a greater involvement in the PPP process.[1]

Private actors play different roles in PPPs: the involvement of private actors was looked at. This also gives us a picture how far various PPP projects have developed. Table 5.3 gives an overview of involvement of private actors in PPP projects.

Six out of eighteen projects (30 per cent) were in an implementation phase. In seven projects private actors are involved in a consultation procedure, while thirteen projects were a joint development. Two projects were even initiated by private actors (Klijn et al., 2006). One of those projects, Sijtwende (Box 5.1), is considered to be the 'best practice' of partnership in the Netherlands. It is striking that this PPP is initiated and managed by a consortium of private actors. Public actors play a less dominant (reactive) role in this PPP.

Table 5.3: Involvement of private actors per phase in 18 selected PPP projects

	Planning phase			Realization phase
Projects	Consultation	Joint development	Private initiative	
Total (18)	7	13	2	6

Source: Klijn et al. (2006).

Box 5.1: The Sijtwende case

Sijtwende is a somewhat special case. It resulted from a long-term inter-administrative conflict between Voorburg (municipality) and the Ministry of Transport (by means of Rijkswaterstaat), which championed a new road track (Verlengde Landscheidingsweg, abbreviated to VLW) through Voorburg. This conflict lasted sixty years! The partnership, therefore, represents a peculiar breakthrough in a public–public controversy. A 'neutral' third party, the private consortium Sijtwende BV, showed itself to be a process manager capable of achieving reconciliation by breaking through the barriers between public organizations. At the same time, it played a role as project manager, in the sense that it developed a creative and innovative multifunctional land use plan.

Continued

The private consortium Sijtwende BV put forward a 'hollow dyke' solution, the Sijtwende Plan. This safeguarded the interests of the Ministry of Transport (the road route) and those of Voorburg (concerns about economic and environmental impact). The 'hollow dyke' rises six metres above ground level and is both soundproofed and landscaped.

The Sijtwende Plan involves a two kilometre length of road most of which is in three lengths of hollow dyke (measuring 1000 metres, 275 metres and 375 metres respectively). Between the three covered sections there will be two junctions. Covering the road in this way increases 22 hectares of land for housing and office building in the area to a functionally useable area of 27 hectares. This multiple exploitation of the area provided financial compensation for the relatively expensive hollow dyke version of the VLW. About 700 new homes will be built on either side, some of them directly adjoining the dyke, but none will be situated directly on top of this structure. The plan also includes about 10 000 square metres of office space and the building of a recreational area, green space and leisure facilities.

The organizational form: contracting or partnership?

Most of the projects in the Netherlands do not have a separate organizational form – they can more or less be characterized as a mutual adjustment through which the construction partners achieve necessary co-ordination on an ad hoc basis without clear organizational structures or contractual relations. Table 5.4 illustrates this. Other research also shows actors' preference for relatively loose forms of organizations (Ham and Koppenjan, 2002; Ecorys, 2002). This is not surprising given the fact that more tightly structured organizational forms bring along more transaction costs. The fact that many projects are not in an implementation phase may increase the tendency to choose loose forms of organization, although in the projects that are in an implementation phase still 50 per cent are being implemented without a special organizational form being employed.

Of course contracts still play an important role in the implementation phase. Large building activities are not started without contractual agreement between public and private actors. Sometimes these contracts are innovative contracts like the contracts that have recently been signed for the road project A59, which is a DBMF contract. But most projects use variations on the classic arm's-length contract.

The available research on PPPs in the Netherlands suggests that whilst the contractual form of PPP dominates the policy discussion, it is the partnership form (often in a rather loosely coupled organizational form) that has so far been dominant in practice. Experience of PPPs is dominated by infrastructure projects or projects in the field of urban restructuring or regeneration. These tend to be rather complicated projects (both in scope and in the sense that they are contested and involve many different actors). Experiences

Table 5.4: Type of organization for 18 selected PPP projects

	Type of (project) organization			
	Public	Private	Public-Private	No separate form
Total (18)	5	4	2	8

Source: Klijn et al. (2006).

in the Netherlands with innovative DBMF contracts remains limited. This is at least an indication that the presumption being voiced before (contract forms for relatively well-defined projects) is not unreasonable.

PPP in the UK: from PFI to partnership?

Public–private partnerships have become a key element in the UK's programme for modernizing public services. PPP has become a broad term, which includes almost any relationship between public and private actors that has the objective of delivering public benefit. In the UK two forms have developed: the Private Finance Initiative (PFI) and Strategic Service Partnerships (SSP).

The rise of PFI in the UK

The PFI arose during the late 1980s and early 1990s in response to a number of factors. The Conservative government had developed policies based on an increasingly pro-market agenda; there were problems in financing capital projects as a result of macro-economic policies (including the government's signing up to Maastricht 'convergence' criteria); there was political pressure for investment in assets in health, education and transport; and there was a lively capital finance market looking for investment opportunity (Spackman, 2002; Greenaway et al., 2004).

In PFI schemes (De Bettignies and Ross, 2004; 4Ps, 2006) four of the main tasks of procuring and delivering capital intensive projects are undertaken in the private sector (Table 5.5).

Before 1992, however, only two river crossings[2] (cf. Box 5.2) and a handful of health service projects in Scotland (see H.M. Treasury 2005, 2006) had emerged. Despite growing political interest in PFI, practice was slow to start – mainly due to bureaucratic and financial obstacles.

The first 're-launch' of PFI took place in 1993. The government created a Private Finance Panel based in the Treasury, but with a mixture of public service and private sector expertise. The purpose of the panel was to promote PFIs and to develop guidance for government departments on their use. The Treasury, formerly hostile to private finance, took on the responsibility for

Table 5.5: Allocation of activity in a PFI project

Public	Private
1. Identification of need and commissioning of supply	
	2. Definition and design of the project
	3. Financing the capital costs
	4. Building the asset
	5. Operating and maintaining the assets to deliver the required service
6. Monitoring performance, making payment, project evaluation and identification of future need	

Box 5.2: The Skye Bridge PFI

The Skye Bridge PFI scheme was negotiated before PFI was launched in 1992, but was signed just after. The capital cost of the bridge was estimated at £23.6 million to be paid back from user tolls until the project had been amortized (expected to be 14–18 years). In the event the bridge cost £39 million. There were weaknesses in its procurement (NAO, 1997), but more seriously there was a significant local opposition to the tolls themselves. The bridge was the only link with the mainland as alternative ferry routes were closed when the bridge opened). The tolls were the highest bridge tolls in Europe. Between 1995 and 2005 £27 million of tolls were collected: the operators expected to collect another £20 million before the PFI ended. In addition, the Scottish Executive would have had to pay £18 million in various subsidies agreed with the bridge operator.

In 2005, after a nine-year campaign of civil disobedience and legal challenges to the tolls, the Scottish Executive announced it had bought out the PFI contract for £27 million – and it was to review all toll bridge arrangements in Scotland.

this new policy – partly using it as a way of exercising control over the 'spending' departments in government. This role was strengthened in 1994 when Private Finance Units were established in each department, and the 'universal testing rule' was implemented requiring *all* capital projects to be assessed for PFI suitability (H.M. Treasury, 1995).

The second re-launch of PFI was in 1995. The government listed £9.4 billion worth of 'priority' projects and promised to eliminate the 'unnecessary bureaucracy' that was preventing PFI schemes from being developed and funded. At the same time the Private Finance Panel started to increase its output of guidance on PFI projects. There was an increase in the number and value of PFI projects signed off. In the same year local authorities established the *Public–Private Partnership Programme* (4Ps) to support PFI projects in local government (which were subject to different accounting rules).

Development of the PFI schemes

From 1995 the number of PFI projects signed each year started to increase. Although the private sector expressed fears about the effect of a Labour victory in 1997 on projects in development, this did not appear to affect their willingness to engage in negotiations. In fact the Labour Party was positive towards PFI,[3] and passed legislation to reassure investors dealing with local authorities and NHS Trusts. The new government brought PFI schemes within the general scope of 'public–private partnerships' that included: complete or partial privatizations; contracting-out with private finance at risk (PFI); and selling government services in partnership with private sector organizations (H.M. Treasury, 2000). The new government responded to continuing criticisms about delays in PFI schemes (see House of Commons, 1996) by commissioning the Bates review of PFI policy. This recommended 27 changes to the organization and management of PFI. All the recommendations were accepted, and a PFI Taskforce (the third re-launch) was established in the Treasury with staff drawn from the UK's financial services industry (House of Commons, 2001; H.M. Treasury 1997a). The Taskforce was time-limited to two years. Towards the end of that period there was a second review of PFI. This recommended the formation of a public–private partnership, 'Partnerships UK' (PUK), to promote PFI and to support specific schemes. Partnerships UK was headed by someone from the private sector and financed by 'success fees' once PFI deals were signed (H.M. Treasury, 1999a).

In parallel, the Office of Government Commerce (OGC) was established. The OGC, based in the Treasury, became broadly responsible for PFI policy whilst PUK (and 4Ps) worked on specific transactions. As Greenaway et al. (2004) observe, these organizations now work in concert to promote PFI and to support each other. PFI was gaining ground in the UK, especially in the

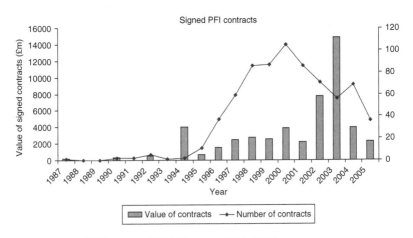

Figure 5.1: Signed PFI projects (H.M. Treasury 2005, 2006)

Box 5.3: PFI roads in the UK

Transport projects (mainly roads and urban rapid transit systems) make up nearly half of all PFI by value (7 per cent of the projects). The Highways Agency uses two main approaches to PFI schemes:

1. A route (and income from a 'shadow toll' or an 'availability payment') is transferred to the PFI vehicle in exchange for construction/upgrading of one section and maintenance of the entire route. The operator has to balance the costs of better construction against the costs of more maintenance *and* loss of traffic revenue. By 2004 there were ten projects like this with a total value of £800 million.
2. A concession is agreed with the successful bidder to build, operate, and maintain a tolled facility (usually a bridge) in return for the toll income *and* income from parallel or alternative tolled routes.[4] The concession runs until the capital costs are fully amortized (twenty years) and then the facility returns (in full working order) to the state. The Dartford Crossing and the Second Severn Crossing were financed this way.

---

period 1995–2001. Figure 5.1 presents the number of PFI projects and the capital value of each year's tranche of projects.[5]

The number of new projects signed in one year peaked in 2000, and the average value of projects appears to have settled around £20 million. Just under half (48 per cent) of the projects (by value) are transport schemes. Other important fields are health (13 per cent), defence (10 per cent) and education (8 per cent) (Shaoul, 2005; H.M. Treasury, 2005, 2006).

Two surveys of PFI schemes (NAO, 2002; Low et al., 2005) observed that PFI provides lessons for other types of procurement:

- Importance of clearly defined performance requirements;
- Financial penalties for failure to perform;
- Innovative governance arrangements (open-book accounting, shared inspections, common performance measurement systems);
- Senior management focus on critical outcomes.

Despite the attention given to PFI contracts in discussions of UK public policy they have never been a *significant* part of the total capital expenditure needed by government. As Figure 5.1 suggests, the number and total value of PFI projects appears to have peaked. This appears to be due to a number of factors:

- The problems involved in obtaining approval for PFI schemes;
- Cherry-picking by the private sector of the more favourable proposals – leaving others unable to complete the early procurement stages;
- The completion of the early investment cycle of a new government;
- The increasing availability of alternative procurement forms (some influenced by PFI practice – see below);

- The application of lessons from PFI to the evolution of traditional procurement routes;
- The problems of 'affordability' as public service budgets tighten and the 'fixed' cost of the PFI charge takes an increasing proportion of spending (McFadyen and Rowland, 2002);
- The relatively high transaction costs of PFI schemes (Dudkin and Välilä, 2005);
- Changing policy priorities that imply a preference for smaller and/or shorter capital investment projects.

PFI has failed to release 'new' money for capital investment in public services. Debt, whether on or off the books, still has to be repaid. And despite being lumped within 'public–private partnerships', PFIs do not demonstrate 'partnership' behaviour any more than classic arm's-length contracts.

The attention for other partnership forms of PPP

In recent years, the standard PFI approach has been supplemented by LIFT (Local Improvement Finance Trust) schemes for local health services (DoH, 2001, 2006) and the 'Building Schools for the Future' (BSF) programme in education (Partnerships for Schools, 2004). In the standard PFI, the 'public–private partnership' dimension is at the interface between the public authority and the 'special purpose vehicle' set up in the private sector to finance and deliver the required (asset-based) service. In LIFT and BSF schemes the public sector holds an equity stake in the 'Liftco' or LEP ('Local education Partnership'). In the case of education this development was partly built on lessons from the failures of some early schools PFI projects to deliver an 'educational vision' (DfES, 2003; Audit Commission, 2003). Both LIFT schemes and LEPs are aimed at supporting smaller capital projects. As with PFI the public authority pays a charge for the use and maintenance of the asset. This involvement of the public sector adds extra complexity with the promise of extra flexibility.

There is still not enough evidence on LEPs (the first of which started in May 2006) and LIFT schemes (only one of which has been operating for over a year). In a review of finance initiatives in health care, however, the Kings Fund (2005) suggested that LIFT schemes suffered from disproportionate transaction costs that would eat into any savings or other benefits.

SSPs, like LEPs and LIFT schemes, are potentially more complex than PFI projects: they are also less well researched. The decision-making, performance, control and accountability characteristics of strategic service partnerships *potentially* place them in opposition to the 'arm's-length' (Coulson, 1998) contractual arrangements that UK public services have traditionally used.

Table 5.6 illustrates the different forms. The *range* within existing SSPs (ODPM, 2004: 71) illustrates a further differentiating factor. The governance structures involved are not simply *different*, they are invariably more *complex.* The traditional contract involves one client and one supplier (perhaps supported by a number of subcontractors in a hierarchical supply chain). A Private Finance Initiative project typically involves one client and one supplier (which may itself be a private sector 'partnership'). An LEP or Liftco involves actors playing more than one role: the public sector and the private sector play client, investor, and service provider roles. A strategic service partnership can involve any number of clients and any number of suppliers.

Table 5.7 illustrates the membership (by overall category) of the 'pathfinder' SSPs identified by the ODPM (ODPM, 2004).

Table 5.6: Governance structures and the complexity of the project

Governance	Specification	Capital funding	Service delivery	Sharing of objectives
Conventional (arm's-length)	Local authority	Local authority	Private sector	Low
Private Finance Initiative	Local authority (output-based)	Private sector	Private sector	Mixed
LIFT / LEP	Local authority / health authority (outcomes) Partnership (outputs)	Private sector / local authority / health authority / central agency	Private sector and public sector co-ordinated though partnership	High
Strategic Service Partnership	Local authority and/or public/private partners	Local authority or private and/or public/private sector partners	Local authority and/or public/private parters	High

Source: Adapted from ODPM 2004: 8.

Table 5.7: Memberships of pathfinder SSPs

	Main partners				
	Local authority	National Health Service	Other sector	Public–private sector	Not-for-profit
Maximum	12	4	7	10	3
Minimum	1	0	0	0	0
Average	3.3	0.5	0.4	1.2	0.2

From early experience with SSPs, the UK government suggests seven key issues (ODPM, 2004):

- Too many partners in the early stages can slow progress;
- Importance of a robust business case, budget and timetable;
- Need for dedicated project management/dedicated project team;
- Small management groups are more effective than large steering groups;
- Careful attention is needed to ensure an integrated structure;
- Complex partnerships need strong leadership;
- Objectives have to be achievable.

These are observations that fit with knowledge of other partnerships (Osborne, 2000; Sullivan and Skelcher, 2002). In the UK the distinction between contract forms and partnership forms has blurred. Central government policy mechanisms, isomorphic forces, and environmental factors have combined to create a patchwork in which 'pure' contract forms continue to be used for supplies (as could be predicted from Williamson) and for PFI service contracts (which would not be predicted). Partnership forms exist across the public sector and show a considerable variety of governance structures (ODPM, 2004a, 2004b).

PPP as reform: the UK and the Netherlands compared

In this chapter we stated that PPP could appear in two different forms: the contractual form and the partnership form. In this section we complete the comparison between the two countries. We will focus on policy discussions in both countries on PPP, review the 'state of the art' in PPP projects and conclude with some conclusions about which forms are dominant.

PPP policy in the UK and the Netherlands

In both the Netherlands and the UK, PPP developed as a consequence of fiscal pressures and (political) discussions about a new and less prominent (vertical hierarchical) role for the state. In the UK PPP was politically presented as a way of meeting demands for investment in public services without, *apparently*, increasing public debt. The policy was aided by a lively capital finance market looking for investment opportunity. In the Netherlands the private sector has remained reluctant to invest in major transport and infrastructure projects.

The explicit policy motives for engaging in PPP in the UK and the Netherlands appear to be similar. In both countries there is a common political discourse of 'value for money', 'improved policy implementation', 'improved service delivery' and 'better risk management'. The procurement of major projects is dominated by the idea of 'innovative contracts' that include the design, finance and maintenance stages traditionally kept by the client. There is also a strong belief that the security of long contracts will encourage private sector innovation. Yet in both countries the 'contract' arrangements are still firmly based in a political context. In the Netherlands there is an active debate about the roles of politicians in relation to setting up and designing PFI projects and the management of the contexts in which they are delivered. In the UK the problems of affordability of PFI charges (particularly in the NHS) and problems arising from the inflexibility of PFI projects (particularly in local government) have remained on the political agenda. Although PPPs have created new ways of *managing* and *organizing* the creation and delivery of public assets they have not de-politicized the spending of public money.

Both countries had difficulties in getting PPP established as a means of supporting public projects. In both countries the earliest and the most significant projects have been in transport and the infrastructure sector. In the UK the flow has extended to education and the health sector (and a move from PFI to more complex public–private structures). In the Netherlands the initial extension has been to the urban planning sector. The slow start in the UK was 'compensated' by a peak flow of PFI projects from 1995 to 2001. The Netherlands, however, seems to have stuck in the 'start-up' phase. In 2004 the Kenniscentrum PPS said that 'The application of PPP is still too incidental'. There were problems with the specification of projects, the definition of performance requirements by public actors, and in making PPPs attractive to private partners. The UK also experiences these problems, but appears to have been more successful in overcoming them. But if we look at both countries from a convergence perspective (see Chapter 2), one can certainly see some convergence in the sense that both countries initiated PPP for more or less the same reason, had initial problems, and although started from a different starting point (see our conclusion further on) seem to be using both forms of PPP more often. One can even see policy transfer from the UK to the Netherlands and recently (with the case of building the Montaigne school) UK-based actors (like Barclays Bank) joining in with PPP projects in the Netherlands.

PPP: state of the art

Although PPP co-operation projects can be found in many areas, they appear to be particularly strong in tackling urban problems (regeneration processes, accessibility, economic vitality, improving the living environment and so on) and transport and infrastructure projects. UK partnerships in health care and education were based on the PFI producing and maintaining the *infrastructure* for services to be provided by the public sector. The more recent UK experience, in which partnerships have been developed for social care services, public service call centres, and tax collection, suggests that PPPs can be developed wherever there is a policy imperative to support them.

In both the UK and the Netherlands the number of PPP projects is growing. In the UK the PFI is clearly a contractual form. The number of PFI schemes appears to outnumber the number of partnership form arrangements (though there is no central register or definition of these). In the Netherlands, however, there are fewer contract form PPPs despite the policy imperatives to create new and innovative contracts between public and private sector. There is 'talk' about innovative contracts and new forms of tendering procedures. In practice, however, there are few examples of innovative contract design. The reality of PPP in the Netherlands is that partnership-like forms, either tightly organized, but most of the time rather loosely organized, are by far dominant up to now. In the UK there is a real possibility of convergence between contract and partnership forms (through health and education partnerships) alongside growing interest in 'strategic' partnerships involving a number of public and/or private parties. Whether these new forms will remain as 'partnerships' in the face of an adversarial culture of contract law, a public sector culture of risk aversion, and a management culture in which the allocation of blame and the allocation of responsibility are practically indistinguishable remains to be seen.

Contracts or partnerships: choice or contingency?

Can the differences between the experiences of the UK and the Netherlands be explained as a matter of choice, of contingency or of path dependency? Contract form arrangements tend to predominate for projects that are relatively easy to formulate (school building, road contracting, and ICT infrastructure projects). Partnership forms tend to occur more with complex projects (urban restructuring and regeneration, service delivery and so on). There remain possible exceptions to this observation: the partnerships for the maintenance and rebuilding of the London Underground have been dogged by disputes about performance monitoring and the allocations of risk and responsibility. Where the partnership is built around long-term contract relationships there is a danger that, as the people who established the partnership move on to other work, those who remain seek the comfort of the contract form in the absence of 'embedded' social structures that legitimate and recreate the partnership form over time.

The differences between the two countries may also be a question of path dependency. In the Netherlands the 'testing ground' for PPP was urban restructuring. There was already an emphasis on partnership forms – and this was not dampened by policy documents and by the Kenniscentrum PPS advice in favour of contractual forms. In the UK, on the other hand, PFI and the range of PPPs were clearly associated with outsourcing and the identification of clear projects that could be specified in clear output terms. This hypothesis would partly fit both the contingent assumption (different forms are suitable for different situations) and the country's different management cultures: consensus and deliberation in the Netherlands; adversity and hierarchy in the UK.

The contingent assumption relies on actor passivity or on actors following 'objective characteristics of the situation'. Active social theories would suggest that the advantages and disadvantages of the two partnership forms can be assessed by actors as the social situation is also a choice of actors. This can be illustrated by a conclusion of a Dutch study of nine PPP projects by Van der Ham and Koppenjan (2002). This concluded that actors either move quickly and choose tendering as the means for implementing a project, or work more slowly to develop partnerships through extensive interactions among possible partners and actors in the wider network. In the first case projects are often narrowly defined and the opportunities for innovation and scope optimalization are often missed. In the second case new ideas are developed, but actors may find it very difficult to manage the resulting interaction process properly (Klijn et al., 2002).

Although the two forms do arise from contingency, this is not a passive process. Actors make choices and assess the current and future benefits of those choices. At each stage of the commissioning or procurement process there may be a reassessment of the choices available until there comes a point at which the actors have to make binding commitments. A contract form is inappropriate when the parties are unclear about what they want to achieve and how they will know they have achieved it. But even in the most loosely connected partnerships searching for added value there will be one point at which it is necessary to develop contract form relationships in order to clarify commitments and responsibilities. For public and private sector actors in both countries the question then arises as to whether the contract form is a manifestation of *part* of the partnership relationship or whether it *becomes* the partnership.

Notes

1. The 18 selected projects contain most of the well-known PPP projects of the last five to ten years.
2. The Queen Elizabeth Bridge (Dartford Crossing) and the Second Severn Crossing. Both these schemes are financed by user fees.
3. 'A Labour government will overcome the problems that have plagued the PFI at a national level. We will set priorities between projects, saving time and expense; we will seek a realistic allocation of risk between the partners to a project; and we will ensure that best practice is spread throughout government. We will aim to simplify and speed up the planning process for major infrastructure projects of vital national interest' (Labour Party 1997).
4. Except for the Sky Bridge where the alternatives were forced out of business.
5. The 2003 figure is distorted by the £1000 million 'Skynet 5' PFI for the Ministry of Defence.

6

'New Public Managers' in Europe: Changes and Trends

Sandra van Thiel, Bram Steijn and Marine Allix

Introduction

New Public Management (NPM) reforms as described in Chapter 1 have affected the profile and functioning of top civil servants. This chapter discusses the combined effect of personnel reforms and the creation of so-called quasi-autonomous organizations. It would seem that as a result of these reforms two different types of 'new public managers' have emerged: *senior public officials* within the central departments and the *top executives* of quasi-autonomous agencies. We expect a number of differences between these two categories. The main aim of this chapter is to investigate these expectations. To do so, we will use data from two surveys of our own (on the Netherlands and France) and secondary sources on a number of countries (Denmark, Germany, Italy and the United Kingdom).

The outline of this chapter is as follows. First we will briefly sketch the main characteristics of personnel management reforms that have occurred since the early 1980s in different Western European countries. Next, we will go into the motives for the establishment of quasi-autonomous bodies and speculate on the effects thereof for the position and job profile of top executives, compared to senior public officials in ministries. Then we will use information from different sources to describe the profile of top senior public officials and top executives, and investigate the differences between them. Data collection on this topic is still in its early stages, so we will not be able to offer information about all characteristics, but there are enough data to give a cross-cutting, representative image of what is happening. In the conclusions we will formulate some questions for future research into this topic.

The rise of the new public manager

In most Western countries public sector reform occurred from the 1980s onwards. To size down and reduce budgets, governments decided to restructure their administrative organization and change the way in which they were working (cf. Kickert, 1997; OECD, 2002, 2005; Christensen and Lægreid, 2003; Pollitt and Bouckaert, 2004). Within government bureaucracies, new management techniques were introduced, usually originating from the private sector like performance indicators and human resource management (cf. Bovaird and Löffler, 2003). This changed the way senior public officials have to manage their organizations and departments.

Next to restructuring and abandoning tasks, parts of the (executive) organization and employees were put at arm's length – resulting in a more autonomous position for the managers involved. As a result, a plethora of public bodies and executive agencies were created (Greve et al., 1999; Pollitt and Talbot, 2004). For example, in the Netherlands in 2006 almost 80 per cent of civil servants at the national level are working in so-called 'executive agencies', while another type of public body (ZBOs) employs more people than all the ministries put together (Van Thiel, 2001). Similar figures can be found for other countries: for example, in Sweden almost 75 per cent of civil servants at national level work in an agency (cf. PUMA, 2002).

It is our contention that as a result of these reforms two major changes with respect to the managerial function have occurred. First, senior public officials have become managers rather than policy advisers (cf. Lægreid, 2003: 145). And second, a new type of public manager has been created: the directors or executives of executive agencies and other types of public body. Together these two categories form what we will call new public managers (cf. Barlow et al., 1996: 7).

Transforming civil servants

To make governments more efficient, market-type mechanisms were introduced, such as internal markets in the public sector (for example, hospitals and schools competing with each other over budgets). Also, co-operation with private sector organizations increased, both in public–private partnerships and through outsourcing of public tasks. This required new skills and routines of senior public officials (Lægreid, 2003) and gave them more flexibility (managerial autonomy) and responsibility (accountability requirements). To acquire these new skills the number of management training programmes increased strongly (PUMA, 2003: 16).

These changes are reflected in the reform of personnel policies in the public sector. These reforms focused on three issues: (i) a reduction of security of permanent tenure by, for example, appointing top officials on a temporary basis and (ii) often on performance-related contracts because (iii) performance and managerial competence became more important criteria in decisions to hire and fire top officials (Pollitt and Bouckaert, 2004).

The implementation of these changes depends on the type of civil service system used in a country. In this respect, two ideal type systems can be distinguished: career-based and position-based (PUMA, 2003; see also OECD, 2005). Table 6.1 presents a global summary of these systems and the aims of the

Table 6.1: Characteristics of civil service systems and their reforms

	Career-based	Position-based
Recruitment	Recruitment based on scholastic background, by examination	Open procedures, applications by candidates from all backgrounds and sectors
Management of senior civil services	Centralized management, pre-structured career paths	Decentralized management
Aim	Coherent civil service; one culture, easy communication and high internal mobility	Wide choice of candidates, promoting competition, innovation and adaptability
Appointment	Appointment to civil service is permanent, contracts are related to positions	Contracts specify individual appointments for fixed terms, sometimes linked to organizational objectives
Disadvantages	• Lack of (external) competition for top positions; • Bias towards generalist skills; • Alienation from society and work floor	• Need for intricate appointment procedures; • Lack of common culture among top executives; • Weak mobility across organizations; • In case of departmental basis; small pool of good candidates
Aims of reforms	• Opening up recruitment process, increase external competition for top executive positions; • Introduce cultural change to stimulate adaptability; • Seeking to introduce management by objectives	• Establish competitive and transparent appointment procedures based on merit; • Re-centralization of management of top executives, for example keeping database of potential executives and central training programme to establish a common culture • Review of promotion and mobility system to encourage mobility across organization
Countries (size of senior civil service)	France (5360) Italy (4800) Spain (276)	Belgium (450) Finland (200) The Netherlands (739) United Kingdom (3500)

Source: Based on PUMA, 2003.

changes that have been planned or implemented. Individual countries may differ from this general picture, and there are of course many 'mixed cases'.

In countries with a *career-based* senior civil service top positions are held by members of an elite, who share a common background and socialization. They change jobs relatively frequently, but in principle never leave the civil service. The main objective of reform in countries with this system is to make top officials more responsive and accountable for their performance. The introduction of competition (from outsiders) and performance-related pay is expected to help achieve these goals.

In countries with a *position-based* senior civil service, vacant senior positions are open to a wide range of candidates, from both the civil service and the market. Personnel management is usually decentralized, that is, left to the discretion of departments. As a result, it can be rather fragmented, preventing mobility across organizations; top officials with specialist skills never leave their policy sector. Reforms in these countries tend to focus on more attention for generalist skills and a common culture, to establish a larger pool of qualified 'leaders' for the public sector as a whole.

The OECD (2005: 182) has pointed out that both traditional ways of organizing civil service systems are under pressure because of their disadvantages. In reality, this means that the two types are converging, with even more 'mixed types' as a result. For example, countries as Belgium, Finland, the Netherlands, Spain and the United Kingdom have made reform of the senior civil service part of the general public sector reform, whereas other countries like France and Italy have undertaken specific reform programmes targeted at the senior civil service (PUMA, 2003: 6). Despite their differences, however, all these countries have concentrated on the implementation of performance-oriented management. This has led to a decentralization of managerial decision-making and a stronger emphasis on the performance and responsibility of individual top officials. Appointments on (temporary) contracts have become more common. Often these contracts (including salary and job continuation) are related to performance requirements. Because of such changes, leadership, change management and human resource management have become important issues in public sector management (Farnham et al., 2005). The extent to which these changes have been implemented is, however, dependent upon country-specific characteristics, like the legal system, the traditional civil service system and the spread of public sector reform in general (cf. Page and Wright, 1999).[1]

The new category: top executives

In the wake of public sector reform many public tasks were delegated to organizations at arm's length to the government. Several reasons were given for such decisions (see Van Thiel, 2001: 9–12 on the Dutch case; Pollitt and Bouckaert, 2004). We will mention three of those reasons here that are expected to have a direct impact on the position of the top executives managing these executive bodies.

First, in some cases it was considered desirable to separate administration from policy. Political interference with individual decisions was not wanted in the case of, for example, payment of benefits or regarding regulatory tasks. Independence would ensure impartiality.

A second motive for establishing executive agencies was the expectation that because of their managerial autonomy these organizations would operate much more efficiently than traditional government organizations. For example, many of these new bodies are allowed to use an accrual accounting system or to retain savings (cf. Pollitt et al., 2004).

A third argument refers to the expectation that the organizations at arm's length will be more customer-oriented. Not only will such bodies be closer to citizens and, therefore, more responsive to customer needs, but it was also argued that customers could exert more direct influence to voice their dissatisfaction in case of poor performance (cf. Le Grand and Bartlett, 1993).

It seems likely that the aforementioned developments have consequences for the job profile and position of top executives of quasi-autonomous agencies compared to senior public officials. First, top executives will have to be managers first and foremost, and be involved in policy-making and politics much less than senior public officials in ministries. This calls for extensive management training and expertise, preferably in the private sector, because that is where most of the newly adopted business techniques originate. Moreover, they operate at a greater distance from the government, which enables them greater managerial flexibility. This should be reflected in their labour position (tenure, salary, and so on). Second, top executives are held accountable for their performance not only by the principal (that is, minister), but also by other stakeholders like clients. Finally, we would expect that the position of top executives would be more comparable to private sector positions than senior public officials' positions. That would fit with the idea that quasi-autonomous organizations operate more like a (private) business.

More specifically, we have the following expectations about differences between both types of new public managers:

(1) Top executives will on average have had more working experience in the private sector than senior public officials (career).
(2) The educational background of top executives will on average be more directed towards managerial studies than in the case of senior public officials (training background).
(3) Top executives will on average spend more time on managerial issues than senior public officials.
(4) On average, top executives will have a legal position less comparable to traditional civil servants than senior public officials (for example permanent tenure, limited salary increments).
(5) Top executives will on average receive performance-related pay more often than senior public officials.
(6) Top executives will on average be less often member of a political party than senior public officials (politicization).

The following sections will deal with these expectations consecutively.

The background of new public managers

Table 6.2 shows some demographic details of new public managers. At first sight there appear to be more similarities than differences between the two types of new public managers: they share the same gender (male), age (over 50) and training background. With respect to the latter it can easily be seen that a large majority of managers have a degree in higher education. More specific data suggest also that law and economics are preferred studies for both types of managers (Nelissen et al., 1996). In France this homogeneity is even stronger due to the important role for ENA in the training of public servants. Although the empirical material is sketchy, this contradicts our second expectation.

Turning to our first expectation, Table 6.2 shows that top executives are still mainly recruited from the public sector, though an influx from the private sector is certainly taking place. Top executives have extensive experience in the public sector, either in the parent department, in the same executive organization or another one, or elsewhere in the public sector. For example, in Denmark most agency directors have worked in the parent department before being appointed (71.1 per cent of all appointments since 1935). Outside appointments are more likely to be from other parts of

Table 6.2: Profile of senior public officials and top executives in European countries

	N	% female	% University degree	Average age	Prior public service	Years in current job
The Netherlands						
Public officials	899	12	96.0	51.5	n.a.	n.a.
Executive agencies	19	18.2	84.2	51.1	89.9%	n.a.
ZBOs	67	14.3	83.3	51.9	76.4%	n.a.
Germany						
Public officials	n.a.	n.a.	96.9	n.a.	95.2%	n.a.
Denmark						
Executive agencies	n.a.	15.9	93.8	54.7	15.9 years	4.4
France						
Public officials	(all)	51.9[a]	n.a.	40–49	n.a.	n.a.
EPS	40	12.5	97.5[b]	53.0	5.2 years	3.5
AAIs	14	13.3	100[b]	62.0	2–4 years	(varied)
SCNs	13	30.0	92.2[b]	54.0	54.0%	6.2

Notes: [a] including all staff at schools. [b] including a degree from a 'grande école'. n.a. not available.
EPS, AAI and SCN are different types of public bodies in France.

Sources: ABD (2003); Derlien (2003); Kettl et al. (2004), Van Thiel et al. (2004), Allix (2005); Survey Data Dutch Ministry of Home Affairs (own analysis – compare Steijn, 2004).

the public or even private sector (19 per cent) than from other ministries (5.8 per cent; Christensen, 2005). For France, the average number of years spent in a job is relatively short. This is caused by the general use of consecutive temporary appointments in public functions (see below). When we look in more detail we find, however, that most respondents have had several jobs in the public domain prior to their current one. In fact, movement between government and business positions is rather frequent (Pollitt and Bouckaert, 2004: 248), as is a strong interdependency between administrative, political and policy-making roles in France (cf. Bezes, 2001). The homogeneous elite, known as the *grand corps*, has a strong corporate identity and an interest in self-perpetuation and self-preservation. This homogeneity is reinforced by the well-known monopoly of the *grandes écoles* for recruitment opportunities into the most powerful posts. The elite colonizes all administrative and top political positions within ministries, but also has the ability to move easily from one sphere to another (administration, party politics and corporate positions), thanks to strong networks. Apparently, most top executives of French quasi-autonomous bodies are also part of this elite. Only 7.5 per cent of all French respondents came from the private sector. In the case of AAIs there is a much higher degree of experience outside of the public sector (41.6 per cent), however, than in the other types of agency. To explain this, it could be hypothesized that the further away a public body is from the ministry, the more often a top executive will come from outside the public domain. The Dutch data support such an expectation; the number of executives with a private sector origin is highest for ZBOs (23.9 per cent) whereas for executive agencies the number is 11.1 per cent (total average for top executives 20.9 per cent).

Recently, increasing numbers of senior public officials are appointed who started their career outside the public sector. For example, in the Netherlands personnel policy reforms led to an increase of the percentage of 'outside' appointments – from 9 per cent in 2002 to 16 per cent in 2003 – although the large majority still came from within the public sector (ABD, 2002, 2003). A similar development is taking place in Italy, where recent reforms (Cassese, 2002) aim to obtain an 8 per cent influx into the highest ranks from outside the public service. With respect to Denmark (Christensen, 2005), there is also a slightly growing tendency to appoint senior managers who have worked in other ministries than their own (30 per cent), but nevertheless they are still seldom recruited from private businesses or local governments. In the German case (Derlien, 2003), more and more senior managers have had experience in other parts of the labour market prior to their public service career (32.2 per cent). This applies, however, mainly to the younger generations; 41.1 per cent of the current higher civil service still has an uninterrupted career in public service. Only 4.8 per cent originates from outside the public service. After early retirement (in their late fifties) it is, however, not uncommon for senior managers to take up a position in the private sector (banks, companies). All in all, there is a rather basic stability over time (1970–94) in German bureaucrats' role of understanding, recruitment and values (Derlien, 2003: 402). This is probably due to the fact that until 1994 NPM reforms occurred mainly at the local level, not the federal.

Comparing our data from Table 6.2 with our information about the career paths from senior public officials within departments, the data support our first expectation. Although the differences are small, top executives originate more often from the private sector than senior public officials in ministries, or at least they come more often from outside the parent department. Technically, our expectation is thus confirmed. Still, in both categories the large majority of top managers has followed a career path in the public sector. This would imply that even in countries with a position-based system, there is an administrative elite in charge of ministries and executive agencies. There are, however, two apparent trends, which might lead to changes in the near future: (i) the percentage of recruitment from the private sector seems to be on the increase (for *both* categories); and (ii) private sector recruitment seems to be larger within organizations that are further away from the central departments.

Functioning within job of new public managers

Unfortunately, we cannot fully investigate our third expectation, because we have not (yet) been able to find information on the job functioning of top executives. This section will therefore only deal with information about senior public officials. Of specific interest is our assumption that the job conditions of senior managers have changed under the influence of NPM. Therefore, we will pay attention to the amount of time spent on management issues and/or the managerial skills of senior public officials.

Each year, the Dutch Home Office holds a large-scale survey on issues related to the job, desired mobility and work orientations of employees working in the public sector (cf. Steijn, 2004). Here we have taken information of this survey on the job characteristics of managers. In the 2002 survey 28 312 respondents were interviewed. Of these, 75 can be characterized as high-ranking senior managers[2] working in sectors relevant for this chapter.[3] For comparison, data about middle managers and 'ordinary' employees are included in Table 6.3 as well.[4]

The seniority of Dutch public officials is quite high. Even more importantly, the data show that they have a loaded working week as they work more hours than stipulated in their contract and perceive a high level of work pressure. At the same time, their job autonomy is somewhat higher compared to other employees, which can explain why Dutch senior public officials are more satisfied with their job compared to other workers and also are less often looking for another job (cf. Nelissen et al., 1996: 97–100). If

Table 6.3: Job characteristics of senior management, middle management and ordinary employees in selected public sectors in the Netherlands (2004)

	Senior management	Middle management	Ordinary employees
Number of working hours (factual)	49	40	35
Mean number of subordinates	117	24	3
Number of years with current organization	19	15	14
Autonomy in job (5 = highest)	4.14	3.94	3.84
Level of work-pressure (5 = highest)	3.42	3.17	2.92
Looking for another job? (% yes)	24%	36%	34%
Job satisfaction (5 = high)	4.24	3.95	3.75

they do, however, they are more interested in a job in another organization; a third even preferred a job in the private sector (overall, this was a preference of 19 per cent of the employees).

What do we know about their performance? A survey in 1995 (Nelissen et al., 1996: 93–7) identified personality traits of civil servants in the Netherlands. At central level most of them see themselves as a statesman (60 per cent) rather than as an advocate or something else. They are dedicated to the programmes that they have to carry out (42 per cent). Hardly anyone would call himself a generalist manager (7 per cent). And when asked, most of them (56 per cent) perceive their own leadership more as participative than hierarchical.

A study into top managers of the Danish public sector corroborates this self-image. It shows that the expertise of top managers is mainly in policy advice and much less on managing organizations to reach maximal performance (Kettl et al., 2004). When asked, they rate their own knowledge of the specific policy domain in which they operate as 74 (on a scale of 100) and their abilities in using (new) management techniques at 63. An evaluation of top managers' involvement by their subordinates corroborates this opinion. Danish top managers are good at offering advice, maintaining the border between politicians and administration, and fostering orderly organizational performance. They are, however, less good at (visible) public leadership within the organization and towards subordinates, and using new management techniques like ICT (Kettl et al., 2004: 38).

In the late 1980s (1987), the German administrative elite saw itself mainly as a problem solver (94.5 per cent), an initiator of new projects (95.2 per cent) and an implementor of policies (94.5 per cent). The roles of facilitator

(3.4 per cent), ombudsman (34.2 per cent) and advocate (53.1 per cent) were least popular. This 'largely emphasizes the classical ideal of the neutral expert civil servant who competently translates political goals into action and impartially serves the commonweal...' As NPM elements, such as the policy/operations divide between ministries and agencies, are not applicable to a highly decentralized system like the German federal polity, 'the "intelligence of bureaucracy" would probably resist such reforms. [U]nder certain conditions, such as during unification after 1990 and since about 1995, mandarins can turn quite managerial' (Derlien, 2003: 420–3). According to Derlien, the increase in political party membership in the 1990s can be seen as an indicator of the increased awareness of the need for economy, efficiency and effectiveness (NPM) as it will help role understanding and streamlining ministries after reforms.

The lack of data on the behaviour within their job of top executives makes it impossible to draw conclusions on our third expectation. However, the data on senior public officials do not appear to corroborate our basic assumption about the shift in job content of senior public officials towards more attention for managerial matters. The self-reports of senior public officials still value policy advice skills as most important (cf. Noordegraaf, 2001, for the Dutch case). There is even a self-acknowledged disinterest in managerial skills. This would suggest that NPM has not led to real changes in the work profile of senior public officials. The earlier findings on the background and history of senior public officials suggested this also.

However, there are two noteworthy observations. First, the German experiences presented earlier show that although senior public officials do not often originate from the private sector, they frequently start working in the private sector after their public career. This effect is reverse to what we expected as a result of NPM influences. Our findings with respect to their job interest also pointed in this direction; their search for a new job extends beyond the parent department. The second interesting observation is presented in the Danish case. Christensen (2005) argues that as a result of the increased need for transparency and accountability, key elements of NPM, senior public officials' careers are cut short more often than before. Both examples show unexpected effects of NPM on the senior public officials' work patterns.

The legal position of new public managers

Relevant changes with respect to the position of senior public officials can perhaps best be illustrated by what has happened in the Netherlands. The Dutch system for recruitment and appointment of senior managers has always resembled a position-based system. Some important reforms, introduced in 1995, made this even more apparent. Until then, most senior public officials made their career through a well-defined path, usually within the same department. Long careers within specific segments of the civil service were the result. The main elements of reform were:

- All senior public officials[5] now belong to a central agency of the Home Office, called ABD; hence they are no longer employed by a specific ministry, but instead fall under the authority of the Home Office.
- Although all senior public officials still have permanent tenure, the maximum number of years in a single position within the civil service is limited to seven years. Senior public officials are expected to have found another job (within the civil service) before the end of that period. This change has led to a competition between senior managers for jobs in the civil service. As a result the medium length of stay within a senior management position in 2002 was only 3.2 years (ABD, 2003).
- Competition for senior management positions within the civil service is open, which in effect means that people from outside the civil service can also apply for them.

These reforms have clearly changed the position of senior public officials within the civil service. They facilitate the development of an *esprit de corps* ('t Hart et al., 2002), which is supposed to increase the emphasis on the managerial aspects of a senior management job and reduce the need for material knowledge of a certain field (but see our earlier findings). Political appointments of senior public officials are frowned upon. The same applies to Denmark, where appointments are based on merit and usually from the own ranks. Nevertheless, like in the Netherlands, the average length that senior managers stay in the same function has decreased from eighteen to nine years on average (Christensen, 2005).

In other countries political appointments of senior managers are more common. Take, for example, the recent changes in Italy. The Italian senior civil service has always had the characteristics of a career-based system as promotions were linked to the length in office. However, major changes were implemented in 1998 and 2002 (Cassese, 2002). A new government can now remove any of the 55 top public officials when they come into office. Moreover, all appointments are temporary, for a period between three and five years depending on the type of position. Interestingly, this seems to have led to an increase in the autonomy and influence of senior public officials, which they did not have before (Cassese, 1999).

The mix of a career-based system with political appointments can also be found in France. Contrary to the Netherlands and Italy, senior public officials are not bound to one policy sector during their career, making for stronger ties between ministries. The influence of elected politicians on the appointment of senior public officials is high. The interwoven nature of politics and administration has less to do with political preferences, but more with the common (training) background of individuals (see above). Senior public officials are not neutral, however, because they are embedded in a

Table 6.4: Appointment of Dutch and French top executives, 2004

	The Netherlands	France			
	Executive agencies (N = 19)	ZBOs (N = 67)	EPs (N = 40)	AAIs (N = 14)	SCNs (N = 13)
Function described as director	95%	70%	80%*	78.5%	84.6%
Appointment by parent minister	84%	35%	77.5%	13.3%	92.0%
Appointment by board	n.a.	54%	7.5%	n.a.	–
Permanent tenure, cf. civil servant	89.5%	32.8%	–	–	100%
Permanent tenure, other labour agreement	n.a.	49.3%	–	–	–
Temporary tenure, based on a contract	–	–	57.5% (3–5 yrs)	93.3% (3–5 yrs)	–

Notes: * also includes director general; n.a. not available.

Source: Van Thiel et al. (2004), Allix (2005).

complex network of loyalty and solidarity within the bureaucratic system at different levels. Through these powers senior managers can exert strong influences on, or organize resistance against, the development and implementation of policies, including NPM reforms (Page and Wright, 1999).

Clearly, the way top executives are appointed differs from the above (Table 6.4). Appointment procedures vary between types of agency. The parent minister always appoints top executives of Dutch contract agencies and French SCN. However, for bodies at greater arm's length the appointment of top executives becomes less and less the prerogative of the parent minister. In the case of French public establishments, 77.5 per cent of the top executives are appointed by the parent minister (and confirmed in the Council of Ministers). In other cases, the prime minister or the president of the Republic is the leading authority, as in the case of AAIs (52.6 per cent). Still, in total 90 per cent of EP appointments are still in the hands of the 'government'. For Dutch ZBOs, appointments are the prerogative of the boards (54 per cent). The minister himself appoints only one out of three ZBO directors.

As employees of Dutch agencies remain civil servants, they benefit from the accompanying legal rights such as permanent tenure. For almost half of the ZBO directors the situation is different; their tenure, salary and other benefits are laid down in collective labour agreements from the private or semi-public sector. Nevertheless, most of them still have permanent tenure (82.1 per cent). The contracts of these top executives are not included in the contract between parent department and executive agency, which contains the output and budget agreements for the organization. Nor is the performance of the organization decisive for the tenure and rewarding of the director.

The French situation is very different, at least for AAI and EP directors. They are appointed on a temporary basis, between three and five years. Nevertheless, they still consider themselves to be civil servants (EP: 90 per cent, AAI: 64 per cent). Those who are appointed on a contractual basis have contracts stipulating objectives that have to be achieved. In the case of public establishments, the directors' appointment is to some degree dependent on achieving the objectives. However, since not all of these contracts entail actual performance measures, it is not entirely certain how parent ministers evaluate the directors' performance. A number of respondents in the survey pointed out that the political aspects of their work and performance are also very important to the decision about the continuation of their appointment, in particular their relation (and trust) with the parent minister or ministry.

To sum up, we expected top executives to have a less traditional legal position than senior public officials. For the Dutch ZBOs this seems to be true; directors are appointed by boards rather than by the minister. Moreover, in half of the cases their legal position is different from that of a civil servant. Also, the uniform discipline on Dutch senior public officials, that is exerted by the ABD, is absent for ZBOs (but not for agency executives). In the UK, top executives and board members are appointed through an independent commissioner (OCPA) to avoid (political) patronage. So, there is (at least partial) corroboration of our fourth expectation.

Interestingly, in countries with a career-based system, such as Italy and France, temporary appointments have become the norm *both* for senior public officials and top executives. In some cases (see below) these appointments are even linked to performance contracts and salaries. This trend fits with the NPM reforms of personnel management and is apparently applied to *all* new senior public officials in these countries – and less so in countries with a position-based system. Our hypothesis is therefore only supported for countries with a position-based system.

Performance-related pay for new public managers

Between 2001 and 2002 the salaries of Dutch senior public officials in the public sector have increased by almost 12 per cent – far more than the salaries of ordinary employees in the public (or private) sector. The data also show that average salaries for top executives are higher than senior public officials' salaries. In 2002 top executives of ZBOs earned about 106 000 euro, whereas the average income of senior public officials was only 90 400 euro (Ministerie van BZK, 2004). Similar figures are found in, for example, the United Kingdom, where the highest paid top executives earn between 150 000 and 225 000 pounds (CPS, 2005) but only 2 per cent of the civil service earn 50 000 pounds or more (plus allowances).

Publications about salaries often generate a lot of debate. However, it is not so much the average income that fuels this discussion, but the fact that an

Table 6.5: Performance-related pay for senior public officials in several European countries

	Variable component of individual salaries	Remark
Netherlands	15.5%	Average bonus component for top managers
France reward	11.6%	% bonuses of total civil servants
Italy	20%	
UK	n.a.	Variable bonuses

Sources: Commissie Dijkstal, 2004; Siciliani, 2004; PUMA, 2003.

increasing number of new public managers earn more than, for example, the prime minister. This is true for 13 per cent of senior public officials and 21 per cent of top executives in the Netherlands. The salaries of new public managers have risen in part because of the introduction of performance-related pay (PRP), which makes the income more variable and allows it to move beyond fixed salaries (like those of a prime minister). Table 6.5 presents information on PRP in four different countries.

Elements of PRP have been introduced in the Netherlands since the early 1990s. In essence this means that senior public officials can rise faster through their salary scales or can get extra bonuses if their performance is 'outstanding'. It is, however, far more difficult to 'punish' senior public officials if they perform poorly. The exact extent to which PRP is implemented for Dutch senior public officials is unclear, but the variable part of the salary seems to be dependent on the job and is higher for more important jobs.

Similar trends can be found in other countries. For example, in 2003 the French government expressed its dissatisfaction with the systems for appointment and payment of top senior public officials (Siciliani, 2004: 5). A scheme of PRP was suggested, but to this day it has not been fully put into practice. As yet, individual performance appraisal determines only a minor part of the overall yearly bonus. Nevertheless, in recent years the level of bonuses has risen more than basic salaries – but with considerable inequalities: the higher the salary, the higher the bonus. The proportion of bonus to total level of reward varies according to the ministry. For instance, bonuses are worth 25 per cent of the total reward in the Finance Ministry and only 5 per cent within the Ministry of Education. More progress has been achieved, however, with the introduction of PRP for top executives in the industrial and commercial public establishments (Siciliani, 2004: 15). PRP seems also to have been applied to a substantial part in Italy (20 per cent of pay), Finland and the United Kingdom (PUMA, 2003). In countries like Norway, PRP instruments have been implemented, but their actual use is still incidental and always with great caution (Lægreid, 2003: 163).

There are only a few differences between PRP developments for senior public officials and top executives. Based on our information, we can conclude that similar schemes have been implemented for both categories of new public managers in both Italy and the Netherlands. In France, more progress has been made with PRP for top executives than for senior public officials, but the literature is inconclusive on the actual difference (Siciliani, 2004). The information on salaries and the introduction of PRP is at this stage inconclusive. In most Western countries it is discussed and plans for implementation have been drawn up. However, progress is slow and varied; in the Netherlands most plans still focus only on senior public officials, because they are more easily disciplined given their legal status. It appears nevertheless that our fifth expectation has to be rejected: there are no real indications that PRP schemes are more often introduced for top executives than for senior public officials. Although actual salary levels are often higher for the former, this difference is not caused by PRP.

Political affiliation of new public managers

According to our sixth expectation top executives will on average be less often affiliated with a political party than senior public officials. Although the relationship between the political elite and the civil service in the Netherlands is less intermingled compared to other countries, membership of political parties or at least a professed preference for parties is quite common among senior public officials. The highest ranking Dutch senior public officials are secretaries-general. Data on their preference (and assumed membership) for certain political parties show that the majority (six out of thirteen; 46 per cent) favour the Social-Democratic Party, a third (four out of thirteen) support the Christian-Democrats, leaving a few Liberals (two out of thirteen) and one Liberal-Democrat.[6]

Derlien's (2003) study of German civil servants shows that membership of a political party has increased strongly among senior public officials; from 28 per cent in 1970 to 59.6 per cent in 1995. The Christian-Democrats have profited most from that increase (four times as much), while the Social-Democrats lost support (by about a third). In 1995 (N = 103), 40.4 per cent were not members of any political party. The remaining 60 per cent belonged to the Christian-Democrats (40 per cent), Social-Democrats (11 per cent) and Liberals (8.6 per cent).

Surprisingly, according to our data political affiliations among top executives appear to be higher in the Netherlands than France. Between one-third (executive agencies) and a quarter (ZBOs) of the Dutch top executives are registered members of a political party, most often either the Social-Democratic or the Liberal party. French top executives are less often members of a political party, at a maximum of 15 per cent. Those who are members of a party are equally divided between the Socialists and UMP. None of the SCN directors, however, belonged to a party.

With respect to our expectation it is clear that additional material is needed. However, it seems that senior public officials are more politicized than top executives (party membership rates are about twice as high), which is in line with our expectation.

Conclusions

While the data are often incomplete, a number of conclusions can be drawn. More research will be necessary to substantiate them.

First, today's senior public officials are much less managers than NPM reforms aimed for. Senior public officials still see themselves mainly as the classical neutral policy expert who advises politicians on decisions and policies. Managerial skills are less valued, and subordinates do not see their senior manager as a 'leader'. There is even some hint of resistance among senior public officials against NPM reforms (cf. also James, 2003). That could explain why the implementation of, for example, performance-related pay has not yet been achieved in most countries we looked at. Where progress has been made with PRP, it would seem that career-based countries such as Italy and France have an advantage because of the centralization and uniformity of recruitment and payment.

A second important conclusion is that the differences between top executives and senior public officials are not as big as we had expected. Both types of new senior public officials come from an administrative elite: middle-aged men with a higher education, often in law or economics, who make their career predominantly in the public domain. Nevertheless, there are some differences, which seem to be stronger as the distance between the executive agency and the parent department increased (for example, in the case of French AAI and Dutch ZBO). These differences concern their appointment (less often by a minister), their prior experience in the private sector (more often the case), their legal position (no civil servant status, higher salary) and their smaller degree of politicization (that is, membership of a political party). All in all, we believe that our distinction between the two types of new senior public officials is therefore useful.

The findings in this chapter have raised some new questions for research as well. For example, part of the NPM reforms is the reduction of indefinite appointments. As a result, we have seen that the average length of time-in-post of senior public officials is reduced. Christensen (2005) offers an alternative explanation for this reduction. He suggests that senior public officials – perhaps as a result of NPM – have become more vulnerable to political incidents, which would suggest that, like top executives, senior public officials are held more accountable for their performance than before. More research is necessary to settle this.

Another interesting observation is that in some countries senior public officials often take on jobs in the private domain after their public career (see, for example, Derlien, 2003 on Germany) – rather than the other way around, which would be more in line with NPM. On the other hand, the fact that senior public officials do cross over the boundary between the public and the private sector also fits with the NPM ideology. Therefore, this observation needs to be investigated further. We only looked into the origin of senior public officials and top executives in this chapter, not where they went working after their current job.

Finally, the difference in salaries between senior public officials and top executives has led to a hot debate, at least in the Netherlands. It remains difficult, however, to draw hard conclusions because the complex bonus systems obscure actual payments. More data are necessary to shed light on this topic.

Notes

1. In turn, the existing legal arrangements and the civil service force have influenced the trajectory of public sector reform (cf. Pollitt and Bouckaert, 2004).
2. We defined this as employees within the highest three salary scales (16–18), who at the same time stated they had supervision over other employees.
3. These include the civil service, the police, the polder boards, research institutes and academic hospitals.
4. Middle managers are defined as employees on salary scales 11–15. Also employees on scales 16–18 without supervision over other employees were defined as middle managers. Ordinary employees are all other employees.
5. At first this applied to all civil servants from salary scale 17 onwards (with 19 being the highest scale). Since 2000 it also applies to those in scale 16 and since 2002 also those in salary scale 15.
6. Taken from: http://planet.nl/planet/show/id = 62967/contentid = 447925/sc = 5fa286.

7
International Benchmarking of Public Organizations: a Critical Approach

Jan Hakvoort and Henk Klaassen

Introduction

The measuring and valuation of the performance of organizations in the public domain continue undiminished as focal points of public interest. Output-oriented and efficient organizations in the public sector are considered self-evident. From the start, companies in the private sector have served as examples, since it is assumed that generally in that category of business there is a good insight in the cost price of the products the organization produces, the cost structure of the organization itself, customer orientation, and so on. Translating the insights gained in the private sector for the public sector seemed more a matter of time than one of problems to be conquered in the course of this transition (Heinrich and Lynn, 2000). Unlike the production in private companies, the production of organizations in the public sector is often difficult to identify, and it is even less easy to completely express it in (financial) ratios. This may be partly explained by the circumstance that the heterogeneity of products in the public sector is greater. A different and more dominant explanation for the measuring – and valuating – problem in the public sector is formed by the various values which together determine the appreciation for what is produced. In the public domain, not only efficiency and effectiveness are concerned, but also values such as accuracy, reliability, verifiability, safety, legal equality and democratic content. That diversity of values has its effect on the day-to-day internal management of public organizations.

The desire to attain output-oriented and efficient organizations in the public sector also means that internal management techniques applied in the private sector have found applications in the public domain as well. Benchmarking, quality models and scorecard methods are examples of techniques that have started to be used in the public domain (Chapters 2 and 3). However, the diversity of values mentioned above raises the question of which problems are encountered when applying private internal management techniques in the public sector, and how these may be dealt with. In addition, however, there are questions such as: Do the differences between public and private internal management warrant separate techniques? What then, are the characteristic differences? The primary focus is on the possibilities and impossibilities of benchmarking in view of the diversity of values in the public sector.

The key question of this chapter is as follows: To what extent does international benchmarking of (production) processes in the public sector yield adequate insights for the benefit of steering and control processes in the public sector?

This chapter is organized as follows. First of all attention is paid to the multi-formity of values and the significance thereof for the application of internal management techniques in the public sector. Subsequently, international *benchmarking* of (production) processes in the public sector will be discussed in more detail. The instrument has evolved from a technique aimed at efficiency inside production processes into a more inclusive instrument that also offers space to other perspectives. When applied internationally, benchmarking shows marked similarities to classic international country-comparative research. The chapter is concluded by a critical analysis of this development.

Multi-formity of values[1] as a complicating factor

In the past decades, much attention has been paid to improving the internal management in public organizations. The introduction of the New Public Management (NPM) model in the UK during the administration of Thatcher gave a significant impulse to this. By now, in many Western countries there is a relatively great number of public administration organizations that have been investigated and organized more efficiently in some way or other. Behind the concept of NPM hides the idea that it should be possible to introduce techniques from the private sector also in the public and non-profit sectors, so as to render their internal management more effective and more efficient (cf. Ingraham, Joyce and Donahue, 2003: 5). Whenever the term 'internal management techniques' is used, people start thinking of economic aspects of managing organizations, limited to the pursuit of such a deployment of means and people as will result in efficient production. This association is self-evident; after all, much of what is being said and written about internal management is about efficiency, whether this concerns the efficiency of production economies or of organizations with a public task. However, such a restriction of internal management in the public sector is too narrow and, as such, incorrect. Efficiency is not the only relevant criterion. If we extend internal management to include effectiveness, a more complete image is shown. By linking both efficiency and effectiveness with internal management, purposefulness and the resulting steering and control of production processes become objectives of the internal management process.

Internal management techniques may be described as analytical aids for the steering and control of production processes of organizations

In the private sector, economic rationality[2] is the dominant factor. It includes a variety of aspects that may be focused on. The most stringent of these is the financial economic aspect. Examples of this are the pursuit of (long-term) profit and continuity of internal management. Kaplan and Norton (1999: 25ff.) acknowledged that in companies, often excessive attention was paid to this strictly financial economic aspect. In their Balanced Scorecard model they mentioned a number of other aspects that should be focused on in internal management: they distinguish a client perspective, an internal perspective and a learning perspective. Although this constitutes an extension of the particular points of interest with regard to internal management, one should consider that these are aspects which, as a result of the attention paid to them, must in the end contribute to economic rationality in the shape of the private organization's pursuit of profit. The customer or client perspective in Kaplan and Norton's model is also interpreted as 'how tempting should we be for clients to realize our vision (objective)?' This is just as true for the 'internal management perspective' they distinguish: 'what do we need to excel at in order to satisfy clients and shareholders?' and for the learning perspective: 'how do we remain capable of permanent change and improvement to realize our vision?'

Inside public and non-profit organizations, the attention to economic rationality has grown. This does not mean that other values (rationalities) do not remain inextricably bound up with the public sector. In other words: multi-formity of values is inherent. Besides economic rationality, democratic legitimacy or political rationality and legal rationality play parts. These rationalities may imply, among other things, that economically less efficient solutions may be chosen over efficient ones. An example may be considerations of legal equality, that is the safeguarding of the accessibility of systems (care systems, social systems) for the less prosperous. In Table 7.1 the differences between the public sector and the private sector in relation to the values in question are represented.

Because of the multiple values, internal management inside public and non-profit organizations is focused on finding the balance between the various values (rationalities). In spite of the fact that in the public sector, attention to economic rationality has grown in the past decades, the other rationalities will always (have to) be focused on, too. In the public domain, if internal management techniques are applied, this cannot remain restricted to aspects that refer to economic rationality. This has consequences for the

Table 7.1: Immanent values in the public and the private domain[3]

Value	Public–private continuum		
	Completely public		*Completely private*
Economic rationality			
• Profit	No immanent value[4]	....	Immanent value
• Continuity	No immanent value	....	Immanent value
• Competitive position	No immanent value	....	Immanent value
• Customer orientation	No immanent value	....	Immanent value
Democratic legitimacy			
(Political rationality)	Immanent value	....	No immanent value
Legal rationality			
• Accessibility	Immanent value	....	No immanent value
• Legal equality	Immanent value	....	No immanent value

use of private internal management techniques inside the public domain. After all, the various values should be considered *together*.[5]

The effect of the presence of multiple rationalities in the public sector versus the dominance of economic rationality in the private sector may be explained with a (fictional) example. Imagine that an analysis of the refuse collection in a town has resulted in outsourcing being considered a logical step to take. There are sufficient private candidates to warrant the stipulation of sharp price conditions for the refuse collection contract period during the tendering procedure. Based on this tendering procedure it is decided that the contract will be granted to a private company. The requisite quality standards are drawn up in the contract, making identical performance by that company a possibility in principle. Is this situation of a public organization for collecting household refuse, with several values taken into account in the organization of the service, equal to the situation of a private organization in which economic ratios dominate? After all, it does seem as though the values (such as accessibility for peripheral customers) can also be arranged preconditionally. However, there are a few catches. It could turn out, for example, that the efficiency profit gained is more than undone, socially speaking, by the (excessively) great demands made of the employees that do the work. If this results in increased absenteeism, employees ending up in the medical circuit for lengthy periods or even permanently, from a social point of view the costs that result from this *do* count. However, from the viewpoint of the company they do *not* count, or to a lesser extent (after all, for this organization the effect in question is an external one).

Provisional conclusion

Improvement of internal management, qualitative improvement of the production process and measuring performance are given systematic attention by the management in the private sector. Also in the public sector the attention of politicians and managers is increasingly focused on the qualitative and quantitative improvement of the products and the provision of services (for an extensive treatment of the use of ratios inside municipalities, see Bordewijk and Klaassen, 2000). Increasingly, internal management techniques used in the private sector are deployed for this. The occurrence of a complexity of values in the public sector may be interpreted as a characteristic difference with the private sector. In addition to this the co-ordination mechanism is different: the budget mechanism versus the market mechanism. Inside the public domain there is no longer a market to serve as hangman.

In the next section of this chapter (strategic) benchmarking will be discussed, since this is one of the quintessential techniques that contribute to an insight in the functioning of organizations inside the public sector.

Strategic benchmarking in the public sector

Introduction

First of all, a number of characteristics of benchmarking will be presented, after which the question of which crucial conditions must be met before a responsible use of benchmarking in public administration is feasible will be discussed. In addition to this, the possibilities and restrictions of the use of benchmarking in comparisons of private and public organizations are discussed. These topics are illustrated with the help of two case examples. The first case relates to an international benchmarking study into disabled policy in Denmark, the UK, the US, Sweden and the Netherlands. The second case concerns international comparative research into the practice of e-government in a number of OECD countries, supplemented by two benchmarking studies.

Benchmarking: a family of internal management techniques

'Benchmarking is the continuous process of measuring products, services and practices against the toughest competitors or those companies recognized as industry leaders' (Camp, 1989: 10). In this classic description of benchmarking as an instrument of the private sector, which stems from David Kearns of the Xerox Corporation, the emphasis is on comparing. As such, benchmarking was an elaborated form of comparative research statistics, which was used a lot in that period (early 1980s) to improve production processes. Over the course of years the concept of benchmarking has evolved from a relatively simple to a rather more inclusive concept. The more complex nature may be seen in a systematic set up, in the continuous nature of the comparison, in the dissimilarity of the organizations that are compared, and in the link to routes for improvement. Benchmarking, as may be applied also in the public sector, can be defined as follows: Benchmarking is a technique in which key data about the production process of goods and/or services inside an organization are compared to data from one or several other organizations, in order to enhance the efficiency and effectiveness of that organization (Hakvoort and Klaassen, 1999: 12; Hakvoort and Klaassen, 2004: 206). This description emphasizes the economic rationality; however, as was stated in section two, other values also play a role in the public domain. These are either explicitly included in the process of benchmarking, or they reappear in the preconditional sense (for example, by making broad public accessibility a necessary condition of the public facilities to be benchmarked, and using this precondition as a basis for investigating the efficiency and effectiveness of the facilities).

At the start of a benchmarking procedure the researcher or the client should take a number of crucial decisions, about: (1) the object of benchmarking, (2) the level of benchmarking and (3) the reference of benchmarking.

Ad 1   The object of benchmarking

The background for use and application of benchmarking is to improve the internal management of an organization. Increasing output and lowering costs are well-known terms in relation to this. Improving internal management has been around since the start of organizations. Moreover, there are many techniques to contribute to such improvement. Absolute standards against which to measure internal management are often lacking, or may be theoretical in nature. A realistic alternative is a comparison through time. Many organizations in the public and the private sphere make comparisons through time: they compare against their own operating results from previous periods. In comparisons through time, the time series technique is used. Therefore, time series analysis is another frequently used internal management technique.

The object of benchmarking in public organizations may be a product or a service, but also (parts of) the process of production. The variety of objects is enormous and very diverse: the number of tax returns processed by an Inland Revenue employee in one day, for example, or the number of students that graduate from each department of education, or the number of parcels delivered in a specific unit of time, or the number of visitors of a museum.

In benchmarking, organizations are compared on the basis of one or several performance indicators. The comparison of organizations can take place both internally and externally. The Association of Universities in the Netherlands (Vereniging van Samenwerkende Nederlandse Universiteiten, VSNU) very regularly investigates the educational and research performance of university education. In principle, all university programmes are assessed once every five years. In the presentation of the research reports of the review committee, which was established for this particular purpose by the VSNU, the various programmes are given a ranking order. The position attributed to each programme is substantiated with considerations, average figures of publication, and course success rates. Such a national comparison of course programmes is an external comparison.

An internal comparison takes place if a university presents a survey of the propaedeutic year and doctoral course success rates of its very diverse programmes as part of the annual budget report. In such a case, success rate figures are used as performance indicators for the various courses.

Ad 2   The level of benchmarking

Benchmarking may be focused on various functions or processes inside an organization. A multitude of function classifications is possible. Direct benchmarking is focused on the primary process. This can be carried out at macro or micro level. In case of benchmarking at macro level the analysis purports a comparison of results of several processes. In a micro level comparison, specific functions are involved. Indirect benchmarking relates to specific functions or processes. Inside this category strategic, operational and process benchmarking are sometimes distinguished. The analysis in strategic benchmarking is focused exclusively on the strategy of others (competitors). In operational benchmarking parts of the work processes are analysed. The analysis in process benchmarking is aimed at improving the total work processes.

Ad 3   The reference of benchmarking

The selection and choice of other organizations in the comparison are very important. Basically, four types of benchmarking may be distinguished (Camp, 1992):

- Internal benchmarking: comparing organizations (operating companies) inside a single parent company; for example, the comparison of the various wards inside a university hospital;
- Competitive benchmarking: comparing products, services and/or goods of a competing organization; for example, a comparison of the various programmes offered by a university of professional education, by the Netherlands Association of Universities of Professional Education (HBO-raad);
- Functional benchmarking: comparison aimed at specific functions (personnel policy or financial reporting); and
- Generic benchmarking: this is a general external comparison that goes beyond the boundaries of the industry in question. For example, the comparison of an invoicing process inside a police district with that of a tax office, or of a university.

The process of benchmarking

Benchmarking is measuring, analysing and improving. It is not just about gathering knowledge, but also about implementing knowledge. Basically, benchmarking follows the same steps that are taken in socio-scientific research. Camp has developed a step-by-step plan in which the various components of benchmarking have been arranged in ten steps. Camp discusses the stages of planning, analysis, integration and action, successively. With a few minor adjustments, the stages and steps in this model may be outlined as follows:

Planning and research

1. Select benchmarking subject.
2. Select benchmarking partners.
3. Determine the method of data collection and collect the data.

Analysis

1. Determine the current gap between performance and methods.
2. Determine desirable performance.

Integration

1. Communicate the results and ensure acceptance.
2. Set concrete objectives.

Action

1. Develop plans of action.
2. Implement plans and guard progress.
3. Test benchmarks against developments.

The steps or stages in Camp's model are clearly distinguished and of a general nature, thus widely applicable. The strength of Camp's model is that a relatively large amount of attention is paid to the implementation of proposals for improvement.

Benchmarking in non-profit organizations

The phased planning outlined in the above is so general that in principle, it may be applied to benchmarking inside the government and non-profit organizations. However, it is very much the question where the boundaries lie. Is every production process, supporting function and societal effect of a non-profit organization suited to benchmarking? To answer that question one would need to take a closer look at the similarities and differences between the use of the model for private organizations and the use of the model for public organizations.

In economic literature the objective of a private organization is often summarized as the pursuit of profit maximization in the long term. Really then, this is the simultaneous striving for continuity of the internal management and for maximization of the profit. In public organizations, the objective in a general sense is not as easily explained: a more extensive range of values plays a part. In this connection, values that are usually mentioned right away are legal equality, legal security and justice, and democratic content; values which, in the design and implementation of the activities of the public organization have to compete with the economic values of effectiveness and efficiency. But there are differences in another sense as well. In many cases, private organizations are not or incompletely confronted with the side-effects of what they produce (for example, by way of negative external effects). Public organizations are supposed to internalize external effects, and consequently, to take them into account when they make their choices of form and implementation.

It requires little argument that 'taking on board' all the values mentioned in the above can lead to considerable complications. In case of a competitive benchmark, first of all the condition should be set that the processes to be compared take place in the same domain (so, either public, or non-profit, or private), to at least guarantee that the same value set is relevant. A second condition is that the measuring level of the various values based on which the comparison takes place is at least ordinal. After all, this is about ranking. Finally, if in a competitive benchmarking more than a mere comparison for each value is required, so as to achieve, for example, an overall assessment, another condition is for the relative weight of the values included to be known.

It should not be concluded from what is mentioned in the above that benchmarking between public organizations is impossible; however, the comparison should be carried out with proper caution. A significant part of the discussion will (have to) focus on the performance desired and on which indicators should be used to portray it.

Possibilities of benchmarking in the non-profit sector

The advantages that private organizations experience as a result of benchmarking also apply to non-profit organizations:

- Stimulating good learning attitude;
- Motivating employees;
- Obtaining external orientation;
- Offering a point of reference;
- Contributing to strategies and implementation;
- Setting objectives;
- Finding and integrating best practices in one's own organization.

Benchmarking provides comparable information about performance, functions and processes inside organizations, against which a non-profit organization may assess its own functioning. Benchmarking shows its value in an organization that is in a process of transition, and where a changed and new strategy has to be implemented. A benchmark study may facilitate the transformation of a proved successful strategy to one's own organization. In the above, a number of conditions that should be set for the successful application of benchmarking have been mentioned. One more condition, concerning the presence of possibilities for steering so as to affect the production (processes) of the non-profit organization, should be added to those. As such an organization is more easily influenced, the significance and sense of starting a benchmarking procedure becomes greater. If a number of factors can be guaranteed when a benchmarking procedure is planned there is no single impediment, assuming the organizations will co-operate, to direct benchmarking being implemented with regard to the primary process of the organization in question. If one or several factors cause problems a more indirect benchmarking method may be sought, that is strategic, operational or process benchmarking.

Limitations of benchmarking in the non-profit sector

Benchmarking renders organizations more transparent: the ratios found in a comparative context provide information about the functioning of that organization. For many non-profit organizations this is information which had not been present before and which – in view of the nature of the organization – had not been deemed necessary, either.

Greater transparency of an organization can pose a threat. After all, the organization's accountability and the pressure to account for one's actions to the outside world grow accordingly. Besides this, the information from a benchmark study may facilitate the process of steering. The latter might be given shape through results-oriented internal management. This may be seen as a threat as well; one from within this time. The culture in non-profit organizations is rarely characterized by 'accounting'.

Another threat is of a very different kind; benchmarking as a justification of poor performance: by comparing one's own poor performance with the even poorer performance of others, favourable results may still be claimed.

A final threat to be mentioned here may occur if benchmarking is introduced into a hostile environment. As a result of the additional information that becomes available, resistance may be evoked – through the process of calling parties to account. Defence lines generate new flows of information. Such accumulation of information may have a negative effect on the life-cycle of ratio systems (negative learning processes).

Benchmarking: comparing various kinds of apples with different types of oranges

Camp's model includes the integration phase. The term 'integration' hides one of the most crucial stages of benchmarking. To portray the performance of an organization, several different perspectives may be chosen. Those various perspectives will result in ratios that each elucidates a characteristic of the organization. For example, indicators about production, means deployed, the transformation process, and so on, may be gathered. Ratios based on those indicators may also be devised, each relating to various aspects such as productivity, effectiveness and efficiency. Naturally, based on such data it is possible to develop courses for improvement (plans of action in Camp's model). However, the partial nature of this method should be acknowledged. After all, the ratios chosen should not be assumed to be completely independent from each other. Changes through improvement routes or plans of action, to change a certain aspect of the performance of the organization, in many cases result in (unintended) changes in other aspects. In other words, aspects may be insufficiently considered in their interconnectedness. In benchmarking, such an approach can never lead to more encompassing improvements, like changes in the composition of the production factors that are being used.

It may be clear that a transition from a partial to an integral approach must be made. A first alternative is working with production possibility curves and ISO cost lines (cf. Blank, 1998: 432–5). This means that minimal cost patterns for the various production volumes are sought. For a given organization, the degree of efficiency may be studied, distinguishing technical efficiency (the extent to which the means deployed are being used) and allocative efficiency (the extent to which the composition of the means deployed is optimal). Besides this, through changing the production volumes it can be determined whether there is scale efficiency (in changing the production volume the deployment of the production means used does not change proportionally).

Insights into the efficiency of the production of organizations may be obtained by Data Envelopment Analysis. With this method, any organization with a certain production may be compared with other organizations that supply the same product. The organization that does this with the smallest deployment of means is most efficient.

Another alternative for an integral approach is to combine benchmarking with what are sometimes termed integral methods. These are methods that incorporate as many aspects of internal management as possible at the same time in the evaluation process, not just products or results. A good example of such a method is the Balanced Scorecard (BSC) method. The essence of the Balanced Scorecard model is that both financial and non-financial data need to form integral components of the information system for the benefit of employees on all levels of the organization. Another example is the INK model frequently used in the Netherlands.

Working hypotheses concerning the use of benchmarking for the evaluation of policy in complex situations

To answer the central question of this chapter, a number of working hypotheses have been formulated. They will be tested on the basis of two international empirical studies. The central question of this chapter is formulated as follows: to what extent does international benchmarking of (production) processes in the public sector yield adequate insights for the benefit of steering and control processes in the public sector? To answer that question the use of a technique, namely benchmarking, is focused on.

The first working hypothesis (h1) is: the use of the instrument of benchmarking in evaluating complex policy issues is effective to acquire an insight into policy performance.

The second working hypothesis (h2) is: the application of benchmarking for a comparison of organizations in an international context and the comparison of countries are possible on condition that a number of crucial principles are observed. Those crucial principles are: at least similar legislation, if possible also reasonably comparable institutional arrangements inside the specific area of policy, and active involvement in the benchmark study of the participating organizations (countries).

The third working hypothesis (h3) is: by using the instrument of benchmarking for complex policy issues, both the strong and the weak points of the policy execution are shown, which is important for the learning and the learning process of the implementing organizations.

Case 1: an international benchmarking study of disabled policy in five countries

Introduction

In 2005 the Danish National Agency for Enterprise and Construction published various country reports of an International Benchmarking Study on Services offered to People with Disabilities.[6] The research was carried out by Ramboll Management research agency, an international research agency with offices in cities in Northern Europe: Stockholm, Oslo, Aarhus, Copenhagen and Hamburg.

In view of the complexity of the topic and the availability of the data, this international study was based on quantitative and qualitative indicators. This combination of indicators prevents one-sidedness of the results obtained and contributes significantly to the validity of the results. The quantitative and qualitative indicators are related to the input, output and outcomes of policy interventions intended for people with a disability.

Selection of countries

In this benchmark study, the researchers studied data pertaining to disabled policy in five countries: Denmark, Sweden, the Netherlands, the UK and the US. The researchers substantiated their choice for this selection on the following grounds. A 'welfare model' in Sweden is nearly identical to that of Denmark; the models of the Netherlands and the UK are reasonably comparable to those of Denmark and Sweden and the US model is very different. In the US, a relatively large number of laws protect the position of disabled people to a significant extent. For the various participating countries, separate 'country reports' were written.

Selection of indicators

The selection of relevant benchmark indicators was restricted by the researchers to the sectors included in the Danish national plan of action for disabled policy. These were the following: housing, employment, education, accessibility of the physical environment, public administration, leisure time and quality of life, and social service. The researchers paid specific attention to the following aspects of the indicators:

- Conceptualization: the extent to which it is possible to accurately formulate the content of a policy intervention or policy measure and the target group for which the measure is intended;
- Data quality: the availability of data, data updates, and sensitivity to policy: to what extent the indicator is sensitive to a policy intervention or policy measure;
- Reliability of the indicator;
- Comparability of the countries;
- The relevance of the disabled policy: the extent to which the intervention or measure is geared specifically to people with a disability;
- The policy model for disabled persons per country; comparability of the policy models.

Collection of data: secondary analysis of existing sources

The empirical data from the international comparative benchmark study are based on secondary information which stems from published data from the government or institutional statistics based on various sources. The comparison between the five countries is based mainly on quantitative indicators. These are focused on input, output and outcomes of public interventions intended for people with a disability. The researchers eliminated indicators from the study if results were incomparable as a result of legislative differences, differences in target groups, measuring problems, lack of data or insufficient quality of data. For each policy sector, a set of two to four indicators were studied. For the factor 'housing' (newly built), for example, the following things were measured:

- Expenditure for the provision of sloping entrance (exit) ramps in new buildings;
- Expenditure for the provision of disabled lavatories in new buildings;
- Expenditure for the provision of lifts in new buildings;
- Expenditure for the provision of disabled car park ticket dispensers at new buildings.

Besides this, for the sector 'existing housing' it was also investigated, based on nearly identical indicators, if and to what extent the disabled policy had actually been realized in the five participating countries.

Below, a definition with regard to the few policy sectors that are crucial for disabled persons is given, of the content of the disabled policies inside each sector. Subsequently, for each policy sector a conclusion has been formulated based on a number of results from the five countries involved in the international benchmark study.

In order to be able to answer the working hypotheses, emphasis has been given to the evaluative remarks of the researchers. Since this is a Danish study, the conclusions have been formulated from a Danish perspective. In this first exploratory international study, Denmark functioned as the benchmark. The data were taken from country reports of Sweden, the UK, the US, the Netherlands and Denmark.

Housing policy for the disabled

The attention to housing was focused mainly on the external facilities of existing accommodation and new houses. Aspects of accessibility to and of accommodations were the main focus. One of the indicators for both current and new accommodations was concerned with the provision of a sloping exit and access ramp to the front door and/or hallway of a house or apartment. Other indicators were: expenditure for special lavatories for disabled persons, expenditure for lifts, and expenditure for car park ticket dispensers.

Conclusions

The Danish regulations include specific rules for the accessibility of buildings, both existing and new ones, and for disabled lavatories, lifts and parking spaces. In the UK, the housing policy process is focused on the independent accommodation of disabled persons. This approach is suited to a new allocation system in the shape of an individualized budget.

In Sweden, disabled policy has been outlined in the National Action Plan for Disability policy, 'From patient to citizen'. Sweden also has a National Ombudsman for the disabled (*Handikappombudsmannen*). This public authority has been given the special task of supervising the realization of the Standard Rules of the United Nations on the Equalization of Opportunities for Persons with Disabilities.

Dutch disabled policy is based on the same pillars as Danish policy, in respect to aspects like equality, compensation and sector responsibility. As far as housing is concerned, policy is focused on the construction of special accommodation and the adjustment of existing houses.

The US has the Fair Housing Act to prevent house owners from refusing to rent or sell houses to disabled persons. The Act also requires house owners to provide reasonable facilities for people with a disability.

Conclusion based on the benchmark study

With regard to the expenditure for specific provisions it may be concluded that the costs for housing provisions in Denmark equal the average costs of the other countries involved in the study.

Employment

With regard to this policy sector, the researchers paid attention to four indicators:

- Occupational participation of disabled persons;
- The percentage of unemployed disabled persons;
- Employment for the disabled through the introduction of flexible (special terms) jobs;
- Expenditure for the realization of flexible jobs.

Conclusions

Denmark has by far the most extensive labour market provisions and the highest percentage of disabled persons working in special jobs ('flexible jobs', as the researchers term them). However, the percentage of disabled persons in the labour market is very similar to percentages in countries like the UK, the Netherlands and the US, whereas Sweden has the highest percentage of employed disabled persons. These facts imply that disabled persons in the Danish job market stay in these special (flexible) jobs, but do not move on to work in normal jobs as a result of this.

In the UK, the overall policy approach to employment is significantly different from that in Denmark. UK labour market policy is based on two fundamental considerations: the non-discrimination principle as outlined in the DDA (Disability Discrimination Act), and the economic revenues of disabled access to the jobs market. Unlike in Denmark, the European directives in this regard apply in the UK.

In the US there is legislation, 'The Americans with Disability Act', to prevent discrimination with regard to selection, hiring, promotion, training, payment, social activities and other aspects of employment. It also requires that employers make adequate provisions for any physical and/or mental restrictions disabled people may have.

In the Netherlands, very diverse measures have been taken to promote disabled integration into the employment market.

Conclusions based on the benchmark study

Let us see what the responsible politicians and administrators in the participating countries may learn from an international comparison. Denmark has by far the most specific provisions with regard to disabled employment policy. This pertains in particular to the creation of flexible jobs. The percentage of disabled persons in the regular job market is mostly similar to the percentages in the Netherlands, the UK and the US. Only Sweden has a much higher percentage of disabled persons in the regular jobs market. This means that in Denmark, a relatively large proportion of disabled persons stay in special positions (flexible jobs).

Accessibility of public transport

For the policy sector of accessibility to public transport, the following indicators were studied:

- The number of platforms accessible to wheelchair users in comparison to the total number of platforms available;
- The number of trains accessible to wheelchair users;
- The number of buses accessible to wheelchair users in comparison to the total number of buses.

Conclusions based on the benchmark study

The results show that disabled accessibility of public transport can and should be improved in all the countries concerned. The Danish results do not differ substantially from those of the other countries. In particular the accessibility to the trains from the platforms requires special attention in all the countries studied.

In Sweden, all railway platforms have lifts for the disabled. No UK data are available for the period 1999–2004. In the Netherlands, plans have been developed and adopted to realize full disabled accessibility of all trains and buses by 2010.

Education

As regards educational provisions the following indicators were taken into account:

- Expenditure for special educational facilities in higher education (bachelor or higher) related to the total number of persons with a disability in the 18–29 age group;
- The number of special educational facilities in higher education (bachelor or higher) related to the total number of persons with a disability in the 18–29 age group;
- The number of persons with a disability who have finished additional studies in comparison to the total number of people with a disability in the 30–64 age group.

Conclusions based on the benchmark study

The Danish facilities (together with the UK ones) exceed the provisions made in the other countries in the benchmark study. In spite of those provisions, Denmark, together with the UK and the US, has the highest drop-out rates. This implies that despite the presence of disabled educational facilities a large number of their users do not finish their studies with a diploma. Politicians and administrators in Denmark (but also in the UK and the US) can learn from this study that special focus on the drop-out rate (early school leavers) is required.

Provisions in the Netherlands are comparable to those in Denmark; however, the Dutch policy instruments are limited in their scope.

In the UK, providers of educational facilities are obliged by law to make provisions and adjustments so that students with a disability have sufficient opportunities to enjoy secondary and higher education.

In Sweden, the general principle is focused on fitting disabled policy inside regular policy. In the schools, support for the handicapped has been decentralized to the local authorities, and regulated in the framework of the Law on Schools.

For politicians and administrators in all participating countries to the benchmark study, the relation between the volume of the facilities and the degree of school success is a significant learning aspect.

Accessibility of government websites

The accessibility of government websites is very important for disabled persons, so that they may remain informed about possibilities and facilities.

Conclusions based on the benchmark study

An earlier benchmark study in 18 European countries was carried out to investigate the accessibility of 172 government websites. The average score of the 18 countries and the 172 websites was between 5.9 and 7.0 on a scale of 0 to 10. The highest scores were found in the UK, followed by Denmark, the Netherlands and Sweden.

Leisure time and quality of life

This policy sector includes disabled facilities regarding television broadcasts and library facilities. In the case of television, naturally these include things such as subtitling for the deaf and direct explanations though the interpretation of news broadcasts for the deaf. The library facilities pertain to the presence of Braille books and books read onto audio tape.

Conclusions based on the benchmark study

The legislation with regard to public television and libraries was researched only generally, and the results do not specify the number of hours of subtitled or interpreted broadcasts for the deaf, or the number of audio books produced.

The benchmark study shows that Denmark and Sweden have a lower percentage of television programmes for the hearing impaired (so with signed explanations for the hearing impaired) than the Netherlands and the UK (cf. Table 7.2). Denmark and Sweden also have a lower percentage of subtitled television programmes than the Netherlands, the UK and particularly the US.

In the Netherlands, the number of audio books published is very small (cf. Table 7.3), but this is compensated by a significant investment in the production of Braille books. In the US, the number of audio books is higher than in the European countries. The percentages in the other countries that took part in this research are on average between those of the Netherlands and the US.

Table 7.2: Number of hours of subtitled television in relation to the total number of hours of television

Country	DK	SE	NL	UK	US
%	30	32	49	71	100

Table 7.3: Percentage of audio books in libraries, in relation to the total number of books

Country	DK	SE	NL	UK	US
%	2.6	2.3	0.1	2.0	4.5

Conclusions about the working hypotheses formulated, based on case 1

The international benchmark study is only a single empirical study; however, it is very informative and useful because it relates to research of a relatively complex policy area with regard to disabled policy. The attention of the researchers is focused on at least eight policy sectors. For each sector several indicators were investigated. The researchers were sensible enough, methodically and technically speaking, to select the countries in such a way that their legislation in the area of disabled policy and their general prosperity levels did not differ significantly. The comparability of the research results had increased reality value as a result of this.

Tentatively and preliminary conclusions may be drawn with regard to the use of benchmarking based on the working hypotheses formulated in the above. First, it may be concluded that the state of affairs around complex policy issues may be studied adequately with the help of benchmarking (working hypothesis 1). Second, the voluminous Danish benchmark study has clearly shown that an international comparison of countries may yield an adequate representation of the state of affairs concerning the performance of organizations (working hypothesis 2). In particular when countries with reasonably comparable prosperity levels are compared, this may lead to new insights in certain aspects. Third, it may be concluded that benchmarking is a powerful and useful instrument for the learning and learning processes of implementing organizations (working hypothesis 3). Politicians and administrators may learn from each other.

Another conclusion that may be deduced from the benchmark study pertains to the different value patters in the various countries. In particular, in Denmark and the UK, values that relate to legal equality are more clearly present than in the other countries. In Denmark and the UK, more emphasis is placed on the accessibility of facilities (schools, among others). This focus is not transformed into better performance of the students in these schools, however, since drop-out rates in Denmark and the UK (and the US) are higher than in the other countries in the benchmark study.

Case 2: e-government practices in seven OECD countries

Introduction

In 2003, the Steunpunt Beleidsrelevant Onderzoek, Bestuurlijke Organisatie Vlaanderen, a policy research centre for administrative organization in Flanders, published a comparable study into the development of e-government in seven OECD countries.[7] The study responds to the current trend of governments having to become 'leaner and keener'. All kinds of (institutional) changes in the public domain were initiated to accomplish this, such as privatization, demand steering and performance measuring. The significance of information and communications technology is central to the report. From the early 1990s, ICT has played an increasingly important role, in the efficient management of data and data exchange between organizations, as well as between organizations and target groups. The report links up to the vision of IBM that there are four phases in the evolution to a fully fledged e-government (Kampen et al., 2003: 8):

• Providing information on the Internet;
• Enabling (single agency) transactions on the Internet;
• Integrating various services;
• Adjusting the provision of services to the demand.

Janssen and Rotthier (in Kampen et al., 2003: 217–18) demarcate the concept of e-government by means of the table given in Figure 7.1, in which they distinguish five domains. The greater the number of domains used in a country, the wider the scope of the concept of e-government is in that country. The authors distinguish the process of automation which supports the entire process of data collection, data storage, data processing, and data use. Automation relates to the many large-scale automation functions in the government organizations, between which no communication is possible.

e-government	
Monitoring the step to the information society **Information society/e-society**	
Automation of one's own processes **Automation**	Changes in the provision of services to citizens and businesses with the help of ITC **e-Administration**
Changes in democratic processes with the help of ITC **e-democracy**	Changes in the relationship between politics and administration **e-knowledge Interchange**

Figure 7.1: The five domains of e-government
Source: Janssen and Rotthier (in Kampen et al., 2003, Chapter 9, p. 218).

Secondly, they distinguish e-administration, concerned with the transition to the electronic provision of services. This is more than just offering the existing services electronically. Janssen and Rotthier mention the necessity of thinking through the existing provision of services from scratch, and adjusting front and back offices to render this form of service provision proactive, integrated and transactional. The third domain the authors distinguish is the provision by means of ICT of a platform for citizens to participate in policy and the development of interactivity between citizens and administrators (in discussion forums, by e-mails to politicians). They call this domain e-democracy. The fourth domain is concerned with the exchange of knowledge between politicians and government (administrative) services. Both have access to information. The final domain that is distinguished is called e-society (information society). This domain constitutes the basis for the other four domains. The government aims to close the digital gap, distribute infrastructure, safeguard privacy, create a regulatory framework, and so on.

In the study, the developments regarding e-government are pictured. For the Netherlands, Finland, the United Kingdom, France, Ireland, Germany and Canada, the administrative characteristics, the ideology and policy in respect to ICT and government and e-government in practice are dealt with in turn. For each country, these main items are divided up further:

- Administrative characteristics in:
  ○ Form of government and administration; and
  ○ Policy and organization.
- Ideology and policy in respect to ITC and government in:
  ○ Government initiatives;
  ○ The role of the private sector; and
  ○ Research groups and the scientific debate.
- e-government in practice in:
  ○ e-administration; and
  ○ e-democracy.

For each country, an image ensues that shows which initiatives were taken, if and how e-government has been placed on the academic agenda, and in which way public services provision is being developed locally and centrally. An important conclusion from the various national studies is that the countries in question did not develop e-government independently of each other. All the countries use a limited definition of the concept of e-government, which concept coincides with the electronic provision of services. Policy in all countries researched is supplemented with a broader scale programme of measures taken against the background of the Information Society.

Benchmark e-government

In itself, a comparative approach as described in the above does not warrant the predicate benchmarking. After all, the leading idea of benchmarking is that it stimulates improvement of one's own performance. This does not necessarily follow from a simple comparison. The international research of the Steunpunt Beleidsrelevant Onderzoek, Bestuurlijke Organizatie Vlaanderen is supplemented with three international benchmark studies: (1) Cap Gemini Ernst and Young, *Online Availability of Public Services: How is Europe Progressing?*[8] (2) Accenture, *e-government Leadership – Realizing the Vision*[9] and (3) United Nations, *Global E-Government Readiness Report 2004, Towards Access for Opportunity*.[10] In this chapter, attention is paid to two of these three studies, since their methodology is comparable. The definitions and the domains that were taken into account differ, which is also reflected in the ranking that results from the analyses.

The Cap Gemini study

Cap Gemini Ernst and Young have done research into the percentage of 'basic public services' available online. In effect, Cap Gemini's study is thus limited to e-administration. A comparison was done of 17 countries and in the area of 20 public services divided in four clusters: revenue services for governments, registration of objects and persons, public services to citizens, and companies and licences. For each of the clusters, the growth of online provision of services in the period from October 2001 to October 2003 is charted. This is presented for the various clusters in Figure 7.2.

Besides for the countries jointly, developments are also pictured for each country separately, with regard to the extent of advancement with which

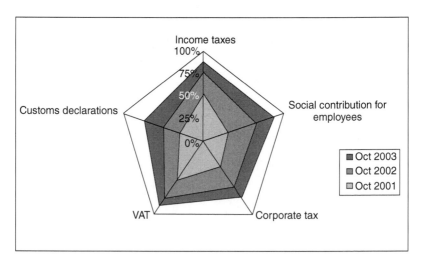

Figure 7.2: Income-generating services

Source: Cap Gemini Ernst and Young, *Online Availability of Public Services: How is Europe Progressing?* 2005, p. 16.

services are offered, and whether they are available completely online. As a result of the various measuring points in time, an image has been created of the development for each country and how the countries relate to each other. Table 7.4 shows the ranking of the countries.

The table shows that in the last two measurements, Sweden was most advanced online; six countries scored 75 per cent or lower. As to the scores for the complete provision of online services Denmark did best, followed by Austria and Sweden. With regard to growth Austria stands out. The comparison of countries leads to the conclusion that the growth of e-government in Europe is still ongoing, although it has declined somewhat. For the complete provision of online services the total score was 45 per cent. This leads to the conclusion that there is still a long way to go in Europe.

Accenture study

Another study was carried out by Accenture: *e-government Leadership – Realizing the Vision*, published in April 2002.[11] This too concerns a ranking of countries. A Service Maturity index was used, indicating the level up to

Table 7.4: Comparison of countries

	Online sophistication				Fully available online		
Country	October 2003 %	October 2002 %	October 2001 %	Country	October 2003 %	October 2002 %	October 2001 %
Sweden	87	87	61	Denmark	72	61	32
Denmark	86	82	59	Austria	68	20	15
Ireland	86	85	68	Sweden	67	67	28
Austria	83	56	40	Finland	61	50	33
Finland	80	76	66	Ireland	56	50	22
Norway	75	66	63	United Kingdom	50	33	24
France	73	63	49	Norway	47	35	35
United Kingdom	71	62	50	France	45	35	25
The Netherlands	65	54	37	Italy	45	35	15
Portugal	65	58	51	Germany	40	35	20
Spain	64	64	50	Spain	40	40	30
Italy	59	57	39	Portugal	37	32	32
Belgium	58	47	23	Belgium	35	25	0
Iceland	56	53	38	Greece	32	32	11
Switzerland	55	49	–	Iceland	28	28	11
Greece	54	52	39	The Netherlands	26	21	5
Germany	52	48	40	Luxembourg	15	5	5
Luxembourg	47	32	15	Switzerland	–	–	–

Source: Cap Gemini Ernst and Young, *Online Availability of Public Services: How is Europe Progressing?* 2005, p. 17.

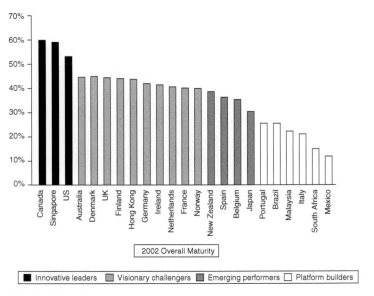

Figure 7.3: Ranking of countries

Source: Accenture, *e-government Leadership – Realizing the Vision*, April 2002, p. 6.

which countries manifest themselves online. The number of services for which governments are responsible and which are accessible online (Service Maturity Breadth), and the degree of completeness with which those services are offered (Service Maturity Depth) are pictured. The product of Service Maturity Breadth and Service Maturity Depth is 'Service Maturity Overall'. This results in a ranking of the countries researched (Figure 7.3).

Besides each country's position compared to that of the others, the Accenture study also represents the developments in each country (comparison of 2001 with 2002 position). The ranking according to Accenture is clearly different from that in the Cap Gemini study. This is most noticeable from the position held in both studies by Germany and Ireland.

Conclusions about the working hypotheses formulated, based on case 2

Based on the international benchmark studies that were carried out in the area of e-government, the following conclusions may be drawn in respect to the working hypotheses formulated earlier.

With regard to working hypothesis 1 (the use of the instrument of benchmarking is effective to acquire an insight into policy performance, in the course of evaluating complex policy issues) it may be concluded that the internationally comparative approach as used by the Steunpunt Beleidsrelevant

Onderzoek does provide a good insight into complex policy issues that can manifest themselves in countries. In addition to this, it prompts the assumption that developments in the various countries do not take place independently from each other. It should be stressed that no actual benchmarking is concerned here. With regard to the two benchmark studies mentioned, one would have to conclude that the insights gained are decided to a great extent by the definitions and demarcations used in the studies. This indicates that the results should be interpreted with the greatest possible caution, and do not simply lead to insights in complex policy situations.

Working hypothesis 2 (the application of benchmarking for a comparison of the performance of organizations in an international context and the comparison of countries are possible on condition that a number of crucial principles are observed) should be rejected. The rankings that result from the studies are so different that they present a very tentative image at best. By and large, the studies result in the same image, but it is insufficiently sharp to be able to reach conclusions for each individual country. In particular the e-government benchmark shows that benchmarks do not always remain restricted to functions that are easy to compare. This means that benchmarks, particularly in combination with a multi-formity of values, do not always show unequivocal outcomes.

As regards working hypothesis 3 (by using the instrument of benchmarking for complex policy issues both the weak and the strong points of the policy execution are shown, which is important for the learning and the learning process of the implementing organizations) it may be concluded that the benchmark studies presented here are too loosely structured to be able to acknowledge the stronger and weaker points of policy execution. However, it cannot be excluded that the results may actually provide an impetus for learning. After all, every positioning in relation to others (other countries) invites further elaboration and as a result possibilities for the adjustment of (policy) processes.

Conclusions

Performance measuring is as ancient as organizations themselves. The classical analysis by way of operational statistics can be seen as a predecessor of internal management techniques such as benchmarking. The renewed attention for comparing the performance of organizations, in the broadest sense of that concept, has given powerful impetus to comparisons of companies and organizations. Benchmarking is not a homogeneous product: it comprises a family of techniques. On the one side of the continuum is benchmarking aimed at identifying efficient production processes, on the other are qualitative comparisons (enabling organizations to learn from each other). A systematic interpretation of the type intended is important when one or the other is used, both for the interpretation of the results and for attaining learning effects.

Inside the public sector, benchmarking has grown into the most widely accepted internal management technique. In comparison to implementation in the private sector, the multi-formity of values inside the public sector requires specific attention when using benchmark studies. Specific analysing techniques may provide a solution. Classic multi-dimensional scale techniques, such as the DEA technique, are a tested solution in this regard.

Of course, the international comparison of public organizational performance in different countries is not an objective in itself, either. To be able to term this benchmarking, the technique must be used with a view to learning from each other by portraying, for example, best practices. Additional advantages could be that it becomes easier to account for one's actions and supervise one's own organization. Formation of an opinion is not the only objective for benchmarking. Adjustment of production processes, making them more efficient, for example, is much more important in many cases. However, as is true of all management instruments, careful implementation is an absolute must. A benchmark study in which, based on the largest possible number of indicators that have not even been screened for their mutual dependency, a comparison between organizations is made, for example, might not only needlessly frustrate management and employees, but also provoke the wrong actions.

The description of international comparative studies in the above prompts a number of conclusions with regard to the instrument of benchmarking. Point by point, these are as follows:

- Country descriptions may be very informative, but they do not always deserve the predicate 'benchmarking'. The descriptions do not really provide clues for measures to be taken (as a result of contextual differences and lack of clarity about a best practice).
- The rankings that result from benchmark studies may depend strongly on the methodology and demarcations chosen, and should be interpreted with the greatest possible caution because of this. The results provide inadequate starting points on which to base concrete policy measures in order to increase performance in the area researched.
- It should be clear what the field of benchmarking is. The benchmark study about disabled policy is clear in this respect. The comparative studies about e-government show that many different functions fall under e-government. In such a case, high scores in a certain area need not indicate great(er) functionality of the total package of services.
- Benchmarking should preferably be started from a need or desire to improve one's own performance, based on which suitable benchmarking partners and/or activities may be sought.

The points above lead to the conclusion that the application of benchmarking in an international context should be undertaken with great caution.

The occurrence of differences in the content and demarcations of the processes to be benchmarked in the various countries will quickly form an impediment to useful comparison (cf. the conclusions of Pollitt and Kickert in Chapters 2 and 3). Differences found between the processes that were benchmarks will then fail to lead to, or result insufficiently in, differences as compared to a best practice. In that sense, international benchmarking also offers outcomes that may be too uncertain to simply learn from.

Conclusions about international benchmarking in the public sector as an answer to the terms of reference of this chapter

- International *comparative studies* are valuable when they aim to portray developments in specific areas of government interference. International *benchmarking* is potentially a valuable instrument for comparison, but in its application requires very accurate elaboration and demarcation of the processes to be benchmarked.
- The biggest problem is the theme of the multi-formity of values, in particular the contextual differences between countries and the institutional and organizational differences in specific policy areas. This is related to the circumstance that the results of an international benchmark study cannot be adequately interpreted in the light of those various value patterns.
- Practical experiences show that many benchmark studies are undertaken, but differences in context are not always taken into account. Organizations and countries involved are not always committed to, thus participants in, the benchmark study. As a result of this, in many cases it also is not possible to derive concrete recommendations from performance comparisons. Instead of the predicate benchmark study, at best such studies deserve to be termed comparative.
- Practice also shows that benchmarks are not always restricted to well-demarcated functions; see section five. Certainly in combination with a multi-formity of values this means that benchmarks do not always show unequivocal results.
- An international benchmark study is not achieved until the organizations and/or countries in question are actively involved in the set up and implementation of the research, and until the institutional arrangements (legislation, organization) and the crucial contextual indicators are reasonably alike.

Notes

1. In this chapter, the concepts 'multi-formity of values' and 'diversity of values' are not distinguished from each other.
2. Rationality and value are interchangeable terms in this chapter.

3. It may be clear, by the way, that the table shows a simplification in opposing public to private. One might even say that the archetypes represented here do not occur in reality, witness the large variety in organizational hybridity. The distinctions in the table were made from a viewpoint of clear positioning.

4. 'Not immanent' in the table means that the value does not have a self-evident position in the functioning of organizations in one of the domains.

5. An example of a technique in which this is explicitly pursued is the multi-criteria analysis. In this technique, scores on various assessment criteria (by way of making the value in question concrete) are weighed so as to bring them together under one single denominator. This method may be applied if a choice has to be made between various alternative policy options, for example.

6. Report, *Dansk handicappolitik I et internationalt perspektiv*, Ramboll Management Edition, Aalborg, May 2005.

7. Steunpunt Beleidsrelevant Onderzoek, Bestuurlijke Organisatie Vlaanderen *Spoor e-government. De praktijk van e-government in zeven landen van de OECD*, J. K. Kampen, D. Janssen, S. Rotthier, K. Snijkers (eds), Louvain, May 2003.

8. Cap Gemini Ernst and Young's *Online Availability of Public Services: How is Europe Progressing?* Web Based Survey on Electronic Public Services, Report of the Fourth Measurement October 2003, January 2005.

9. Accenture, *e-government Leadership – Realizing the Vision*, April 2002, 88 pp.

10. United Nations, *Global E-Government Readiness Report 2004, Towards Access for Opportunity*, New York, 2004, 182 pp.

11. Accenture, *e-government Leadership – Realizing the Vision*, April 2002, 88 pp.

8
Will ICTs Finally Reinvent Government? The Mutual Shaping of Institutions and ICTs

Vincent Homburg and Ig Snellen

Introduction

For at least a couple of decades, governments have implemented a rather heterogeneous set of private sector management techniques known as New Public Management (NPM) (see Chapters 1 and 2). In the previous chapters, it has been shown that NPM takes many forms and shapes, and is implemented in a variety of ways in diverse institutional contexts.

For about a decade, governments were confronted with yet another wave of reforms that look less institutional or managerial, but rather technological in nature. This new wave of technological reforms is referred to as 'e-government' (Bekkers and Homburg, 2005; Chadwick and May, 2001; Gascó, 2003). E-government refers to the application of information and communication technologies (ICTs), notably Internet technologies, inside and surrounding public administration (for a more elaborate definition, see below). In literature and in practice, there are some very interesting claims about e-government in relation to NPM reforms. For instance, in 2000, Symonds projected that '[r]einventing government, a fashionable but premature idea a decade ago, is at last being made possible by the Internet' (Symonds, 2000: 17). Dunleavy and Margetts (2000) claim that e-government has overtaken and superseded NPM, thus claiming e-government and NPM are rather compatible phenomena. Furthermore, Bellamy and Taylor claim that '[t]he patterns of organizational change which are so commonly associated with the information age are remarkably consistent with the patterns associated with current forms of managerialism in public administration' (Bellamy and Taylor, 1998: 37; see also Heeks, 2001). In practice, it seems that some of the core concepts of NPM reforms, like client-orientation, joined-up government (Bogdanor, 2005) and so on, are indeed unequivocally enabled and inspired by ICTs (Fountain, 2001). For instance, in the US, one of the international forerunners of e-government applications, visions on e-government emerged in the context of the National Partnership for Reinventing Government (National Performance Review, 2000). In the 1990s, the Clinton/Gore Administration viewed e-government technologies as vehicles with which re-engineering government could be instrumented. In fact, application of ICTs was at the heart of the NPM inspired National Performance Review of 1993. This line of thinking was developed further later on in the first decade of the new millennium (National Audit Office, 2002; National Performance Review, 2000). In fact, the Access America Programme can be regarded as an update of the National Performance Review, with the noteworthy addition of the Internet (which, of course, was not mentioned in the first NPR reports). In general, in the above reports, there is a strong belief that ICTs in general can assist in the creation of customer-focused public bureaucracies (Chadwick and May, 2001; Fountain, 2001).

The suggestive comments by authors like Symonds, Dunleavy and Margetts, and Bellamy and Taylor, and the anecdotal evidence from reforms in the US hint at convergent patterns when technological and NPM reforms are combined. Given the heterogeneous character of NPM (see Chapters 2 and 3), this raises the question of whether, and if so, why, technological reforms produce convergent change in continental European contexts, and whether and why technological reforms that are implemented in concurrence with managerial reforms actually result in convergent patterns of reform in various institutional contexts. The question that is addressed in this chapter, therefore, can be stated as follows: *To what degree does the combined application of managerial and technological reform in public administration result in convergent patterns of change, and how can this be explained?*

The central question is addressed in a number of ways. First, the role of technology in relation to institutions and institutional reforms is analysed using theoretical notions of technology. Second, national e-government policy documents are analysed in order to scrutinize and reflect on the envisaged use of technology in reforms in various institutional contexts. The focus is on e-government policies of the UK, Denmark and the Netherlands, enabling a comparison of impact of reform in the UK and in two continental European countries. Third, implementation issues in actual e-government initiatives are analysed and reflected upon.

This chapter is structured as follows. First, the concept of e-government is explored and defined. The next section discusses the concept of technology in relation to institutions. Then, visions of reform in national e-government policies and implementation issues and information resource management challenges are analysed. Conclusions are presented in the final section.

E-government defined

In general and loosely stated, e-government concerns the use of ICTs in public administration. Traditionally, ICTs have been used in public administration in clerical and supportive functions like finance, budgeting and personnel record keeping. It has only been for about two decades or so that ICTs are used to support primary processes of public administration (for example, automated processing of administrative orders) and to enable exchange of information between various public sector bodies, and between government as a whole and citizens. The rise of Internet technologies has boosted especially the use of ICTs for purposes of inter-organizational communication and exchange of information between public sector organizations on the one hand and citizens and corporations on the other hand. For instance, many public sector organizations nowadays feature websites through which citizens and corporations can interact with public administration. Although many of us are aware of these kinds of electronic public services, actually and rigorously defining the concept of e-government in not an easy task: the concept itself seems to be more based on pragmatic experiences and visions (European Commission, 1996, 1997, 2000; National Audit Office, 2002; National Performance Review, 2000; OECD, 1998, 2003; Prime Minister and the Minister for the Cabinet Office, 1999) and management consultancy (Accenture, 2002; Cap Gemini Ernst and Young, 2003) than on a solid theoretical view. For instance, Gruening thoroughly analysed fourteen schools of thought on public administration and public management and concluded: '[T]he *use of information technology* seems to be a characteristic ... that has no specific theoretical roots. It is strictly a pragmatic idea, used where it is useful' (Gruening, 2001: 17). In general, the conclusion that the use of ICTs in organizations has no theoretical roots can be contested (Gazendam, 1993; Homburg, 1999), but the way in which ICTs are dealt with in public administration theories, and in NPM writings particularly, certainly lacks theoretical rigour.

Various authors have emphasized a variety of types of electronic interaction between governments and citizens that can be subsumed under the heading of e-government (Chadwick and May, 2003; Grönlund, 2003):

- Government-to-citizen interaction, with which governments address citizens and corporations as customers of public services. In practice, this type often takes the form of citizens receiving information, contacting civil servants and/or performing transactions using a website as a one-shop-no-stop delivery channel. Fountain provides the example of an International Trade Data system that provides businesses with licences and permits that are required under international and federal legislation (Fountain, 2001).
- Government-to-government interaction, which basically is the electronic coordination and exchange of information between several, often internally compartmentalized agencies or departments. This type of interaction is the technological counterpart of the concept 'joined-up government' (Bogdanor, 2005; Pollitt, 2003).

• Government-to-voter interaction (online voting or e-voting). At this moment, online voting takes place in, among other places, Australia (Australian Capital Territory), Brazil, Canada, Germany (Niedersachsen), New Zealand, and the US (California) (Aarts, Leenes, and Svensson, 2001). In many cases, e-voting occurs alongside postal voting and traditional voting.

• Government-to-citizen interaction. This type of interaction often takes place in discussion forums, and is aimed at participation of citizens, interest groups and other stakeholders in the policy process and decision-making about, for instance, urban and rural planning projects like the reconstruction of a neighbourhood, a shopping mall or the planning of a railroad. Grönlund mentions examples of local electronic forums in the Swedish city of Bollnäs, where citizens engage in electronic discussions with the local politicians (Grönlund, 2003).

• Apart from these forms, which are all targeted at proactive and responsible citizens, there are some services that target the less benevolent aspects of citizens' behaviour. E-government services can also be used for criminal prosecution, fighting fraud or enforcement of legislation. For example, in many countries internal revenue services (tax agencies) are frontrunners in the application of e-government. One of the more important motives for tax agencies to use e-government services is to promote compliance of taxpayers by supplying them with accurate and more compelling information. In the US, the PATRIOT Act has resulted in increased use of ICTs by Intelligence and Security Agencies for the purposes of collection and sharing of information on potential terrorist activities (Regan, 2004).

In this chapter, we focus on (1) all above patterns of interaction between governments and external stakeholders and (2) the interaction inside government (government-to-government). We therefore define e-government as the use of information and communication technologies, especially Internet and web technology, by a public organization to support or redefine existing and/or future relations with 'stakeholders' in the internal and external environment (Bekkers and Homburg, 2005).

Technology and institutions

In the academic NPM literature, but also in the practice of government reforms, ICTs are often seen as enablers (sometimes even causes) of desired or desirable changes in public administration. For instance, in the British White Paper *Modernizing Government*, it is stated that '[I]nformation technology is changing our lives: the way we work, the way we do business, the way we communicate with each other, how we spend our time. New technology offers opportunities and choice' (Prime Minister and the Minister for the Cabinet Office, 1999: 45). Likewise, the Canadian International Development Agency

(CIDA) enthusiastically propagated the use of ICTs in the Philippines by stating that 'ICTs will facilitate greater efficiency and effectiveness in delivering services to the public' (World Summit on the Information Society, 2006). The above claims are examples of how abstractly and deterministically policy-makers talk about technology, reducing technology to a material cause. In doing so, they largely ignore (1) the role of human agency in *shaping* the design or use of technology (Orlikowski and Barley, 2001), and (2) the contexts in which effects are to be noted (either the UK or the Philippines, in the above examples). Seemingly, human agency is limited to the choice to use ICTs and specific e-government implementations; once adopted, technologies presumably work their effects on the machinery of public administration unambiguously.

A view on the role of e-government in modernization and reform programmes as expressed above, in which technology is depicted as a material, *physical* artefact, is contested in a strand in the literature known as social shaping of technology (SST). SST emerged from a critique of crude forms of technological determinism, which holds that (1) the nature of technologies and the direction of change were unproblematic or predetermined, and (2) technology had a necessary and determinate impact on work, organizations, government systems and societies as a whole. The SST literature, on the contrary, argues that technology does not develop according to an inner technical logic, but that technology in general is a *social* artefact as much as it is a *physical* artefact, patterned by the conditions of its creation, its use and the context in which it is implemented (Fulk, Steinfield and Schmitz, 1987; Williams and Edge, 1996).[1] Most scholars working in the line of SST seek to explain how interests, perspectives and institutions shape the design and meaning of technical systems; in other words, they put emphasis on the role of agency in technological change.[2]

Using a SST perspective, it is possible to question *general* uses of technologies in NPM initiatives. According to general SST principles, it can be stated that the design of any technology – and thus, its uses and ways in which technologies are integrated into everyday practice – mirrors the taken-for-granted understandings and assumptions of reform programmes in whose context technologies are implemented. For example, in NPM initiatives that emphasize customer orientation and responsiveness, one might expect other kinds of Internet applications (that is, web-based transaction services, track-and-trace facilities), than in initiatives that stress consultation or public accountability (in which cases one might expect Internet discussion forums, or web-based league tables, respectively). Obviously, rather comparable or similar Internet technologies can be embedded into different institutional settings in different ways, occasioning different outcomes (Barley, 1986; Orlikowski and Barley, 2001). Since technology may shape institutions, as well as is capable of being shaped by institutions that surround public administration, what is traditionally considered as 'the technology' and its 'institutional context' is often hard to demarcate. This renders any claim about superiority of technological reforms over managerial reforms problematic. With respect to the research question of this chapter, and the claims about the eventual realization of reform programmes using technologies, a 'social shaping of technologies' perspective sheds new light on the discussion about technological and institutional reform.[3] By scrutinizing e-government using an SST perspective, e-government is conceptualized as much emergent, evolving, embedded, fragmented and provisional as NPM is. Obviously, the question is not if and how technological reforms supersede NPM or make management reforms irrelevant; rather, the question is how, in specific institutional contexts, specific e-government initiatives are shaped, how technologies are crafted and used in particular ways, and how technologies, once adapted, in turn shape institutional processes and managerial capabilities. In the subsequent section, this – until now, rather conceptual – question is addressed empirically.

Analysis of e-government strategies and practices

Introduction

In order to analyse what kinds of effects are actually yielded when managerial and technological trajectories of reform are combined, below two alternative research strategies are employed.

First, national e-government policies of three European national governments are analysed with respect to their view on technology, envisaged ambitions, goals, and implementation strategies of technological and institutional reforms. In exploring possible linkages between technological and NPM reforms, we draw on the analysis of e-government strategies in the UK, Denmark and the Netherlands. These three countries represent a variety of national administrative regimes (Esping-Andersen, 1996; Kitschelt, Lange, Marks, and Stephens, 1999; Pollitt and Bouckaert, 2004). The UK has been chosen as a representative of the Anglo-Saxon world in which NPM as e-government reforms originated. The UK can be classified as a unitary, centralized state with a majoritarian executive government (Pollitt and Bouckaert, 2004). Kitschelt (1999) refers to the UK as a liberal welfare state. Denmark and the Netherlands, on the other hand, are classified as unitary, communitarian decentralized states (Adler and Henman, 2005). Kitschelt refers to Denmark as a social democratic welfare state, whereas the Netherlands are classified as a corporatist state (Kitschelt et al., 1999). The Danish case is especially interesting because this country – like other Scandinavian countries – has a long-standing tradition in using ICT in public administration. The analysis of e-government strategies serves to analyse discursive convergence of technological and managerial reforms.

Second, actual implementation practices are analysed by reviewing studies of government-to-government structures in various European countries in various sectors. With this analysis of actual implementation practices, convergence beyond discursive levels (that is, decisional and operational) is analysed and reflected upon.

National e-government policies: antecedents of reforms

In the UK, initiatives to put ICTs at the centre of a concern to modernize public administration are stimulated by the Cabinet Office, especially the Office of the E-Envoy and the Central Information Technology Unit (CITU) (Chadwick and May, 2003). A key aim is to emulate private-sector ICT approaches and stimulate market mechanisms ('choice') in delivery of public services to customers and business. 'The British public has grown accustomed to consumer choice and competition in the private sector. If our public service is to survive and thrive, it must match the best in its ability to innovate, to share good ideas, and to control costs. Above all, the public service must deliver efficiently and effectively the policies, programmes and services of government' (Prime Minister and the Minister for the Cabinet Office, 1999: 35).

In the *Modernizing Government* White Paper (Prime Minister and the Minister for the Cabinet Office, 1999) and in *E-Government: a Strategic Framework for Public Services in the Information Age* (Minister for the Cabinet Office, 2000), e-government is portrayed as an aspect of modernizing government which has only one purpose: to make life better for citizens and business. The emphasis lies on the improvement of electronic service delivery in such a way that it delivers what people really want, fully exploiting government's information resources. Citizens are portrayed as intelligent and 'empowered' consumers, while government is seen primarily as a service organization:

> People are aware of the possibility and benefits of excellent service, and they expect it in all dealings with business ... The challenge for the public sector is that the same growing expectations will be applied to government services. (Minister for the Cabinet Office, 2000: 8)

The distinctive role for e-government reforms in the context of the modernization of government is that they should virtually (that is, not by means of changes in organization structures or administrative hierarchies) reintegrate the administrative machine. E-government reforms are portrayed as a remedy against the disaggregation and decentralization that had happened under Next Steps. For instance, in the section on 'Information age government', it is stated that:

> The Government must bring about a fundamental change in the way we use IT. We must modernize the business of government itself – achieving joined up working between different parts of government and providing

new, efficient and convenient ways for citizens and businesses to communicate with government and to receive services. (Prime Minister and the Minister for the Cabinet Office, 1999: 45)

In other words, e-government initiatives are seen as vehicles to implement joined-up government and foster service delivery. An important impetus for making this happen is a corporate ICT strategy which encourages the convergence and interconnection of ICT systems of individual (central and local) public service agencies. Such a relatively centralist approach (materialized in, for example, a 'Government Secure Intranet') boosts cross-departmental working, makes the public sector work more coherently, provides a clear basis for sharing data between departments and, in general, to 'help government to become a learning organization by improving our access to, and organization of, information' (Prime Minister and the Minister for the Cabinet Office, 1999: 46).

Concluding, it can be stated that in the British modernization programme, there is a distinct role for ICT use and applications. As announced in *Modernizing Government*, and as is further elaborated in *E-Government: a Strategic Framework for Public Services in the Information Age*, technology is crafted and shaped rhetorically to enable actual client orientation and joined-up government (JUG). Both client orientation and JUG are supposed to be achievable by means of well-co-ordinated, government-wide information strategies.

In Denmark, e-government policies have been initiated by central government (notably the ministries of (1) Finance and (2) Science and Technology) and regional and local administrations.

In the 1990s, policy documents drafted by intergovernmental working groups and ministries portrayed ICTs in the context of a more open, transparent and decentralized society. For instance, in 1995, the globalized network society is portrayed as follows.

The numerous global networks with their debates, databases and dissemination of information do not lend themselves to control. They invite both anarchy and refreshing debate. (Ministeriet for Videnskab Teknologi og Udvikling, 1995)

Equivalent visions are sketched in subsequent White Papers. In these documents, attention is paid to the role of ICTs in fostering decentralized network societies. For instance, the first target of the 2002 White Paper *From Vision to Action Info Society 2000* is that: 'e-government should actively contribute to the development of a network society' (Digital Taskforce, 2002: 6).

In general, until about 2004, the focus was on transparency, interaction with citizens, free access to government information and on measures to prevent social polarization into a two-tier society of ICT winners and ICT losers.

Since about 2004, a notable change has occurred. Projekt Digital Forvaltning (Project E-Government), developed by a cross-government council, emphasized service delivery as the primary aim for e-government: 'Digitalization must contribute to creation of an efficient and coherent public sector with a high quality of services, with citizens and businesses at the centre' (Digital Forvaltning, 2004: 4).

The guiding idea behind the Danish e-government strategy in terms of implementation is and has been throughout the last decade, that the responsibilities for the implementation of e-government should lie as decentral as possible. For instance, there is a variety of boards and councils involved in the implementation of e-government information strategies. In the foreword of the 2004 White Paper, the responsibilities of individual public authorities for their transition are stressed.

Concluding, it can be stated that in Danish e-government initiatives, throughout time, there is a shift in emphasis ranging from support to open, decentralized grassroots initiatives with support for personal development and free access to information, to a situation in which electronic services are emphasized, yet still in the context of a rather decentralized government apparatus. Tasks and responsibilities for e-government initiatives are spread over various ministries and between local and central levels of government. Specific centralization tendencies seem to be lacking in e-government strategies.

In the Netherlands, various policy documents (Ministry of Economic Affairs, 1999; Ministry of the Interior and Kingdom Relationships, 1999, 2000) have been drafted in which a national e-government policy takes shape. The most important policy aims as formulated in *Action Programme for Electronic Government* (Ministry of the Interior and Kingdom Relationships, 1999) and *The Digital Delta* (Ministry of Economic Affairs, 1999) are increasing the accessibility of government, improving the quality of public services and enhancing the internal efficiency of government. As such, these initiatives and policy proposals reflect customer-orientation and a focus on delivery of services. Customer-orientation and service delivery are to be achieved through the establishment of thematic, demand-pattern driven virtual services counters, with themes being 'living and building', 'care and welfare' and 'business'. In all of these counters, several (semi-) government organizations will have to work together. An important project, which is focused on the improvement of the internal efficiency of government, is the realization of authentic basic registers, in which public data that will be shared by several parties are stored.

In a subsequent document *Contract with the Future* (Ministry of the Interior and Kingdom Relationships, 2000), the scope of e-government is broadened: the political participation of citizens is also mentioned as an area that deserves attention and stimulation. Although in general, the image of the citizen as an intelligent consumer of public services is prevailing, and the importance of electronic service delivery is stressed, there is also reference to electronic services that allow for an open and 'horizontal' dialogue between citizens and governments. There is explicit reference to the importance of digital interactive policy-making practices, and electronic voting. A key element of e-government that is being mentioned is the use of so called digital playgrounds (*digitale trapveldjes*). Digital playgrounds refer to digital community projects in which citizens of relatively deprived neighbourhoods are trained to use ICTs and to gain access to the Internet. With these kinds of projects, one aims to increase the social capital in specific neighbourhoods.

From the various national policies on e-government, it is possible to reconstruct the 'rhetoric' of technological reforms in terms of observed risks, challenges to be tackled, and view on the nature of the redesign of the relationships between government and its surrounding stakeholders.

In all e-government reform initiatives studied, there is a tendency to put emphasis on public service delivery through electronic means, and to promote interoperability in order to actually realize joined-up government.

There are, however, also some notable differences. First, in the UK e-government strategies, interoperability and actual JUG are believed to be achieved by means of a well-coordinated, government-wide centralized information strategy. In the Dutch and especially Danish policies, it is stated that such an approach is not practical and is also objected on normative grounds. In these countries, there is emphasis on consensus-based implementation strategies involving an apparent myriad of councils and boards. Second, whereas all national e-government approaches put emphasis on (electronic) service delivery, especially in the Dutch initiatives, there are also references to interactive policy-making (that is, the citizen is not only portrayed as a consumer, but also as a 'citoyen' or 'good citizen') and electronic voting. In the Danish e-government policies, there used to be references to uses of technology that promote grassroots democracy in which technology fostered open debates, transparency and personal development of individuals; in more recent documents (Digital Forvaltning, 2004), however, these objectives have disappeared and more emphasis is put on the importance of service delivery.

In short, there is some discursive convergence in the sense that in all e-government policies, there is emphasis on the application of ICTs in order to deliver public service electronically and, in order to make this happen, to improve communication and exchange of information between various departments and agencies inside governments. The direction of reform, the view of technology, envisaged uses of technology and the way in which technologies are assumed to be shaped by prevailing societal developments and norms, however, are fundamentally different. In the UK e-government strategy, technology is crafted and shaped rhetorically to enable fundamental client-orientation and joined-up government through centrally co-ordinated, government-wide information strategies. In the Danish and Dutch visions, on the other hand, technology is assumed to be less malleable and control of technology is achieved through all kinds of partnerships between levels of government.

National e-government practices: implementations of reforms

The analysis of strategies from documents has revealed partial convergence, at a rhetorical level. In order to analyse to what degree convergence exists at decisional and/or operational levels, technological reforms behind the concept of 'joined-up government' in various countries are analysed. The term 'joined-up government', which is frequently used in policy documents and organizational practices, is mirrored in the term 'government-to-government' interaction (G2G) in the e-government literature and practice. Moreover, the degree to which existing ICTs allow for actual exchange of information between various organizations is denoted by the term 'interoperability'.

From the analysis of e-government strategies, it has come to the fore that various ways to actually achieve JUG or G2G can be envisaged, ranging from using government-wide relatively centralist strategies, to rather decentral, consensus-based approaches in Denmark. A recent European study (Millard, Iversen, Kubicek, Westholm and Cimander, 2004) has investigated in what ways interoperability (which is presumably conceived as a precondition of actual JUG) is actually achieved. The authors investigated best practices of G2G reorganizations in several service clusters in Austria, the Benelux countries, Finland, France, the UK, Greece, Iceland, Ireland, Italy, Norway, Portugal, Spain and Sweden. This particular study includes case studies taken from the sectors of income tax, car registration, citizen certificates, family allowances, student grants, social benefits, building permissions, enrolment in higher education, citizen portals, social contributions for employers, corporation taxes, customs declarations, business registration, environmental-related permits and business portals.

The authors found a myriad of approaches and implementations of G2G e-government initiatives. For example, they identified the digitization of student grants in Denmark as a success story, because only the virtual service counters (websites) were implemented on top of the existing patterns of information exchange between relatively autonomous organizations, their workflows and legacy systems. Another Danish case, the delivery of social benefits, was said to be successful. In this particular case, few or no changes to existing, well-functioning organizational structures and levels of integration between systems were necessary for the aim of interoperability. In the Netherlands, car registration was found to be successful; digitization of the service has led to changes to the working steps for civil servants and citizens, but this has not involved many changes to the actual organization of back-offices and the information systems therein. On the other hand, enrolment in higher education in the UK was also found to be successful. In this case, various legacy systems had to be incorporated and this was successfully achieved through the use of data standards and conversions, and by ensuring scalable, flexible, resilient and secure systems, including the centralization of relevant data structures by the agencies concerned (Millard et al., 2004).

In general, the authors identified various configurations with which interoperability and joined-up government were actually achieved and enforced:

- By means of digitization of organizationally unchanged back-offices; in this configuration, existing inter-organizational linkages are digitized and automated, and/or virtual web-based counters are erected on top of existing legacy technology. In this configuration, existing organizational workflows and exchanges are more or less cemented as it is.
- By means of fundamental redesign and centralization of back-offices; in this configuration, service delivery and philosophy of service design and service production.
- By means of simultaneous centralization of back-offices and decentralization of front-offices.
- By means of modularizing common back-office components over broad areas, while retaining flexibility and possibilities to adapt to specific requirements.
- By means of clearing houses that enable the exchange of information from various sources without the need to necessarily integrate data sources. Clearing houses are organizations that enable data exchange and data interoperability by providing intelligence which registers and routes data remaining in existing, decentralized databases. Clearing houses are configurations that enable interoperability through other means than centralization, and allow for communication of otherwise incompatible data standards, languages, semantics and syntaxes.

The authors could not, however, identify ultimately superior implementation strategies. They stated that:

> [o]ne of the clearest conclusions emerging from the present study is that state structures, and institutional, legal, regulatory and cultural factors, can be extremely important in determining the nature, cost and success of eGovernment. As has been demonstrated earlier in this report ... progress often depends on whether or not there is a history of back office integration and cooperation, but not necessarily through centralized structures. (Millard et al., 2004: 61)

The authors furthermore conclude that in realizing e-government initiatives and reforms, policy-makers should carefully consider existing organizational and technological conditions, which they assume reflect local institutional regimes and cultures. Millard et al. therefore recommend that 'different countries across Europe need to develop their own paths as each has unique identities, cultures, legal systems and institutional structures' (Millard et al., 2004: 61).

Conclusion

This chapter started with the proposition that e-government as technological reform could realize the change potential inherent in the rhetorical claims of the Anglo-American NPM literature. After having scrutinized e-government reform strategies, and having reviewed international patterns of interoperability (JUG/G2G) reforms, we conclude that views that express that technology can actually make NPM work, are too simplistic to capture the complicated reality of technological and managerial reforms.

First, we contested the narrow-minded, technological determinist view of technology that is inherent to the claims about coincidence of technological and managerial reforms in public administration. In many cases, technology is seen as a strict enabler or sometimes even cause of desired or desirable reforms in public administration. In many cases, claims about e-government as instrumentation of managerial reform are susceptible to the criticism that technology is depicted as having an autonomous, exogenous influence. We argued for a different view of technology, as expressed in a 'social shaping of technology perspective' in which ICTs are seen as social and physical artifacts simultaneously: they are physical in the sense that they are designed and implemented in order to meet specific requirements and serve purposes, but they are also social in the sense that technologies allow and constrain specific behaviours, and shape and are shaped and selected by the institutions that surround public administration. Consequently, the distinction between technology itself and institutional context in which technologies are implemented, is relatively hard to demarcate.

The 'social shaping of technology' perspective was clearly visible in the analysis of national e-government strategies of the UK and Denmark. In both strategies, explicit references were being made to administrative reforms, but the trajectory and NPM elements adhered to contrasted sharply. Interestingly, in both strategies, technology was portrayed in such a way that it could support the specific trajectory of reform. In other words: in those strategies, prevailing views of reforms are enshrined in envisaged uses of technologies.

The idea that specific uses of technologies can support various trajectories of reform was also noticed in the study of back-office interoperability strategies of various clusters of service delivery in various European countries. In various countries, specific mechanisms were chosen in order to realize joined-up government: either back-office digitization without redesign, deep reorganization, application of clearing house constructions, depending on the specific state structure and institutional, legal, regulatory and cultural factors.

Concluding, we deny that e-government can be seen as an unequivocal instrumentation of unequivocal NPM reforms. With e-government strategies, specific elements of NPM are highlighted with specific envisaged or actual uses of technology. As such, we conclude that the divergence of NPM practice and concepts throughout various institutional contexts is probably enlarged by using information technologies. As such, these conclusions are consistent with earlier studies on uses of ICTs, which showed that technologies tend to be applied in such a way that they replicate and even enforce existing institutional structures.

This makes a case for the *reinforcement thesis* which has been suggested numerous times in studies on effects of ICTs on organizational structures, inter-organizational relations, and so on. The reinforcement thesis states that technologies tend to be applied. For example, with respect to the reinforcing forces of ICTs on bureaucratic structures in the 1970s, Nohria and Eccles stated that '[c]omputer systems and software adopted the "architecture" of bureaucracy ... Not surprisingly the language of information systems became the language of bureaucracy' (Nohria and Berkley, 1994: 120). In our contemporary administrative reform practice we see that especially the communicative qualities of ICTs, notably Internet technologies, can be used to redesign information relations in and surrounding public administration and thus, at first sight, to instrument managerial reform. The direction of reform, however, is far from unequivocal, and largely depends on existing state structures, pre-existing institutional structures, and legal, regulatory and cultural factors. A single marriage between New Public Management as a managerial innovation and e-government as a technological innovation is a fallacy: e-government and NPM are far more contextually bound than is apparent at first sight.

Notes

1. In this chapter, we use a rather liberal connotation of social shaping of technology, without following particular consensual orthodoxies claiming distinctiveness of subdisciplines like social construction of technology, political economy of technology, or sociology of knowledge (Williams and Edge, 1996).
2. Note that SST includes work by social constructivists, but is not equivalent to social constructivism.
3. Note that this question is relevant for the NPM literature as well as for the academic e-government/information system literature. This latter literature has traditionally ignored regulative processes, normative aspects and cultural frameworks that shape design and use of ICTs and, therefore, has yet to make much use of more recent developments in public administration theory that include themes of convergence/divergence, path dependence, and so forth.

9

Hospital Performance Indicators: How and Why Neighbours Facing Similar Problems Go Different Ways – Building Explanations of Hospital Performance Indicator Systems in England and the Netherlands

Christopher Pollitt[1]

Aims

1. Taking a key element within the NPM (performance indicators) to show how neighbouring countries facing broadly similar problems treat this in very different ways (that is, more divergence than convergence).
2. To compare, contrast and assess different theories that might explain the divergence.

A performance orientation is generally taken to be one of the key distinguishing features of the NPM (see Chapter 1, and Pollitt, 2003). This chapter examines the operational manifestation of a performance orientation – sets of performance indicators (PIs) – in two neighbouring countries – England and the Netherlands. It examines alternative explanations for the fact that the developmental trajectory of PIs in the chosen sector – hospitals – is very different in the two countries. Thus the main aim is not to give an exhaustive account of the PI systems themselves (which will be only lightly sketched), but rather to interrogate *explanations* for what appear to be large differences.

This chapter links to a number of other parts of the book. Most obviously, it is hoped some further light will be shed on the issues of convergence and divergence which were first raised in Chapter 3. The comparison of England and the Netherlands in Chapter 4 is repeated here – but this time for hospital PIs rather than the steering of executive agencies. This chapter can also be compared with the analysis of benchmarking (a particular form of performance measurement) in Chapter 7.

Background

Performance measurement and performance management are key elements within most definitions of the NPM. The NPM emphasis is supposed to be on results – on outputs and outcomes rather than rule following or the control of inputs (Blair, 2002; Christensen and Lægreid, 2001: 19; Pollitt, 2003: Chapter 2).

A closer focus on results is arguably particularly important in the most expensive and complex public services, such as health care and education. These are also services which touch upon the lives of almost all citizens. This chapter will, therefore, examine the development of performance indicators for hospitals in two neighbouring countries, the Netherlands and the UK.

Both countries face similar problems – rising public health care expenditures due to demographics, changing health care technologies, increasing public expectations and some doubts about the quality of care. Both countries are relatively wealthy and both have been exposed to NPM ideas and practices. Each knows what goes on in the other's health care sector – the potential for transfers of management technology appears to be high. But beyond that the similarity stops. The trajectories of the two hospital systems have been very different. The UK was a pioneer of PIs for hospitals (first national data set 1983) and has developed an extremely elaborate and sophisticated system. The Netherlands has been slow to develop hospital PIs (the first national set was approved in 2003) and has thus far chosen a much less ambitious set. It is also the case that the development of the Dutch hospital PIs has been far less tightly led and controlled by government than it was in the UK, and that the Dutch data sets have thus far been primarily intended for 'internal' use by professionals and managers, not for public league tabling, as has been the practice in the UK. In the Netherlands there appears to have been a conscious wish (at least by some parties) to avoid the 'name and shame' tactics employed by the New Labour government in the UK since 1997, and to leave hospitals with control over how they present their own data (Berg et al., 2005). Whether the Dutch can actually avoid league tables appearing is another question – the press and consumer organizations have already published rankings.

How can we explain these large differences? There are a number of possible reasons:

- Perhaps the Dutch are just slow? Now they have started, they will need to catch up with the global trend to NPM, as exemplified in countries like the UK, Australia and New Zealand.
- Rational choice theorists might argue that differences are due to some species of 'embeddedness' and path dependency. For example, it might be proposed that once the UK had started on its trajectory in 1983, there was positive feedback from developing the system further and negative feedback for any move to 'go back'. The Netherlands did not start then, because it faced a different set of incentives and penalties, which favoured the choice of a different strategic approach. However, now it *has* started with hospital PIs, we may expect a similar self-reinforcing trajectory.
- Differences in political cultures and political systems – the Dutch are more consensual and gradualist (that is they don't actually *want* to 'catch up'). Creating a wide base of consensual support is regarded as just important as – or at least a necessary first step towards – getting effective action.
- Differences in organizational structures – the Dutch health care system is much less centralized than the UK NHS, it is insurance-based rather than tax-financed, and it is more of a public/private mixture. For all these reasons it is less amenable to central direction.

Some (but not all) of these theories could be used in combination.

Background: hospital PIs in England

The first national set of health care PIs appeared in England and Wales in the autumn of 1983 (Pollitt, 1985). The introduction of the first PI set was strongly driven by central government. The Conservative government of the day was facing the aftermath of a severe economic downturn, and at the same time was publicly committed to strict control of public expenditure. Equally, it was aware that upward cost pressures in the NHS were very great, not least because of demographic change (an increasingly elderly population) and technological change, and also the constant improvements and innovations in medical technologies (Harrison, 1994: Chapter 3). The introduction of PIs was specifically linked to efficient resource use. Performance indicators, the ministry said, would:

> enable comparison to be made between districts and so help Ministers and Regional Chairmen ... to assess the performance of their constituent ... authorities in using manpower and other resources efficiently. (Department of Health and Social Security, 1982: 2)

In the rush to install the new system the government of the day appears to have made extensive use of previous academic data collection carried out for a rather different purpose – an academic attempt to build a model that would predict gross failures of service at particular hospitals.

The PI initiative should not be understood as a freestanding innovation. In fact it was part of a rapidly developing package of measures by which the government attempted to gain better control of NHS costs and subdue some of the consequences of professional medical autonomy. Other measures included the imposition of 'efficiency scrutinies', a review of the NHS estate and, most important of all, the introduction, for the first time of (usually non-medical) general managers in all hospitals and health authorities (Harrison, 1994).

Over subsequent years the PI package underwent constant changes (for the purposes of this chapter it is not necessary to list and explain all the indicators, a task that would in any case easily occupy a whole book!). By 1985 the original set of just under 150 indicators per health authority had grown to 425. In the mid-1980s a search also began for more clinical indicators of 'avoidable deaths' (as originally proposed in Charlton et al., 1983). By 1989 roughly 2000 Health Service Indicators were being published, based on new, standardized ('Korner') data (Roberts, 1990). After another ten years, the exercise had become a highly publicized set of annual league tables in which hospitals were awarded three, two, one or no 'stars', and which carried significant consequences for both the public image of hospitals and the career prospects of their chief executives (see, for example, http://ratings2004. healthcarecommission.org.uk). The PI set had also slowly come to include more measures of clinical effectiveness, and of patient satisfaction. Thus, for example, one could pick out the indicators shown in Table 9.1.

Table 9.1: Examples of selected UK hospital PIs (clinical and patient-oriented)

Hospital	Indicator	Current national figure	Current hospital figure
Good Hope	Deaths within 30 days of surgery	2.922 (per 100,000 patients)	3.322
Wirral	Deaths within 30 days of surgery	2.922	1.967
Good Hope	Inpatient survey: respect and dignity	82.3% (response to patient questionnaire surveys)	83.4%
Wirral	Inpatient survey: respect and dignity	82.3%	81.6%

Source: Department of Health website http://www.doh.gov.uk/performanceratings/2002, accessed 20 December 2002.

One can see from this particular selection from the national database that on the clinical indicator of deaths within thirty days of surgery, Wirral hospital scores better than both the national average and Good Hope hospital (which is slightly poorer than the national average). The patient survey questions concerning the perception of having been dealt with in a dignified and respectful manner show a similar picture – Wirral scoring better than Good Hope, and the latter being below the national average. This kind of 'league tabling' is exactly what some of the architects of the current Dutch scheme have been striving to avoid. On the other hand there have already been more particular and limited comparisons between Dutch hospitals, such as one on waiting times.

Whilst the above example only scratches the surface of a large and complex data set, it is already considerably more detailed and nuanced than most of the media debate about these NHS hospital PIs. The public and political argument tends to be conducted in terms of the headline score of each hospital as zero, one, two or three 'stars'. These stars – as in a hotel guide – compress a whole of mass of data about very different aspects of performance into a single summative score. What exactly this 'means' is exceedingly hard to say.

Background: hospital PIs in the Netherlands

Twenty-two years after the launch of the pioneering NHS PI set, the first Dutch national performance indicator framework became operational. Early in 2003 the Dutch Health Care Inspectorate (an autonomous section of the Ministry of Health, Welfare and Sport) had decided to develop a set of hospital indicators covering patient safety and clinical effectiveness (Asbroek et al., 2004). This was thus a very different starting point from the NHS system, which had begun by focusing on costs and efficiency, and only later developed significant measures of clinical effectiveness and patient satisfaction.

Not only was the starting point different, so was the process by which the launch was arrived at. Whereas the 1983 set for the NHS had been developed in a rush within the health ministry, the Dutch Inspectorate set as a prerequisite that they would secure the co-operation of the Dutch hospital associations and the Dutch Medical Specialists Association (Orde van Medisch Specialisten). There was also extensive academic involvement from the Department of Health Policy and Management at Erasmus University Rotterdam and the National Institute for Public Health and the Environment (RIVM). Eventually it was agreed that the development of the indicator set should be a joint venture, and that the indicator scores would not be published as a national league table, but by each individual hospital, in its own preferred way (Berg et al., 2005). This gives each hospital the opportunity to offer its own qualifications and comments on its 'scores'. (The indicators can be found on www.prestatie-indicatoren.nl.)

It was not the case that prior to this initiative nothing was happening in the Netherlands. It was rather that the Dutch response had definitely *not* been a central government-led national system. There had been a quality movement in acute care from the beginning of the 1980s, occasionally spurred onwards by media attention to certain failings and scandals. However, it mainly had the character of a series of 'in-hospital' local and professional initiatives, and the degree of implementation had been variable. A National Organization for Quality Assurance in Hospitals (the CBO) had been founded back in 1979, but it had not adopted a strongly patient-oriented mission until 1998 (www.cbo.nl, accessed 17 May 2005).

By the mid-1980s the Dutch government faced considerable dissatisfaction with the existing system of hospital care. The existing, top-down rationing arrangement seemed to be generating continuing conflict while failing to achieve efficient resource allocation. Therefore the centre-right government set up an independent committee – the Dekker Committee – to report. This committee recommended an ambitious, market-oriented reform based on a combination of regulated competition between providers and mandatory national health insurance (but no performance indicators!). At first these proposals received almost unanimous political support, but by 1993 the attempt to implement a version of these proposals had collapsed in political and organizational disarray (Helderman et al., 2005: 198–9). One may contrast this collapse with Mrs Thatcher's 'internal market' reform of the NHS in 1989, a fundamental change that was imposed in the teeth of adverse public opinion polls and bitter opposition from virtually all the health care professions. In the shadow of this developing failure, a series of meetings (the 'Leidschendam' Conferences) took place, involving government agencies, national associations representing the hospitals and other institutions, professional associations and patient organizations. These generated a framework for creating quality standards, and this was subsequently given legislative backing in the form of the 1996 Care Institutions Quality Act. This legislation afforded individual institutions considerable leeway in how they pursued quality, although it obliged them to collect certain categories of information. In short, we again see a typically Dutch process of consensus-formation taking place through discussion between a variety of social actors, with the government playing only a partial role. We also see a process of policy formulation that plays out over rather longer time periods than would be usual in the UK.

First explanation: the Dutch are laggards

Perhaps the Dutch are slow, and just need to catch up? One occasionally hears this form of explanation on the lips of management reformers. It usually comes from a worldview which assumes that there is a new model of public management, superior to previous forms, a 'best practice' which is rapidly diffusing through the world and which all countries that aspire to 'stay up' or 'be modern' will sooner or later have to adopt. In short, there is one solution, and one track (which could be called 'NPM' or, more recently, 'good governance') and towards which all must converge.

Yet, as we have seen in Chapters 2 and 3, this kind of convergence model does not accord with the facts in many continental European states. Very deep-seated differences remain between the management reform trajectories of different countries, and important states such as France, Germany and Italy have never really bought the 'reinvention/NPM' package anyway (see Chapters 2 and 3, and also Pollitt and Bouckaert, 2004).

It is not necessary to dwell for long on this model of one track/inevitability. It is a weak analysis – indeed, it is hardly an explanation at all. To accuse some individual or organization or country of being a laggard does not by itself *explain* anything. And, more specifically, to accuse the Dutch hospital system of lagging behind its British equivalent would be, to put it mildly, contestable. Once the underlying convergence model is exposed its simple functionalism, a-historicalism and downright inaccuracy are obvious. Even international bodies such as the OECD, which once mildly flirted with NPM convergence, have now embraced a more nuanced message of legitimate and necessary diversity (compare the account in Premfors, 1998, with the more recent OECD outputs such as OECD, 2003).

Second explanation: rational choice

For more than two decades now rational choice theory has been extremely popular in economics, political science and business studies. It is certainly able to offer explanations as to why governments resort to certain types of management reform, including the creation of executive agencies and their subjection to systems of performance targets (see, for example, James, 2003). However, it is much less used in comparative analysis. Indeed, the restrictiveness of its central assumptions (for example, that all bureaucrats 'maximize self-regarding and hard-edged utilities in making official decisions' – Dunleavy, 1991: 174) might make it seem a poor candidate for explaining national or organizational *differences*. Furthermore much (not all) rational choice analysis tends to concentrate on current incentive structures and the way actors try to maximize their utilities, a focus which backgrounds or excludes historical and contextual factors. Pierson (2004: 9) puts it like this:

> Most important is the way in which micro modeling exercises that are centered on strategic interactions among individuals encourage a highly restricted field of vision, both in space and time. Among the things that tend to drop out of such exercises are issues of macro structure, the role of temporal ordering or sequence, and a whole host of social processes that

play out only over extended periods of time and cannot be reduced to the strategic 'moves' of 'actors'.

Some scholars have, however, sought to ameliorate the seemingly abstract and context-free nature of applied rational choice theory in ways that would make it more suitable for the comparative analysis of differences between particular contexts. One strand in this modification has been the attention given to notions of 'embeddedness' (Granovetter, 1985) and 'path dependency' (Pierson, 2004). This elaboration of the theory allows rational choice theorists to get beyond their usual focus on actors strategically calculating their present interests with no regard to history, because it allows for the possibility that earlier decisions (perhaps decisions actually unknown to current actors) may structure current choices, so that the costs of departing from previous trajectories or paths seem to get higher and higher or, to put it another way, there is steadily positive feedback in favour of remaining on the same path set in some previous period ('path dependency').

How might this work in the case of hospital PIs? No one yet seems to have made a full-scale application of path dependency concepts to the particular subject of this chapter, but a possible line of argument can at least be sketched. To begin with, the UK government had solid, rational reasons for adopting PIs in 1983. In rational choice terms it was the principal (and paymaster) trying to get a tighter grip on a hitherto rather autonomous group of agents (health authorities and hospitals). The need to tighten control at that time has already been explained – there was something of a public expenditure crisis and, if left to themselves, health care expenditures seemed liable to rise at worrying speed. PIs were one tool, along with the installation of general managers and various other initiatives, in the attempt to monitor costs and improve efficiency (Harrison, 1994).

Without necessarily realizing it, however, the introduction of PIs had set the UK government on a particular path. To begin with, having PIs was an announced policy and, therefore, politically difficult to reverse. If there were weaknesses in the first set of PIs (and there were plenty – see Pollitt, 1985) then the least costly response was not publicly to admit defeat by abandoning the idea, but rather to take steps to improve and elaborate the PI set. And this is exactly what happened – new indicators were introduced, and existing measurements were refined; data collection was standardized to improve reliability and the presentation of the data was steadily improved. As time went by the government began to move to introduce direct measures of clinical performance – something that had been almost totally absent from the first set in 1983. Unsurprisingly, this led to tensions with the medical profession, but these were gradually overcome, so that the purpose and scope of the PI set developed to include indicators of quality of care as well as the efficient use of resources. As all this development continued a community of PI specialists – managers, statisticians, academics – grew up around what was a major annual exercise. Naturally, this community added its voice to those already demanding more or at least better measures. At each stage it was easier to go forward to greater sophistication than to go back to having no PIs at all – this is the 'positive feedback' to which path dependency theorists refer. By the time we get to, for example, the advent of the New Labour government in 1997, the political cost of abandoning PIs would have been rather high. 'What are they trying to hide?' one can imagine critics saying, had the government tried to drop the annual PI exercise. The rational choice was to continue it, but to repackage the exercise in ways that allowed two gains. The first was the further tightening of controls over hospitals, their managers and (by proxy) health care professionals (another move by the principal to monitor the agents). The second was for New Labour to tell the public that *their* indicators were better than ever before (in this case the agent – the government – claiming to *its* principal – the electorate – that it was being transparent and efficient). And that is exactly what they did.

So what was the situation in the Netherlands during these UK developments? Why did the Dutch choose differently? Whilst the Dutch government also faced demographic and fiscal pressures in the mid-1980s, their initial reaction represented a contrasting strategic choice. Starting with far more of a public/private mixture in the acute sector, the Dutch government initially (1986–93) put its faith in market-type reforms (the Dekker Report) to generate higher efficiency. They were not starting with a state-controlled system to anything like the same degree as the UK government (see fourth explanation, below), so the more *dirigiste* route initially adopted in the UK (measure performance, insert general managers, introduce widespread mandatory contracting-out) was unappealing for key political actors, if not downright unfeasible. As a group of Dutch academics put it:

> Although the state has a major constitutional responsibility for the efficiency, accessibility and quality of health care, it is not equipped to accomplish these responsibilities under its own strength. (Helderman et al., 2005: 194)

In rational choice terms, the Dutch government faced similar environmental pressures but a rather different set of incentives and penalties, because of a differently structured system. During the 1980s, at the critical juncture, they set off down a different path. Later, from the mid-1990s, they returned to an attempt to regulate the largely private provider system, but that was again viewed as unsuccessful. Since 2001 Dutch governments have once more turned to regulated competition, although it is too early to decide how well this 'replay' of Dekker will turn out. Overall, one might say that the different institutional arrangements in the two countries embody different rationalities (although this would be rejected by some rational choice purists, as straying too far from their original, individual actor frame of reference).

Third explanation: cultural and political system differences

There is a substantial tradition, in comparative political science and comparative public administration, of explaining observed national differences in terms of the different architectures of politico-administrative systems (for example, notably, Lijphart, 1984, 1999) and/or in terms of cultural differences (for example Hofstede, 2001; Mouritzen and Svara, 2002). Standard works ascribe different trajectories of management reforms mainly or partly to different national systems (Pollitt and Bouckaert, 2004). Thus (and this example is highly relevant to the case of health service PIs) the Netherlands, as a strongly consensualist and fairly corporatist political system is far less likely (or able) to rush ahead with 'hard-edged' or controversial reforms than the aggressively majoritarian, centralized and individualist UK (Pollitt and Bouckaert, 2004: Chapters 3 and 4). Politically and culturally, the Dutch need to discuss new ideas at length, and seek agreement between all the major stakeholders (in our case the hospital associations, the medical profession and the government). Sharply judgmental use of indicators (for example, publicly to pick out certain hospitals as poor performers, as happens in the UK) would be unlikely to secure an appropriate level of acceptance, in the absence of which a multi-party governing coalition would find it risky to push ahead. In the UK, however, a single party government, with a majority, has less need to do deals, especially where the matter is one of securing economy and efficiency in the direct expenditure of public funds. To use the technical language of political science, there are fewer 'veto points' in the UK political system.

Pitched at this systemic level, therefore, one would expect to find a less aggressive, more negotiated use of all kinds of management reforms in the Netherlands, and one would expect to find this across many sectors. The differences we have observed for hospital PIs would be reproduced with respect to other reforms, such as privatization of public bodies, the introduction of market-type mechanisms (MTMs) to the public services, and the use of comparative test scores and other indicators to reward or punish individual schools. And in fact, if one compares the Netherlands with the UK, this expectation is largely confirmed (Pollitt and Bouckaert, 2004). There are many examples other than the hospital sector where the UK government has pushed NPM-style reforms much harder, faster and sooner than did its Dutch counterpart (for example, privatization of state utilities, compulsory competitive tendering, performance league-tabling in local government, education and the police, performance-related pay for all kinds of public servants, the creation of closely measured autonomous executive agencies, and so on – see also Chapter 4).

Fourth explanation: differences in the organization and financing of health care

This fourth explanation is similar to the third explanation, in that it focuses on structural and contextual factors rather than the individual motives and strategies which are central to the rational choice perspective. However, it is pitched at a lower level – sectoral rather than national. In essence, the argument is that the acute health care sector has certain structural characteristics which make it more (UK) or less (Netherlands) amenable to a national system of performance indicators. These characteristics may be summarized as in Table 9.2.

The sources of finance for health care are very different in the two countries, as Table 9.3 illustrates. It might be argued that the greater diversity of finance in the Netherlands, including the more substantial component of private insurance, is reflected in a greater need for consensus about reforms. The Treasury/Ministry of Finance is not calling the shots to anything like the

Table 9.2: Anglo-Dutch differences in the organization and finance of the hospital system

	UK NHS	*The Netherlands*
Organizational structure	Single, centralized system reporting to the Department of Health	Pluralistic system with different social groups supporting different subsystems
Source of finance	Predominantly financed from central non-hypothecated taxation	Predominantly financed from hypothecated insurance payments (many different companies and systems, with a 'floor' scheme subsidized by central government)
Ownership	Mainly public, small but growing for-profit sector	Mixed public/non-profit, plus a small for-profit sector

Table 9.3: Sources of funding as a percentage of total health care expenditure, 1998

	Government funding	*Social security funds*	*Private out-of-pocket*	*Private insurance*	*Other*
NL	4.1%	64.5%	8.0%	17.5%	5.9%
UK	73.5%	9.8%	11.1%	3.5%	2.1%

Source: OECD data: adapted from Blank and Burau, 2004: 63.

same extent as in the UK. In the Netherlands there is compulsory state health insurance for all employees whose income falls below a certain threshold. The government sets contribution rates. Additionally about one-third of employees have to take out additional private insurance to cover acute health risks (Blank and Burau, 2004: 66–7). This does not mean that the government is not involved in these aspects at all. It does play an active role in setting prices (though this is beginning to change with the latest attempt at managed competition) and in regulating private schemes, including legislating for standard packages and risk pooling for certain high risk groups.

There are also some interesting differences in trends between the two countries. Over the thirty-year period we are considering the share of public funding in the total health spend rose (with fluctuations) in the Netherlands, but declined in the UK (see Table 9.4). However, the effect of this was to bring the absolute levels of public funding closer together, since the UK started with a very high share and the Netherlands with a much lower one.

Of course there are other characteristics which the two systems *share*. In both countries individual hospitals are extremely complex organizations, providing a wide range of services (many of them non-standardized) and employing a remarkable variety of occupational groups, including some of the most highly skilled professionals. These shared characteristics make it very hard to devise a few key performance indicators which will adequately and accurately sum up the quality of care or, indeed, the overall efficiency of the hospital in question. So finding a useful set of indicators that will command confidence from all the major stakeholders is a major challenge – in both countries.

The Netherlands and the UK also have in common some broader features of the health care system. They both spend a lot on the elderly – respectively 41.2 per cent and 43.0 per cent of total public health spending in 2000 (Blank and Burau, 2004: 7). Both have rising numbers of this 'expensive' elderly group, with the Netherlands rising from 11.5 per cent of the population in 1980 to 13.6 per cent in 2000, and the parallel UK figures being 15.0 per cent and 15.7 per cent (Blank and Burau, 2004: 3). Both are

Table 9.4: Public funding as a share of total health care expenditure

	1970	1980	1990	1998
NL	61.0%	69.2%	67.7%	68.6%
UK	87.0%	89.4%	84.3%	83.3%

Note: The 68.6 per cent of public funding shown for NL in 1998 comprises 4.1 per cent direct government funding plus 64.5 per cent social security funds – see Table 9.3 above.

Source: OECD data: adapted from Blank and Burau, 2004: 26.

exposed to very similar pressures as a result of the relentless (and expensive) advance of medical technology, which constantly widens the range of available diagnostic approaches and treatments and may help raise patient expectations.

Combining explanations?

Combining different theoretical approaches is a common and sometimes fruitful academic strategy (for example, Pierson, 2004; Pollitt, 2001). However, we do not wish to adopt the naive position of concluding that if all the relevant theories are put together a single, rounded explanation will result. To say that different theories afford different perspectives on reality is one thing. To say that they can all be put together is another. The position taken here is that theories can only be combined (used together) if their underlying epistemologies are reasonably compatible.

Thus it is argued that our third and fourth theories can be readily combined, but our second and third and our second and fourth are much more problematic bedfellows. Both the third (cultural and political system differences) and the fourth (organizing and financing) are theories which emphasize the importance of systems and institutions as constraining and enabling structures which tend to 'point change in a certain direction', and make other kinds of change extremely difficult to achieve. They both allow individual actors room for manoeuvre and credit them with a variety of possible motives, but they also stress how individuals have to 'work with the grain', if they are to maximize the probability of their reform ideas becoming accepted. The fourth theory 'nests' quite comfortably within the third, because the specific characteristics of the sector are themselves influenced by the broader characteristics of the system. Thus one might say that the specific NHS characteristic of centralized finance and government control is in part a sectoral reflection of the more broadly central executive-dominated nature of the British political system. Similarly, the somewhat corporatist or 'pillarized' pattern of the Dutch health care sector, and its behavioural norm of consensualism are both echoes of the wider Dutch political system as a whole.

The second theory (rational choice) is very different from the third and fourth. Not only does it lay most of its stress on individual actors and their strategies (rather than on institutions), but it also offers an extremely simple (supporters will say 'elegantly simple') model of how these individuals behave. This particular set of epistemological assumptions is too far from those of theories three and four to be easily integrated with them. However, a crucial step for rational choice theorists is to accept (or not) that different institutional arrangements create substantively different patterns not just of incentives and penalties, but also of rules for the game. Those rational choice theorists who *do* accept this produce work which is much more compatible with structural arguments such as those used in the third and fourth explanations. Those who do *not* remain limited in their ability to explain national differences, because of the essentially decontextualized and a-historical nature of their tool kits.

Discussion and conclusions

Although this chapter began with an emphasis on the very different trajectories followed in developing hospital PIs in the Netherlands and the UK we should note that this is by no means *only* a story of difference. For we must also explain why, twenty years after the UK, the Netherlands has decided to 'buy in' to this particular concept.

Nor must we *assume* that the big differences we have noted between the two national systems will remain in perpetuity. Just as the shares of public spending within total health care spending seem to be converging, just as the UK seems to moving towards a larger private sector presence in the acute field (more resembling the 'mixed' Dutch system), so the Dutch indicators could begin to be used more as they are in the NHS. The corporate entities that created the Dutch system may not be able to continue to control it. Media and public pressure may lead to the production of league tables and to more uniform and competitive arrangements for publicizing hospital PIs – there are already some signs of this. That would be one version of the positive feedback/path-dependent trajectory suggested under our second theoretical approach. It is virtually impossible to go back, so one goes on, and going on draws in new players and new uses for the performance data, and leads to continuing modifications of the PI set. So this will be a point worth watching.

Similarly, the centralized approach hitherto practised in the UK may begin to dilute as the private sector presence becomes more important there. One could conceptualize this as an increase in the number of veto points in the UK system, so that it more closely resembles the Dutch arrangements. Central government, by degrees, would lose its power to dictate the rules of the game. It would no longer be possible to apply a top-down, uniform system to a growing variety of organized private for-profit and non-profit interests.

The above are speculations about the future. We should be on firmer ground explaining the recent past. Here a combination of theories three and four appears to perform rather better than theory two (rational choice). Theory two does reasonably well in explaining the adoption of PIs at a particular point in time, as a rational response by powerful actors to external pressures on the system (cost pressures and legitimacy issues). But it is not particularly convincing in explaining the very different timings and trajectories in the two countries. The Dutch government also faced a fiscal crisis in the early 1980s, but they did not – one is tempted to say *could* not – go down the same road of central controls of hospitals as was adopted in the UK. And when Dutch PIs did appear, they were 'produced' by a different set of actors than had been the case in the UK.

These differences are rather more convincingly explained by the more 'structural' theories three and four. Or, at least, they are better explained in general terms. When we want to look in more detail, however, the combination of three and four seems to have its own problems. To begin with, there is a problem of the level of explanation. Which is more important in this case – the characteristics of the overall political system or the particular features of the acute health care sector? Both seem to contribute, but in what proportions? For example, is the multi-party, 'post pillarized', 'polder model' nature of the Dutch political system more important in explaining the gradualist Dutch approach to PIs, or should we look to the particular relationships between the hospital associations, the insurers and the representative organs of the medical profession?

Another point for discussion is that both theories three and four bundle together 'harder' structural influences (like the electoral system or the role of the Dutch medical specialists association) and 'softer', cultural factors (such as the famous Dutch predisposition to consensually negotiated problem-solving). A closer analysis might try to separate out structural and cultural elements and weigh them separately. One test would be a situation in which radical structural change was introduced, so that the number of veto points increased or decreased. Structuralists would then predict that policies in that country would change, and probably change quite quickly. Culturalists might argue that, since cultural norms are the strong frame within which policy agreements are arrived at, change would still be incremental and slow, because just changing institutional structures does not yet change norms of appropriateness. Unfortunately, it is hard to think of a sufficiently big structural change of this kind in either the Netherlands or the UK during the period under study, so this test must await future developments. What would be required would be, for example, a change in the electoral system, or in the basic pattern of corporate interests in the health care sector.

In conclusion, then, we can say that there are several ways of explaining the similarities and differences in the evolution of hospital PIs in England and the Netherlands. Simple-minded assertions that the two countries are either completely different or following identical tracks will not hold water. Rational choice theories appear to have the potential to offer actor-centred accounts of why PIs are adopted at a particular moment in time, and perhaps also why, once adopted, they are very hard to get rid of. On balance, however, the structuralist theories do a better job of explaining the trajectories of development over the past quarter century or so. They posit broadly similar external pressures being mediated in contrasting ways by fundamentally different national and sectoral institutions of health care governance. However, they are also less precise than rational choice theories about which mechanisms are involved, and at what level of analysis. To sum up, Dutch and English neighbours have gone different ways, mainly because they live in houses with very different internal layouts.

Note

1. I am very grateful for detailed comments on earlier drafts of this chapter which I received from Wendy van der Kraan and Roland Bal, both of the Instituut Beleid en Management Gezondheidszorg, Erasmus Medical Centre, and from Steve Harrison of the Department of Government, University of Manchester. I trust it is obvious that they share no responsibility whatsoever for my interpretations.

10

New Public Management and Evaluation

Frans-Bauke van der Meer

Introduction

In the last four decades governments and governmental bodies in Western countries have come under increasing pressure, both societal and financial in nature. The quest for efficiency, efficacy, responsiveness, flexibility and accountability of government is a dominant one. As outlined in the introductory chapter, this has given rise to numerous innovations both in public organization and in policy-making and implementation. These innovations aimed at improving government in some respects in order to accommodate 'external' and 'internal' pressures.

Not all these innovations are considered successful. Some are replaced by others within a few years' time, in which case a change of direction (for example, on a centralization–decentralization dimension) is not uncommon (Pollitt and Bouckaert, 2001: 149–52). In other cases innovations are supplemented with other ones, for example autonomization followed by a growing intensity of central control (Bekkers 1998; Van Thiel and Pollitt, Chapter 4). On the other hand there are successes, at least in the eyes of some actors involved (see Pollitt in Chapter 2 and Kickert in Chapter 3). Such 'best practices', however, may be copied elsewhere with mixed results (for example, Hakvoort and Klaassen, Chapter 7). Moreover, authorities and agencies are frequently criticized (for example, in cases of a disaster) for procedures and practices they have long taken for granted. It may be concluded that, although many procedures and innovations are considered 'necessary' and 'unavoidable', not enough is known about their working and impact (cf. Teisman and Van Buuren in Chapter 11).

In this chapter I will discuss what evaluation does and what it can contribute to insight into the dynamics and effects of (new) public management reforms. To do so, I pose three key questions:

(1) How is evaluation actually applied in relation to NPM reforms?
(2) How are evaluation results used and how can their impact be understood?
(3) How can evaluations in and of NPM reforms be improved?

The theoretical framework that I will present to help answer the second question will also be used to explain the state of affairs in relation to the first question. Moreover, it will be used in combination with empirical observations to support the conclusions with respect to question 3.

Before going into the three questions in turn I present some observations on the broader context of reforms in the public domain. In my view this is relevant for the present subject, because evaluation of specific measures or of specific (classes of) reforms should take into account relevant boundary conditions and goals or requirements that are not explicitly included in the focal measures.

Challenges for public management

NPM-type reforms in the public domain are quite widespread (Kickert, 1997; Pollitt and Bouckaert, 2001). Although the label NPM refers to a rather heterogeneous set of innovations and practices (see Chapter 1), it can be said to comprise the utilization of private sector management techniques and organizational forms in the public sector. NPM innovations seek to improve efficiency and quality of public administration and service delivery by decentral autonomy and output control, frequently regulated by management contracts. The underlying rationale seems to be that an incentive structure that rewards efficient production and measurable output enhances motivation and creativity of individuals and groups and can replace much efficiency reducing hierarchical control. Moreover, the decentralized nature of the new arrangements is thought to enhance flexibility, responsiveness and tailor-made solutions: a demand orientation, which is presupposed to be the main guide of private sector management. Taken together NPM reforms are expected to trigger a better use of public sector resources.

NPM reforms are by no means the only type of reforms with which public and semi-public agencies are occupied. Nor is the underlying rationale of NPM the only rationale about improvement in the public domain. A second type of innovation focuses not so much on government or public sector production per se, but on joint production of policies, public works and services with private sector enterprises and/or societal organizations (Teisman and Verheij, 1996; Tops and Weterings, 1998). The aims are in a sense similar to those of NPM innovations, viz. improving efficiency and quality of public production. But here (semi-) public agencies are not the sole producers. Here too, there is a parallel with private sector strategies, where organizations initiate joint enterprises to realize projects, develop new technology or penetrate new markets. The main rationale, however, is quite different from the NPM type. The problem is not that the public sector uses its resources in a suboptimal way, but that government lacks key knowledge, financial and other resources to realize many projects and solutions to societal problems. Government is only one among many actors in a societal network of interdependencies. Only by co-operation can effective results be hoped for.

A third set of new strategies in public management seeks to involve citizens and societal organizations having an interest in certain policy issues or domains. This participation (Edelenbos, 2000) may include the phase of problem definition, generation of possible solutions, a role of citizens and societal organizations in policy implementation and evaluation, and a shift in responsibility towards the citizens or private initiative. By definition, there is some overlap with the second type of public management innovations since hereto, non-governmental actors are involved in the production of policy and policy outcomes. However, there are other rationales for such participative strategies. One of them starts from the notion that societal problems often cannot be identified in an objective and unambiguous way. The public task, then, is not so much to solve 'the' problem, but to search for ways to accommodate different problem definitions at the same time (Teisman and Verheij, 1996). By involving individuals and groups having an interest in at least some of these definitions, the searching process is part of its solution. In and by interaction with other actors (among them governmental ones) actors may change or broaden their problem definitions and/or come to conceive of new solutions. Thus, eventual outcomes may in part be created by and gain the support of stakeholders. The role of government is mainly a facilitating one in producing solutions and support (De Bruijn et al., 1998).

Now, it is important to notice that these different rationales and steering practices, as well as classical hierarchical approaches, are applied simultaneously, often by the same actors, sometimes within a single policy initiative.[1] Thus, it is not only worthwhile to ask how successful individual public management innovations are and how valid their rationales are, but it is also interesting to see how different types of reforms influence each other and how their rationales interact in practice, for these interactions influence behaviours and outcomes. Therefore, evaluation should take account of them.

Evaluation as an instrument in NPM practices

In the framework of NPM-like innovations evaluations play an important role. Assessment of performance or output and comparing it to initial targets or contractual commitments is central to the philosophy of this type of approach. Moreover, the felt need for public accountability of (autonomized) agencies has given rise to numerous review procedures and control mechanisms, which also involve the collection and judgment of data on performance and results (see, for example, Sanderson, 2001, who describes local practices in the UK). Such practices contribute to an 'evaluative state' (Sanderson, 2001: 303) or 'audit explosion' (Power, 1994) in which performance measurement and accountability constitute the dominant perspective (see, for example, Chapter 4).

Although there are differences between countries with respect to the quantity and specific characteristics of performance evaluations (for example, Christensen et al., 2003), there is a clear tendency, at least in the Anglo-Saxon and Northern European world towards more and more quantitative performance assessments. This holds both for 'internal' management reports and external audits (Pollitt et al., 1999; Wollmann, 2003).

With respect to the utilization and impact of these evaluations four observations can be made. First, they influence and direct actual behaviour. Since performance indicators generally are known before the actual performance takes place, they can and will guide this performance (Van Thiel and Leeuw, 2002). If the performance of academic work is assessed by counting the number of publications in international refereed journals, the number of such publications and the time devoted to producing them will rise. In a sense, the impact precedes the actual evaluation. But there are also ex post impacts as, for example, the allocation of new budgets is based on evaluation results: consecutive action is constrained or enhanced or redirected by such reallocations.

Second, this type of evaluation may give rise to unintended or perverse effects. This is a consequence of the fact that performance indicators used generally are only partial operationalizations or proxies of the goals aimed at. This phenomenon is known as the performance paradox (Meyer and Gupta, 1994; Van Thiel and Leeuw, 2002).

 Third, frequently, especially in the relation between 'principal' and 'agent' the amount and the specificity of data produced by agents are so large that their impact is greatly reduced by the overload or ambiguity it creates for the principal (Hazeu, 2000). The steering capacity of the principal may actually be reduced by the massive introduction of performance data.

Finally, the fact that evaluations in this context focus on accountability may produce 'defensive' reactions by evaluated units in the sense of denying the validity of evaluation outcomes or seeking excuses beyond control (Sanderson, 2001; Teisman and Van der Meer, 2002). Such reactions reduce the opportunities for learning since the question of possible improvements is evaded.

Evaluation of NPM reforms

In view of the impressive amount of evaluations produced in relation to NPM-like management, it is remarkable that NPM reforms as such, including the evaluation procedures involved, are evaluated far less systematically (Pollitt, 1995; Pollitt and Bouckaert, 2003; Forbes and Lynn, 2005). Broadbent and Laughlin (1997) observe much resistance in UK government towards such evaluations, for budgetary and other reasons. Still, in the meantime there have appeared a number of studies. The edited volume by Wollmann (2003) gives an impression, although it is not always clear whether its reviews pertain to evaluation as an instrument within NPM or to an evaluation of the reforms as such. In part this can be excused for it should be noted that there is no sharp demarcation between these two categories of evaluation.

There appears to be a grey zone in between in which NPM reforms are evaluated within the logic of NPM itself. For example, the success of a reform may be measured by the extent to which performance data are produced, and not so much by a related increase in efficiency or responsiveness. In part this may be due to methodical problems such as a poor measurability, or lacking ex ante data. But even apart from that, there often seems to be a remarkable inclination, especially in audit institutions, to focus on administrative control and documentation instead of on eventual results.

A study by Boyne et al. (2003) is interesting, not only because it tries to assess intended outcomes of public management innovations in the British education, health care and housing sectors, but also because it devotes attention to unintended effects with respect to equity. Interestingly, this last variable appears to be the only one with an unequivocal, and negative, result. Broad and open evaluations like this one seem to be the exception rather than the rule.

Dynamics of evaluation

After this rough sketch of practices of NPM evaluation, I now venture into a theoretical reflection about why evaluation practices are shaped in the way they are, when, why and how their results are used and how their impacts are generated. Next, I will use this theoretical framework to contribute to an understanding of the dynamics of evaluation in and of NPM (see boxes) and to develop ideas for its improvement (see following sections).

I propose to view evaluation in terms of sense-making processes (Weick, 1979, 1995). The simple and somewhat naive argument to justify this approach is that evaluation aims at sense-making. It is about assessing what is or has been going on, how this has come about, how the findings have to be valued and about how we might think of possible improvements. But, although the previous sentence may reflect the ambition of evaluators and/or their principals, we should realize that it may not be shared by all actors involved in the evaluation process. Some may see it as an irrelevant time and money consuming bureaucratic practice or as a threat to their autonomy or professional discretion. Some may loyally contribute data, but not hope or intend to learn something from it. However, these other actors are still engaged in sense-making. They attach meaning to the evaluation process and its outcomes. For our present purpose this is not interesting in itself. The key argument for viewing the dynamics of evaluation in terms of sense-making processes is the thesis that the interplay of the different sense-making processes in the actions and interactions of actors determine the shape, the outcome and the impact of evaluations. I will elaborate this thesis in a number of steps below.

First, in the stage of initiating an evaluation a large number of choices are made by commissioners and evaluators. Amongst these are substantive choices, such as: What exactly is to be evaluated? Which criteria are to be used? Which types of data are required? There are also methodological choices: How are data to be collected? How are they to be interpreted and related to each other? Finally, there are organizational or administrative choices: Who is to perform the evaluation? Who is to be involved in what roles? Who should take cognizance of the results and act upon them?

How are such choices, which constitute the 'script' for the evaluation, made? Presumably they are the result of interactions (consultation, negotiation) between the actors involved in this stage. This interaction takes place in the context of already existing frames of meaning and patterns of practice. I call such patterns of thinking and acting *repertoires* (Van der Meer, 1999; Van der Meer et al., 2000). To the extent to which there is consensus among the actors involved, the definition of the evaluation will reflect the common repertoire. Where there is dissensus, negotiation, compromise and use of 'power' will come about, often resulting in vague or ambiguous formulations. But even then, the resulting design reflects sense-making form repertoires. Agreement is reached by means of (implicit) answers that actors give to questions like: What is acceptable? What are driving forces? What opportunities are left for influence or manipulation in a later stage? Thus, sense-making in interaction gives shape to the evaluation.

Commissioners of NPM related evaluations, who frequently are co-initiators or sponsors of the reform, and the evaluators they hire generally will have a strong belief in the rationale behind NPM reforms. Therefore, in thinking about evaluation they will, for example, tend to start with the idea that a result-oriented structure will evoke maximal motivation and productivity (both quantitative and qualitative). Thus, in their view evaluation should assess results and measure these in terms of success or accordance with preset goals. The agent should then be rewarded accordingly. Within the NPM rationale this argument with respect to evaluation seems to be self-evident. From this perspective there is little reason to doubt the rationale itself, which may explain why NPM reforms are seldom explicitly evaluated. And when they are, evaluations tend to focus on the extent to which organizations involved bring NPM procedures and provisions into practice and far less on what the eventual impacts of the reforms are.

Second, in carrying out an evaluation, again sense-making and interaction take place. In this stage typically other actors become involved. Often commissioners will be involved less, but others, such as managers and other personnel of evaluated units, clients, citizens, partners, and so on, are interviewed, are requested or required to produce data, or are even asked for their own opinions and assessments as in participative or responsive evaluation (Abma, 1996; Taket and White, 1997; Ryan and DeStefano, 2001). Obviously, these new actors have to make sense of what is asked of them, even if they take the evaluation for granted and adopt an a priori positive attitude. They do so by utilizing their own repertoire, which may differ considerably from the repertoire of the initiators of the evaluation. Moreover, the new actors will also make sense of the evaluation as such: What are its aims? How valid will the results be? What consequences may the results have? This sense-making will of course influence their responses. This may be called 'strategic' behaviour, as long as it is not synonymous with disloyalty. It is clear from this argument that the evaluation is considerably influenced by sense-making processes in this stage. It might even be said that the evaluation often is redefined during its course.[2]

> Professional employees in a unit involved in some sort of contract may make – from their professional perspective – a rather sharp distinction between the quantified output criteria mentioned in the contract and 'real' quality, which is hard to measure. If so, they may consider it fully legitimate to score on the output criteria as quickly and artificially as possible in order to save time for the real thing or to induce an 'accurate' evaluation, although the indicators are invalid from a professional point of view (Green, 1999).
>
> Also, managers of agencies will have their own impressions and make their own assessments of the functioning of their organization and its efficacy. These images may not fully correspond to the picture that emerges from the data to be included in the evaluation, for example, because the evaluation data do not reflect relevant changes in external conditions as they are experienced and interpreted by the manager. This may trigger the manager to provide additional data, to present data in other ways, or to supply extensive comments to the data. However, he may also refrain from such actions if he fears that these will be interpreted as defensive window dressing by the principal.

A third step in my theoretical argument is about the impact of evaluations (cf. Van der Meer, 1999). Here again the notion of sense-making plays a key role. The influence of evaluations and evaluation results on actual behaviour (talking, rewarding, changing, acting) is determined by how they are interpreted and valued by actors involved. Besides that, the influence of evaluation on actual administrative and organizational behaviour depends on the way its outcomes become embedded in the web of other factors influencing this behaviour (Weiss, 1990). It is important to note that in this stage generally there are far more actors involved than those who commissioned the evaluation. Although the latter may sometimes have the power to make decisions with respect to tasks, personnel, budgets, rewards, or organizational structures and procedures, they are by no means the only actors whose sense-making matters. I have already pointed out the possibility that evaluation evokes perverse effects or defensive reactions if that seems to be useful or self-evident from the perspective of evaluated actors.[3] Moreover, evaluated actors may try to 'improve' their actions in anticipation of or reaction to evaluation. The way in which they proceed in this connection will again depend on how they interpret both their own behaviour and the evaluation and its outcomes. Finally, also the commissioners of the evaluation or those with formal power to make decisions on its consequences have to make sense of the evaluation results – explicitly or implicitly – before they can act upon it.

In NPM contexts evaluations frequently focus on performance measurement and comparing quantified results with ex ante targets so as to enable accountability. Thus, evaluations may lead to reallocation of budgets or revision of contracts. These attributes may well have quite different meanings for the actors involved.[4]

A typical principal might feel the evaluation gives him control and enables him to bear an overall responsibility without the necessity of going into implementations details. He may, furthermore, feel secure even if he does not fully understand the details of the evaluation; because he holds a strong belief in the rationales behind NPM. The general picture of success or failure suffices (cf. the fact that surveillance is often delegated to independent overseeing bodies). Sense-making and consecutive action seem straightforward, although additional information supplied (see previous box) may cause some equivocality. But if 84.7 per cent of Dutch passenger trains are 'on time', while the contract requires 86.5 per cent, that is a failure.

For a manager of an implementing agency the evaluation results may be far more ambiguous. He may have doubts about the validity of the results, he has to think of explanations and he needs to invent internal measures and external strategies to deal with the situation shown or induced by the evaluation. In this sense-making and strategy development process there is far more at stake than the straightforward comparison of targets and realization. It determines to a large extent how the organization will 'learn' from the evaluation, but it also determines the negotiation strategy with the principal, which may eventually influence the decisions the latter will take.

Professional employees are often in a position in which they do not need to react directly to evaluation outcomes. However, they are confronted with possible management measures. Their assessment of the validity and relevance of the evaluation and of the sensibility and force of the management measures will influence their behaviour. They may feel forced to 'conform', although perhaps in 'perverse' ways, or they may feel their professional status and factual autonomy is large enough to virtually negate the evaluation results and/or the management measures. Also, if their 'results' are successful, this may enhance their immunity from critique in later episodes.

A following theoretical idea connecting the dynamics of evaluation processes to sense-making and interaction is that third actors play a role.

Evaluation is not a sense-making process that takes place in isolation between principal and agent or between evaluator and evaluated, but in a context full of other actors, such as competitors, clients, citizens, interest groups, parliament, press, and so on. Such actors may formally or informally influence the focus or criteria used in evaluations. They may also react to evaluations (or their various follow-ups). If these third actors (are considered to) have power or are thought of as 'important' by the focal actors, their reactions may contribute to an indirect influence evaluations may have on these focal actors. Moreover, third actors may adapt their own behaviour on the basis of their interpretation of evaluation outcomes.

> Suppose, some targets are set for the personal safety policy in a certain neighbourhood and an evaluation report shows that safety has increased, while at the same time many inhabitants of the neighbourhood feel less secure than they did a year ago. They may protest and seek media coverage for their problems. Or they may realize that they can influence (that is more realistic from their point of view) performance indicators, for example, by reporting incidents more frequently to the police. The first reaction may, for example, trigger a decision to include subjective experience of inhabitants in next year's performance review (as is actually done in the Rotterdam safety monitor). The second reaction may lead to a lower score in the following year, which may trigger measures that are not actually warranted by worse performance (cf. Van Thiel and Leeuw, 2002, for similar examples).

Many, if not most policy processes are multi-actor in nature, because the policy is formulated or negotiated in interaction and co-operation between different administrative bodies and layers, and often also with private and societal organizations. The same holds for many 'implementation' processes. In these cases, what has been said about third actors above applies in a specific way. Like citizens, clients and media, co-producers can influence evaluation and will react to their outcomes (or not) and thus co-determine the set-up, conclusions and impact of evaluations. More specifically, in cases of co-production it is not a single actor who defines and commissions evaluations. Different actors may do so at the same time, thus producing concurring evaluations with potentially contradictory results, which will not necessarily contribute to substantive improvements or better co-operation. An interesting aspect in this connection is the question of who initiates an evaluation, along which lines and especially who is evaluated? Even apart from the substantive conclusion of an evaluation these elements may strongly influence sense-making processes of the different actors and hence their reactions.

> Dutch spatial developments actually are a co-production of different governmental bodies, private enterprises, environmental and other interest groups and citizens. If the central government or the Spatial Planning Bureau commissions an evaluation to assess to what extent the general goals formulated in the Spatial Policy Bill are realized, municipalities may experience this as an effort to increase central control, especially if they are not given the opportunity to insert their goals, limitations and assessments in the evaluation process (see Van der Meer and Edelenbos, 2006, for a detailed analysis and some options for dealing with these complications).

This theoretical argument gives rise to the presupposition that the design, the outcome and the impact of evaluation are products of complex interaction processes, in which sense-making from a diversity of perspectives takes place. Then, insight in the relevant repertoires and knowledge of the interaction patterns between relevant actors helps to understand the dynamics around evaluations and their impacts. Based on such understanding, ideas for more effective evaluations and evaluation arrangements may be developed.

How to evaluate public management reforms?

Above, I hypothesized that the relative lack of comprehensive evaluations of NPM reforms is due to the self-evidence that their rationales have for their promoters. Of course, from an 'external' perspective, such as developed in this chapter, evaluation of NPM reforms as such is very desirable. In this section I develop some ideas on what such evaluations might look like. The following section is devoted to the question how evaluations of NPM innovations – and also evaluations within the framework of NPM practices – can be done in a way that enhances utilization of evaluation results and their impact. For both themes I use the theoretical argument developed before.

In the preceding discussion of the dynamics of evaluation I advanced the thesis that actual developments on the behavioural level (design of the evaluation, steps in the evaluation process, and (re)actions in relation to its outcomes) are mediated by sense-making among actors involved in the consecutive phases. These sense-making processes are connected to actor repertoires and their interaction patterns, hence they will be situation or position or sector specific.

This argument is not only relevant for evaluations of management reforms but may also be applied to the dynamics of the reforms themselves (cf. Teisman and Van Buuren, Chapter 11). This is relevant in the present context, since it has consequences for the way in which evaluations of public management reforms can and should be undertaken. The argument runs as follows.

NPM reforms are designed on the basis of specific rationales (which could be denoted as repertoires). Their actual shape and their impact on actual behaviour, however, depends to a large extent on the sense other actors make of the reforms. This would imply that the meaning of such innovations may differ between actors and that their impact and 'success' is context dependent. To phrase it differently: the effects of an innovation do not only depend on characteristics of that innovation, but also – and primarily! – on the meaning it acquires from actors' perspectives and on the interplay of interpretation-related actor behaviours. Thus, a typical evaluation question should not be whether new arrangement X is 'good', or 'better' than arrangement Y, but how arrangement X works in a specific context[5] and why (see also Pollitt et al., 2004). Evaluations should indeed search for explanations of the functioning and effects of public management innovations since this may provide new input in sense-making and learning processes, contributing to ideas for improvement. Moreover, the analytical argument can potentially be generalized to other settings, which is generally not the case for substantive findings. When a successful example of contract management is found (irrespective of the criteria that are used to arrive at that judgement), a key question should be what conditions and mechanisms produced that result. Insights like these are necessary to be able to link evaluation results to other settings.

The theoretical approach advanced in this chapter also implies that knowledge of the perspectives (repertoires) of actors involved (in whatever role) as well as of their interactions is necessary for explanations to be found. Therefore, interviews with actors in different roles and positions – or other forms of their participation in the evaluation process – are required to reconstruct their repertoires and be able to explain their (re) actions and thereby the functioning and eventual effects of the management structure or strategy under review. It should be noted that this thesis is not based on a normative choice for democracy or empowerment (however honourable such a choice would be), but on an analytical argument on the dynamics of evaluation and public management innovations.

It should also be noted that involvement of stakeholders in the evaluation process may influence and enhance the impact of the evaluation since participants are more aware of the fact that there is an evaluation. Therefore, they may be more inclined to acquire knowledge on its content and conclusions, to recognize more elements, and to feel more committed to act upon the evaluation outcomes. In fact, resulting changes in actor sense-making and behaviour may also influence the functioning and effects of the public management innovation(s) under scrutiny. The direction of these changes depends on how evaluation results and other experiences in the evaluation process are linked by actors to their existing ideas and practices (Van der Meer, 1999). That is why the idea that participation produces support seems to be too simplistic, both with respect to the evaluation process and with respect to the public management innovation evaluated. It is quite conceivable that a negative attitude towards a public management innovation is reinforced or induced in the process for some actors. And even if actors' attitudes change in a positive direction the question remains exactly what it is that they support: their (changed) image of what the innovation is about is decisive.

Thus, although I have argued that some form of interaction with stakeholders in the evaluation is required for sensible evaluation of public management innovations, it should be realized that in doing so the object of investigation might change. Or, to put if differently, the evaluation process becomes an integral part of the functioning of the innovation.

Towards effective evaluation

The ideas on the dynamics of evaluation outlined above also provide clues to improve the efficacy of evaluations, both of and in NPM innovations. The first question here is: how can we define and assess the effectiveness of evaluations? A number of levels of impact come to mind (cf. Hupe and Van der Meer, 2002: 14):

(1) Actors evaluated and other stakeholders take note of the evaluation.
(2) Actors use evaluation results in considering changes in policy, management, working processes, and so on.
(3) Actors support the conclusions of an evaluation.
(4) Actual changes in policy (implementation) or management as suggested by the evaluation.

However, on reflection this scheme is problematic.

First, although level (1) seems to be valid on the level of the network as a whole – it is a necessary condition for any impact to materialize – it is not so at the level of individual actors. Through chains of interactions in the network the behaviour of some actors may change, partly as a consequence of the evaluation, without these actors having any knowledge of the evaluation (indirect impact).

Second, level (4) may come about as a consequence of other processes than the evaluation. In fact it is generally very difficult to attribute actual changes to a single cause or even to estimate the contribution of a given cause.

Finally, levels (3) and (4) are not necessarily higher or better than level (2). Criteria, conclusions and recommendations given in an evaluation reflect, as I suggested above, in part a specific perspective or repertoire. Thus, evaluation results or other experiences in the evaluation process may acquire other meanings for other actors, making sense utilizing their own repertoire. Although the evaluators may judge this negatively, from any other stance it may be considered a potential contribution to new ideas, new innovations and hence learning.

Therefore, my thesis is that the only *general* criterion for effectiveness of evaluation is the extent to which it contributes to learning processes in the network of relevant actors/stakeholders. The extent to which this is the case can be related to the number or the diversity of actors learning (or reporting to learn) something from the evaluation, or to the measure to which new concepts or 'facts' from the evaluation are used in consecutive discourse. 'Learning' might also be measured by the extent to which actors attribute actual changes – or decisions not to change – to the evaluation or to concepts and 'facts' produced by the evaluation. Finally, learning can be measured by the extent to which evaluations trigger interaction and debate in the network.

One could point to the fact that many evaluations, especially in the context of NPM, do not primarily aim at learning, but rather at control and accountability (see Sanderson, 2001; Teisman and Van der Meer, 2002). However true that may be, my argument would be that the efficacy of accountability oriented evaluation depends on the extent to which and the way in which it is included in sense-making processes of and among actors involved. If no actor reads something new in the evaluation, if its results are no object of debate and if no decisions (not) to change behaviour can be related to the evaluation, the evaluation has not been effective.

Thus, the key question becomes how learning from evaluation can be enhanced (cf. Thoenig, 2003).

The theoretical argument in this chapter suggests that at least some actors should both recognize the evaluation (outcomes) as sensible from their existing repertoire and as new. If the first condition is not met, the evaluation is simply noise to them; if the second is not met, there is nothing to be learned (except the fact that there is nothing to be learned, which consolidates existing repertoires and may decrease opportunities for future learning). The 'connectivity' of evaluations – the extent to which they are connectable to existing repertoires of different actors, thus inserting new elements in these – depends on both their contents and the interaction processes in which they are embedded. Actors commissioning or performing evaluations can enhance connectivity by gaining knowledge of actor repertoires, related preoccupations, dominant questions and so on, to which the evaluation design can be adapted. Alternatively they can involve second and third actors in the process of designing the evaluation.

It should be realized that the preconditions for connectivity and learning are generally different for different actors, since their repertoires and positions in interaction patterns differ. By consequence, it will not be possible to design evaluations that maximize learning for all actors at the same time. Actors have different interests and questions. Especially in the case of co-productive or participative policy processes, actors should be allowed, enabled and stimulated to perform or commission their own evaluations, thus feeding their own learning processes. This may also reduce perverse behaviour or defensive reactions (however these may be defined).

But it should also be realized that policy and management results eventually are produced in the interplay between all actors. If evaluation is to stimulate and improve their co-operation, it should also help their mutual debate and collective learning processes (Gray and Jenkins, 2003). Efforts should, therefore, be undertaken to enable linking of and confrontation between different evaluations, done by different actors at different levels, and to supplement them with joint (multi-actor) evaluations (Teisman et al., 2002; Van der Meer and Edelenbos, 2006). In the latter case collective learning and mutual co-operation can already take place in the design phase of the evaluation.

Conclusions

In this chapter I dealt with some issues concerning evaluation of and in NPM innovations. Evaluations in support of accountability constitute a core element of NPM philosophy and arrangements. Still they may have unintended and even perverse effects. It was also observed that NPM arrangements as such are far less systematically evaluated. To explain this state of affairs and to develop directions of improvement, I proposed a theoretical framework in which 'sense-making', 'interaction' and 'repertoires' are the core concepts. By conceiving of evaluation as a sense-making process in interaction between actors in a network, both the design and the impact of evaluations can be explained (as well as the lack of evaluation or the lack of impact). Moreover, the argument gave rise to some ideas about shaping evaluations of public management innovations as such. These can be summarized as follows:

- The success and impact of public management innovations are not only determined by characteristics of the innovation; evaluations should therefore be contextualized.
- Evaluations of public management innovations should include (context dependent) explanations for their functioning and effects, both for context related learning and for generalization to other contexts.
- These explanations require knowledge of actor repertoires, which implies some sort of participation of key actors and stakeholders in the evaluation process.
- Evaluation of NPM innovations influences the functioning and impact of these innovations, that is, evaluation becomes part of the innovation.

Finally I derived some conclusions with respect to enhancing efficacy of evaluations (both of and in public management innovations):

- Learning is the only general criterion for evaluation effectiveness.
- Connectivity of evaluations in relation to actor repertoires determines their learning potential. Thus enhancing evaluation efficacy requires enhancing connectivity which in turn requires interaction with stakeholders.
- Since different actors have different repertoires and learning needs, a multiplicity of evaluations should be favoured, performed by different actors, at different levels and with different core questions. However,

these evaluations should have enough connectivity to contribute to mutual debate and co-operation. Also multi-actor evaluations should be an element of the set of evaluations in a network.

A focus on learning and actor involvement in the learning process is not new in the world of evaluation. On normative grounds or just to enhance utilization diverse forms of participative evaluations have been developed (Stake, 1983; Guba and Lincoln, 1989; Cousins and Earl, 1992; Abma, 1996; Patton, 1997; Preskill and Torres, 1999; Van der Meer and Edelenbos, 2006). However, the rationales of these forms of evaluation seem to have long been seen as incongruent with the NPM paradigm. Still, gradually new connections between these different 'repertoires' seem to come into being, especially in situations in which the fact that policy outcomes result from the interplay between many actors cannot be missed (Teisman and Van der Meer, 2002). For example, the authors in a volume edited by Gray et al. (2003) struggle with the role of evaluation in collaborative arrangements. On the one hand there is a felt need for assessment of results of collaboration and of the success of collaborative arrangements by means of 'objective' and independent measuring; on the other hand the necessity to explicitly involve the actors in the network is underlined, although not all contributions are clear about what their roles should be. The framework proposed in the present chapter may help in this respect.

To be sure, further research is needed to test the theoretical notions advanced in this chapter, especially their application to NPM innovations and related evaluations. Also the recommendations should be tested and evaluated in their own right. This chapter intended to provide a framework and some first steps to perform such research and to arrive at evaluations that more effectively support the process of learning by experience on an organization and network level.

Notes

1. For example, in the new Dutch law on care ('Wet Maatschappelijke Ondersteuning') all four rationales can be found:
   - hierarchy: the municipalities are made responsible by law for societal care.
   - coproduction: care should be delivered as much as possible by private organizations.
   - participation: care clients should participate in formulating care policies; clients should take responsibility for organizing their own care as much as possible.
   - new public management: care delivering organizations are contracted and evaluated according to agreed performance measures.
2. Cf. Dawson (1996: 233-62) who makes a similar analysis of the implementation of planned change.
3. In fact, the labels 'perverse' and 'defensive' are interpretations and valuations based on sense-making processes themselves. There are few actors considering

themselves perverse or defensive. This precisely exemplifies the diversity of sense-making in these processes.

4. Cf. Schein (1996) on typical differences in 'culture' between operators, technicians and managers, linked to their tasks, knowledge and position.

5. The specific context is not trivial either. Actors may have different perceptions of or convictions about what the relevant context is.

11
Implementing NPM: a Complexity Perspective on Public Management Reform Trajectories

Geert Teisman and Arwin van Buuren

Introduction

Several of the earlier chapters indicated that NPM reforms are implemented in a variety of ways and have different effects in various European countries. The conclusion that the shape and effects of reforms vary according to the institutional contexts in which the reforms are implemented, seems to be valid. The implementation of the same type of reform in different contexts such as, for instance, the introduction of benchmarking methods (Chapter 7), the application of public–private partnerships (Chapter 5), and the creation of agencies for the production of public goods and services (Chapter 4), result in a whole range of new management approaches, organizational arrangements and outcomes.

The institutional explanation for varieties of output and outcomes

The question is then posed, from where does this variety of output and outcomes arise? A well-known and frequently used explanation for differences in implementation and outcomes is the institutional approach (see Kickert, Chapter 3). The main argument of this approach is that every country has its unique political-administrative history and that a unique past has created a specific political and administrative context (Pollitt and Bouckaert, 2004; Peters, 2004; Kettl, 2005). From their own unique starting point governments will develop their own style in dealing with reforms, even when these reforms are gaining attention all over the world, as in the case of NPM. This contextual explanation is sometimes limited to the political-administrative characteristics of countries, but sometimes also extended towards system-specific characteristics of a specific organizational field (see Chapter 9, in which Pollitt shows the value of combining more explanatory theories for analysing the implementation of performance indicators in the health sector of different countries).

Institutional theories help explain the large variety of NPM reforms in different countries. However, they offer a relatively static account of the implementation of specific NPM reforms. The unexpected and largely unpredictable dynamics of implementation processes are not part of the explanation. There are many developments that influence the course of a NPM reform trajectory, which are difficult to explain from an institutional perspective. In this chapter, we want to complement the institutional explanation used in this book with a perspective derived from complexity theory. This enables us to focus upon the unexpected dynamic processes in implementation trajectories that, for example, can explain the rich variety of public–private partnerships in spatial planning in the Netherlands, or of performance contracts between different ministries and their executive agencies in the United Kingdom (cf. Chapter 5).

The added value of a complexity theoretical explanation

A more detailed analysis of *the course* of implementation processes, from which NPM tools get their shape, provides additional explanations for the variety of output and outcomes in trajectories, not only between countries, but also within countries and even within a single organization. By focusing on the *dynamics* of implementation processes, an additional explanation for differences in the results of NPM reforms can be identified. We admit that the initial conditions in every country, but also in every region or policy field, are of considerable importance for the way reforms are implemented. We, however, wish to supplement that with the idea that implementation is not only a function of these contextual starting conditions and the characteristics of the reform as such, but also is strongly influenced by emerging and rather coincidental events and behaviours during the implementation process.

We assume, therefore, that the outputs and outcomes of reforms are partly explained by inherent characteristics of reforms like benchmarking, public–private partnership and sourcing out to agencies, partly by the initial conditions shaped by the cultural heritage of the country, region and policy field, but also to a considerable extent by process dynamics in the implementation.

Implementation is conceptualized as a process of resistance, learning and couplings. The processes of resistance and learning are often influenced by all kinds of coincidental events occurring within parts of the policy system and with intentions that have little whatsoever to do with the reform or the initial cultural conditions. To speak about these coincidences we use the term 'interconnections'. It is our assumption that the output and outcomes of reforms result partly from incidental, unexpected, and, on the other hand, from planned interconnections with (political, administrative, or societal) events and developments that cross the implementation path of reforms.

The way public managers deal with emerging events when implementing reforms also contributes to the shape reforms finally obtain. The dynamics of processes, therefore, should be considered as a third explanatory dimension besides the dimensions 'reform' and 'institutional context'. We assume that this dimension has more explanatory power in modern complex and dynamic societies, where developments and policy changes are often stumbling over each other.

We elaborate this third dimension of explanation from the complex adaptive systems approach developed in physics and biology, and recently applied to the management sciences (Mittleton-Kelly, 2003; Haynes, 2003; Teisman, 2005). A complexity perspective can add important insights to an institutional perspective, especially where it challenges the notions of linearity and predictability. The focus is more on the (co-)evolutionary nature of implementation processes. From the outset, there are new concepts on public management (NPM) and an existing set of initial (cultural) conditions, but after the process of implementation starts, it will take place in a complex, highly interconnected world of several organizations, a whole bunch of actors and processes, as well as a variety of environments. Implementing a reform is not adding one element to an existing situation or adapting an existing situation to a new philosophy. It is a co-evolving and iterative process between a reform and the situation in which this reform gets its meaning and shape (see Sanderson, 2000, who develops a complexity perspective on policy evaluation).

We can use the metaphor of a policy window proposed by Kingdon (1984) to illustrate the importance of the third dimension. Kingdon assumed that the implementation of reforms could be compared with a rocket that has to be launched in order to reach a specific location in space. He argued that the energy needed and the direction the rocket finally gets will depend not only on the quality of the rocket and the lift off, but also on the orbits of the different planets in the context of the course the rocket takes. Together with Kingdon's assumptions, however, we assume that it is not only the well-known planets and their courses, but also all kinds of unknown objects (like the rubbish from earlier attempts) the rocket will face, as well as interferences with other rockets launched earlier, later or from other places, that will have considerable impact on output and outcomes of reforms.

From this perspective we argue that the results of implementing NPM reforms depend upon the specific dynamics of the different landscapes (that is, arenas or policy communities) in which public organizations are active and the subsequent value systems in which they have to fit. In complexity theory, organizations, decision processes, service delivery chains, and so on, are seen as complex evolving systems, interconnected with other systems in a wider and dynamic environment. Implementing a NPM reform means adding a new element to a specific system, and thus, not only changing the behaviour of this system, but also the way in which this specific system is seen by, and interacts with, its environment. Out of this co-evolutionary trajectory between the different parts of the system (organization, process, chain) and its environment, the concrete (but never definite) shape of the NPM reform emerges.

From this perspective the introduction of elements of NPM generates an emerging pattern of shaping and reshaping the NPM reform within public organizations. This occurs as a result of the dynamic co-evolution between this reform trajectory, the traditional ways of doing in the organization, and the ever-changing behaviour of the environment. This co-evolution is the result of the many interactions between the interconnected elements of the context of the NPM reform on the one hand, and the role that is played by this NPM reform in shaping its own environment on the other.

In this chapter, we will introduce the theory of complex adaptive systems and translate its main concepts to public management. This will enable us to demonstrate how NPM reforms and their implementation can be seen from the perspective of complex adaptive systems. The importance of notions of interconnectivity and co-evolution in public management reform will then be illustrated with an analysis of the implementation of Green-Blue Services (public–private contracts between farmers and government) in the Netherlands. This account will be complemented with some international comparisons based upon secondary case material from different countries and different sources.

In the final section of this chapter we will then return to the insights complexity theory can add to the institutional approach. We conclude that the implementation of reforms like NPM depend upon the interconnections that are made with other changes that, partly coincidentally, take place in the context in which a reform is introduced. Complexity theory delivers useful concepts to make more insightful detailed analyses of implementation processes of reforms. This is, however, only a first step and many research questions still have to be answered.

Complexity theory

Complexity theory focuses on the dynamics of the interrelated development of systems. To put it a little more provocatively: complexity theory tries to understand changes that cannot be explained from the past, but must be understood in terms of emergence and creation. It incorporates more of the chaotic aspects of the physical and social life and departs from the idea that main events can be explained from main causes.

Inspired by chaos theory (Gell-Mann, 1995; Nicolis and Prigogine, 1989; Waldrop, 1994), complexity theory forms the social application of this 'new science' (Merry, 1999). Core assumptions of complexity theory are:

(1) Systems (organizations, processes, and so on) are inherently dynamic and in a state of constant flux. They are inherently chaotic, because of the unpredictable behaviour of their components' elements (organizational units, employees, actors within a network) and their

interconnectedness with other systems on lower, higher and equal levels (Holland, 1995).

(2) Their interconnectivity has the implication that changes within one (part of a) system have (largely unpredictable) effects on other (parts of the same or other) systems, due to the own interpretation of this event by these elements or systems. The development of a system is thus a dynamic co-evolution between elements within a system and other systems (Van den Bergh and Gowdy, 2000; Van Buuren and Edelenbos, 2006).

(3) Complex evolving systems tend to develop out of a rather chaotic mess towards temporary equilibriums. Equilibriums provide temporally 'stable' situations, but normally will change over time again. If systems cannot keep themselves in a specific state of dynamic equilibrium, they tend to enter into a new state of chaos (they are not able to develop a unifying identity from which they can influence their environment in a predictable way) or fall back to inertia (they are not able to adapt to changing circumstances).

(4) Irregularities and chaos are judged on their merit in explaining dynamics, not condemned as things that should not be allowed. When systems can cope with the variety in their environment, and develop themselves and their subsystem to a new dynamic equilibrium situation, they can make a system leap towards a higher level of effectiveness and sustainability. The theory of autopoiesis, however, also teaches us that adaptation can be superficial without a real change. This type of adaptation can easily lead to inertia.

(5) Small changes within the current state of affairs within a system, or within its environment, can have large and unforeseen effects on the course of development afterwards. The idea of small differences and large effects is based on the idea that unpredictable interconnections between elements of a system can create either positive or negative feedback. These feedback mechanisms can lead to a development that fits within past cultural expectations (because changes are damped out due to negative feedback), but also to innovations that contribute to new cultural characteristics – because changes are multiplied by positive feedback (see Van Buuren and Gerrits, 2006).

Complex systems are different from each other in many respects, but they are also highly comparative on a more general level. In particular, their co-evolutionary development in a complex and dynamic environment is an important characteristic. As a consequence of their interconnectedness, the actions and strategies of (elements of) systems influence each other. This does not, however, occur in a linear and mechanistic way. Other elements or systems interpret these signals in their own way and react in their own manner. Out of chains of action and reaction, unpredictable co-evolutionary processes emerge.

Complexity theory and public management

Complexity theory can be utilized to analyse the practices of public management and its reforms, as well as to derive directives concerning these actual practices (Haynes, 2003). Governmental organizations can be seen as complex adaptive systems and constellations of interacting elements, which are interacting with a dynamic environment of other organizations (White, 2001). Medd (2001) cites Cilliers (2000) and his description of complex systems, which can be used to describe policy processes. In this vision, a policy process:

- 'Consists of a large number of elements which in themselves can be simple' but which 'interact dynamically by exchanging energy or information'. The 'effects of these interactions are propagated throughout the system'.
- Has 'many direct and indirect feedback loops'.
- Can be characterized in terms of 'open systems – they exchange energy or information with their environment – and operate at conditions far from equilibrium.
- Has a 'memory, not located at a specific place, but distributed throughout the system' and 'thus has a history'.
- Has emergent properties, that is, 'behaviour of the system is determined by the nature of the interactions, not by what is contained within the components. Since the interactions are rich, dynamic, fed back, and above all, non linear, the behaviour of the system as a whole cannot be predicted from an inspection of its components'.

Complexity theory focuses on the nested characteristics of organizations and processes. Agencies are composed of actors, are part of ministries, which are also part of the larger central government, which is part of a political system, which as such, is part of international systems. They are viewed as interdependent and part of multi-layer governance. Agencies, to go on with this example of a subsystem, are also embedded in several intertwined organized implementation or innovation networks that are less recognized. Many members of the agency are multi-included in several networks and it is especially this multiple character of inclusion that creates tensions between the policy implementation of a single organization and broader processes of policy development.

Often managers try to reorganize their organizations in search of more effective implementation of reforms. Successful reform trajectories that generate intended effects, however, cannot only be explained by the internal logic of this reorganization. From the perspective of complexity theory they also depend strongly upon the existing logic of the complex systems in which the reform is implemented. The moment managers reorganize their organization they often are aware of the importance of the context. *This, however, is a 'snapshot' awareness. The changes afterwards are not taken into account.*

Since agents, or actors, within a policy system act according to their own schemata with which they interpret external messages (like a reform proposal), they will respond to the messages/reform in a variety of ways, depending on their internal sense-making process. Sometimes, a response reinforces the implementation of a reform (positive feedback), and other times the response transforms or extinguishes the initial meaning and shape of a reform (negative feedback). Both types of feedback can occur together and create a highly dynamic process, as well as a variety of outcomes. This variety cannot be explained by the type of reform, nor the institutional context, or by the implementation scheme of the reform as such. In order to focus upon the 'coincidental go together' of series of developments we highlight two terms from complexity theory: *interconnectivity* and *co-evolution*.

It is a core characteristic of complex systems that they are highly interconnected, both internally (the component elements) and externally (the system with other systems). Therefore, the behaviour of the different (elements of) systems influence one another. The development of a system thus depends upon the interactive behaviour of its component elements, and that of the systems outside of its environment. Development within complex systems is always the result of co-evolving (elements of) systems. A system influences its environment, but is also influenced by this environment.

Reforming the public sector: introducing NPM

In their search for more efficiency and effectiveness, European governments have introduced many NPM and NPM-like reforms (Pollitt and Bouckaert, 2004). In Chapter 1 a number of general characteristics of these reforms were mentioned. They are meant to make government more lean and mean, to rationalize the delivery of public services, to introduce market-like mechanisms and to streamline internal procedures. In general, NPM is oriented towards the introduction of mechanisms that stimulate a more efficient and economical way of working in governmental organizations.

NPM reforms do not only consist of changes of organizations. They also include changes in procedures, processes, chains, or network relations. Implementing market-like contracts implies changing the relation between public organizations or their constituent parts. It can also mean changing the relations within a service delivery chain (cf. Chapter 8). Implementing public–private partnerships changes the relation between public authorities and private investors, but also the way in which they interact and co-operate (see Chapter 5). The creation of executive agencies implies other types of relations and working procedures between the parent department and the agency (as demonstrated in Chapter 4).

Thus the introduction of new organizational forms, new contractual arrangements, new performance indicators, new market-like mechanisms, takes place in existing systems, with their own dynamics, standard operating procedures, values and interpretation schemes (schemata in terms of complexity theory). The shape of a specific NPM reform in practice depends upon the way its implementation trajectory emerges on the waves of the developments in the different (parts of) systems in which it is introduced. This emerging trajectory depends on the dynamic behaviour of the specific landscapes in which it has to find its place.

Each of these settings has its own values and dynamics. For example, in the political arena gaining the support of voters, getting media attention, getting more grips on the public sector and realizing visible successes are important ambitions. Within the bureaucratic organizations all sorts of managerial and co-ordination problems play a role. The administrative top executives want to 'steer' the department and have other ambitions besides the NPM reform itself. The ministerial top wants to minimize the probability that failures are made. The organization in which the NPM reform is implemented also has its own organizational processes that require attention. The actors within these processes all have their own values with regard to the organization, what it has to do and how it has to do its tasks. Finally, NPM reforms obtain their shape and meaning within the daily working processes of street-level bureaucrats, who implement parts of the reform in their concrete actions and decisions.

By explaining the outcomes of this 'search for fitness' of a new management concept, we have to know how this tool becomes interconnected with elements and developments within its implementation context, as well as the different landscapes that affect its shape and meaning. This context is dynamic and interconnected, and interactions between different elements can cause totally unexpected effects, due to ignorance about its specific characteristics. Introducing market-like mechanisms can produce a stream of positive feedback in which the market 'hollows out the public service' (Rhodes, 1997). It can also produce a stream of negative feedback in which the bureaucratic culture disrupts the implementation of market mechanisms, thereby minimizing the actual impact of the market mechanisms. Political responses to management reforms can undo its effects, but can also have an accelerating effect (Pollitt and Bouckaert, 2004). This depends on the way in which the reform becomes interconnected or disconnected with other decision-making processes, strategic choices of actors, existing procedures or cultural habits of the context in which the reform is implemented.

Compared to other studies of the theme 'NPM and complexity theory' (Haynes, 2003; Rhodes and MacKechnie, 2003; Blackman, 2001), our analysis is rather new. Most of these studies are primarily prescriptive and deal with the question of how NPM reforms are compatible with the recommendations about management and policy that stem from the theory of complexity.

Other studies try to explain how organizations can use complexity theory to sustain themselves in a dynamic environment. Using complexity theory, as we do, to analyse the way in which NPM reforms are implemented, has not yet been pursued elsewhere.

We will use an in-depth case analysis from the Netherlands to illustrate our argument. Herein we focus on the presence and effects of connections between the specific reform and other developments in the environment. By doing so we will show the explanatory value of the complex dynamics of the different settings in which a reform is implemented. The results of the Dutch case are corroborated by findings from other European countries (secondary sources).

Green-Blue Services in Dutch spatial planning: the case of Reeuwijk

A rather good illustration of the importance of interconnections between different policy developments and a NPM reform is the case of the spatial reallocation of Reeuwijk, a Dutch municipality between Rotterdam and Utrecht. The NPM reform consists of introducing a market-like system to stimulate farmers to deploy their land to reach such public goals as water retention and nature development. Compared to traditional measures (dispossession of land by governments, instructions about ground water level and about the way in which farmers have to deal with unique flora and fauna), these financial instruments seek to stimulate the economic logic of farmers and provide them with more opportunities to adapt their business strategy and incorporate these 'Green-Blue Services'.

Reeuwijk faced severe problems related to water management in the early 1990s. Due to salt water seepage, the surface water contains a large amount of chloride. The growers need clean water for their plants and trees. The Water Board wants to improve the water quality in its jurisdiction. The low level of many meadows causes problems for the farmers, because of high surface water levels and the resulting problems of the accessibility and deployment of this land. Moreover, the Province of South Holland wanted to develop more nature in agricultural areas. Therefore, the Province looked for possibilities, together with the Water Board, to enlarge the water retention capacity, thus enabling it to cope with calamities (extreme rainfall, high river water levels).

In 2003 they came up with a rather radical solution to the different problems in the polder. Large water basins were proposed in order to improve the water quality, enlarge the retention capacity and indirectly improve the nature quality. However, that would mean the end of business for many farmers in the polders. Geophysical research showed that this proposal was not feasible because of high costs and many technical risks. It also became clear that the inhabitants of the area were strongly opposed to this proposal. Consequently, the proposal was withdrawn.

To find a new solution that was broadly supported, a joint search was initiated by public officials from the Province and Water Board and citizens (joined together in a Working Group that included farmers, growers and inhabitants of the polder). However, the governments' ambitions remained largely the same: improving the water quality (reducing the amount of salt in the surface water) and enlarging the nature areas. The ambition of the farmers was rather simple: they wanted to continue their business in the polder. Only a creative solution could solve the problem, which required combining nature development, water management and agriculture in an innovative and fine-tuned way. A standard approach was not suitable to solve the persistent problems in the polder and to leave alone the existing business. Therefore, a search for a 'new' solution began.

An external process manager was hired to facilitate the joint process of fact finding and decision-making. He introduced 'Green-Blue Services' as a high quality package deal. Farmers received financial compensation for the loss of the agricultural value when they allowed their land to be used to conserve water (Blue Services), or for landscape development (Green Services). The Green-Blue Services were presented as a new market-oriented policy instrument in water management. These policy instruments fitted into a bottom-up governance approach in which citizens and businesses were actively involved to realize public goals. The persons who provided these services were repaid for this and they could increase their compensation by improving the way in which they fulfilled the requested service.

With Blue Services farmers are involved in the management of water. Their land is used to conserve water in times of high water or calamities. In some periods the farmers accept higher water levels in order to reduce seepage pressure and to improve the water quality. In this way, water management is combined with traditional agricultural activities and more functions are given to agricultural land. With Green Services farmers are involved in the development of nature. In return for market-like financial compensation, farmers manage their land in a nature-friendly way to give flora and fauna better opportunities to survive and multiply. The idea of Green-Blue Services may have been new, but particularly the theory about Blue Services fitted well with the Dutch tradition of co-operation between citizens and government in its history of the fight against water. The more market-like and decentralist orientation can be interpreted as a place- and time-specific use of the NPM ideology.

In the case of Reeuwijk the Working Group discussed the proposal intensely. The final proposal aimed to meet all the interests of all the actors involved. Farmers and growers tried to find an acceptable solution to continue their businesses, but wanted to accommodate the ambitions of the different governments as well. They knew that non-intensive management of their pastures would contribute to nature development. They also knew that higher surface water levels would mean a reduction of chloride in the water, and thus an improvement in the water quality. But they also required a financial compensation for the loss of agricultural value (loss of grass production and less possibilities to drain off fertilizers).

The Green-Blue Services proposal was not simply approved by the Province and the Water Board. The latter did not have any experience with Blue Services. The Water Board was afraid that it gave away authority to the farmers; since water management is the core responsibility of the Water Board itself. Blue Services were considered to have only small impacts and such small-scale measures did not fit their policy ambition to introduce large-scale, rational and efficient water management. In their search to reduce the amount of salt in the surface water, they aimed at measures with large impacts. This policy strategy of the Water Board provided important negative feedback to the proposal of the Working Group.

The nature department of the Province was also not very eager to agree to the proposal of the Working Group. They preferred more large-scale measures to invest in nature development. They were not convinced of the quality of the nature projects proposed by the Working Group. They questioned the contribution of Green Services to the overall quality of nature in the polder.

In sum, the proposal of the Working Group did not seem to fit well with the policy environment. However, a new development within the province opened up a new possibility to make an interconnection and to enlarge the chance of success for the proposal of Green-Blue Services. With support of the Ministry of Agriculture, the province worked on specific 'area contracts' with so-called peat meadow areas. These areas have the same problems with regard to sow drop; bad water quality, decreasing possibilities for agriculture, and so on. The area around Reeuwijk is part of such a peat meadow area. The province tried to develop public–private management agreements with private actors to safeguard these areas from further deterioration. This development coincided with the process of the Working Group. Due to the political deputy of South Holland who was responsible for both projects, it was agreed that the Green-Blue Services proposal would be incorporated – as a separate and autonomous part – into the definitive area contract for the peat meadow area of Reeuwijk. This co-evolution between these two developments and the possibility to interconnect them was an important success factor for the proposal of the Working Group.

However, this agreement was not enough to get sufficient – financial – support for the proposal of the project team and the inhabitants. To that end, the project manager from the Province (also participating in the Working Group) found a creative connection between the Green-Blue Services and a much larger project. He proposed to the province to integrate the proposal in the so-called Wet Axis through the Green Heart (the green area of the western part of the Netherlands). This project is financed by the national government, and thereby ensured that there were enough financial resources to implement the proposal.

Still today, however, much remains uncertain. The political representatives of the Water Board, the Province and the municipality of Reeuwijk agreed in January 2006 on a rather broad and vague proposal and ordered a subsequent study in 2006. The municipality of Reeuwijk was the main driving force behind this decision, in view of the coming City Council elections (March 2006). They were afraid of a possible political shift that could generate negative feedback to the proposal of the Working Group. Another political majority could be much more negative about the proposal than the existing majority. So, the process was hastened and a rather vague proposal was approved.

The actual implementation of the Green-Blue Services depended upon two other crucial aspects: (i) the co-operation of the other farmers within the polder, and (ii) the co-operation of the Water Board in the near future. The land of the polder has to be reallocated to enable the execution of Green-Blue Services. This requires (voluntary) co-operation from the farmers. Without co-operation reallocation will become a timely and costly operation. There will probably not be enough money to pay for the costs of an involuntary reallocation. The second threat is the scepticism of the Water Board. Only when evidence grows that the fight against chloride in surface water can only be won with small-scale and specific measures will the policy philosophy of the Water Board change. Although more evidence regarding this has been brought forward, it takes time for officials and administrators to acknowledge this.

Most recently another unexpected development has arisen. The proposal is thwarted by another policy proposal for a new road through the polder. The municipality of Reeuwijk is looking for investors in this road, and thus wants to concentrate businesses along this roadway. This has the consequence that some areas along this road may be used for accommodating growers, who need a good accessibility for their company. Should, or rather when, this proposal be approved, the reallocation of the farmers will become much more difficult. At the time this chapter was written (early 2006), the Working Group has attempted to postpone the decision on this road in order to safeguard its own proposal.

An important condition for the success of the Green-Blue Services proposal is that it should be connected to other developments in its environment. The Working Group in Reeuwijk and the participating officials (especially of the Province) made fruitful connections between this concrete project and other policy processes (interconnectivity). But there were also many more coincidental events that were very important (co-evolution) including: the totally unexpected results of the study towards the feasibility of the retention basins; the way in which the outcomes of the coming elections were estimated; the developments in national policy ambitions regarding the 'Green Heart' of the Netherlands, and so on.

Unfortunately, the proposal of the Working Group lacks a connection with another regional project, the new road through the polder. This could cause problems when the reallocation of the polder has to be executed. It remains to be seen whether it will be the road or the proposal of the Working Group that will fit better with the ambitions of politicians.

The findings of this case illustrates that the introduction of NPM reforms depends largely on process specific characteristics. The proposal of the Working Group did not get much support before it was connected with other policy initiatives. Political support is important for the implementation of the Green-Blue Services proposal. This support is obtained in a more indirect rather than direct manner: by connecting their own proposal to other – more appealing – proposals the Working Group gained a sufficient level of political support. Experiences from other countries corroborate this conclusion, as we will demonstrate below.

Experiences in other European countries

Next to political support, financial means and support from governmental agencies are also necessary conditions for success. The importance of these conditions can, however, vary over time. A detailed case study of housing policy in Dublin (Rhodes and MacKechnie, 2003; Haynes and Rhodes, 2004) has shown that four dimensions were of crucial importance for the implementation of initiatives in this sector: a political, a financial, a social and an innovative (how 'sexy' a proposal is) dimension. However, Rhodes and MacKechnie conclude: 'Not only does the relative importance of these dimensions vary across different types of initiatives, but it varies across time for specific initiatives' (2003: 73–4). The environment in which a reform is implemented is dynamic and changes continuously. The way in which an initiative gets meaning depends largely on the specific circumstances at the moment of launching. The OECD makes a similar conclusion in a study of the implementation of results-focused management: 'Few significant public sector initiatives are independent, most of necessity must interact with a range of other initiatives and programs, government and otherwise, as well as with environmental considerations including social and economic aspects, and the perspectives of multiple stakeholders' (OECD, 2002: 47).

Andreescu (2005) has noted the importance of dynamics in implementation by referring to it as 'negotiated evolution'. She studied the way in which NPM reforms have changed the role of human resource managers. Under the influence of NPM, this role has developed from strict personnel administration to more strategic partnership (see, for example, Chapter 6 on the role of public managers in general). Looking more closely at this very generic trend, however, Andreescu also observed that many contextual factors were of high importance.

> For the HR function to become more strategic, far more is needed than the HR director to simply decide that the department 'will be' strategic. Rather, the role the HR function takes on will be the result of a continuous process

of negotiation with other groups within the organization and will be achieved by a process of 'negotiated evolution' which involves credibility building, agenda management, continuous delivery and other influencing techniques. The HR function operates thus within a complex system of interdependencies and conflicts over the form, ownership and implementation of the HR agenda – and no single group is in full control. (Andreescu, 2005: 27)

A third and final example from other countries can be found in a study of system innovation and transitions (Elzen, Geels and Green, 2004). For example, the transition towards a more sustainable agrifood chain in Switzerland was only possible by way of a co-evolution of several reforms and developments in a variety of subsystems of society (Belz, 2004). The growth of organic farming was only one so-called niche development. Integrated production was another one. Changes in the preferences of consumers was a third important development and the retail chains functioning as a gatekeeper between consumer and farmers were a fourth important subsystem. Finally governments are indicated as an important group of proponents of change. Belz concludes that 'the mutual reinforcement and alignments between these three social groups provided the momentum for the transition towards a more sustainable agrifood chain' (Belz, 2004: 112). Implementing reforms, therefore, should not be conceptualized as something that has to be done, but much more as a process of co-evolution between existing and new attempts to change the course of development in a certain area. In addition to the well-known institutional approach focusing on the implementation of a specific reform in a more or less stable and knowable institutional context, complexity approaches highlight this element of co-evolution.

Discussion and conclusion

Implementation trajectories of NPM reforms are dynamic and unpredictable. Several examples in this chapter, and in this book, have demonstrated this. The interconnectivity of different elements and processes of public domains, and often even from outside the public domain, is the driving force behind dynamic and sometimes chaotic processes. The implementation of NPM depends on the way it is shaped in the process in which it gets form and meaning. Moreover, it makes use of the interconnected character of its context. This two-sided relation makes implementation of reforms highly interactive. On the one hand, interconnectedness makes a solid implementation difficult. On the other hand, however, only by becoming interconnected with relevant developments in their context, can the successful implementation take place.

These dynamics of the different settings make the outcomes of a reform trajectory unpredictable and unique for each case. The outcome of implementation trajectories is context-specific and process-specific. NPM reforms are influenced by their context, but also influence their context. It is only when reforms fit with their context, and become interconnected with other developments, that they will survive and succeed. An important success factor for the implementation of NPM is to recognize the interconnectedness between the many elements around a concrete policy process: the many (units of) involved organizations, their actions and specific dynamics, other policy processes and ambitions, and so on. Only by seeking fruitful connections with these dynamic elements, can the chance that a NPM reform is actually implemented be enlarged.

Thus, NPM reforms are in their final shape (although their shape is never definitive) not only context-specific but also 'process'-specific: they reflect the dynamics of their implementation process (cf. Chapter 3). Implementing NPM reforms in largely comparable contexts does not mean they will be similar after their implementation. Therefore, the process through which they obtain meaning and functionality is important. Linkages are difficult to handle by public managers who implement NPM reforms, but at the same time they are important sources for progress.

For example, in the Sijtwende case that is presented in Chapter 5, the authors show that the PPP itself facilitated the necessary connections between a locked-in public policy domain and a private entrepreneur offering a way out. The public resistance against PPP was (temporarily) lessened only because it created a way out. The PPP did not result from an implementation strategy of the existing PPP policy of the Ministry of Finance. By bundling the different ambitions of the public actors involved and filling up the gap between the different administrations, the private party stumbled more or less into a PPP that afterwards became the most quoted example of PPP in the Netherlands. The temporal and coincidental co-evolution with some changes in the bureaucratic environment of the project created a fit and helped to overcome earlier resistance.

This chapter has highlighted the importance of the *process* of implementation. This process is part of a set of co-evolution developments. The output and outcome of reforms result for a considerable part from the way in which a reform proposal is connected to neighbouring developments. Reforms are transformed and translated in a process of co-evolution with developments in its context, and by doing so their ultimate shape and meaning are determined. As such, complexity perspectives add important insights to institutional perspectives and help managers and researchers to develop a dynamic, adaptive and process-oriented perspective on implementing NPM reforms.

12
Conclusions

Sandra van Thiel, Christopher Pollitt and Vincent Homburg

Introduction

From the late 1970s on, Western bureaucracies have been confronted with clamours for change and reform, as politicians were looking for a leaner and more effective administration. Under the heading of New Public Management a range of apparently universal business techniques were applied to public sector organizations. In this volume, a number of these reforms have been discussed, including the creation of executive agencies, public–private partnerships, personnel reforms and the use of performance measurement instruments. This served two purposes. We wanted (i) to show the range and diversity in the actual implementation of specific NPM techniques in a number of (continental) European countries and (ii) to offer an explanation for differences and adaptations of the predominantly Anglo-American ideas of NPM in continental European countries. Now the time has come to sum up our findings.

To that end we will first review the range of differences and diversity in the implementation of NPM, as found in the previous chapters. This will call for a reappraisal of the universality of the concept of New Public Management. Next, we will review the different explanations for the complex patterns as put forward between these covers. This exposé will also help us to identify some future research needs to conclude this chapter with.

Diversity and divergence

To some commentators and politicians, the idea of globally converged, universal and generally applicable management techniques is intuitively appealing. It may indeed be tempting to assume that particular courses of action are inevitable, because many other countries are pursuing them – or, are *talking* about them. Why should one be left behind when everyone seems to be adopting reforms?

The actual experiences with NPM reforms as discussed in previous chapters, nevertheless, have often shown highly differentiated developments. Take, for example, the creation of executive agencies in the UK and the Netherlands, as discussed in Chapter 4. While there are similarities in the way in which these agencies are controlled by parent departments (through contracts, performance measurement and liaison officers), there are also many differences. For example, the preference for the agency model has different origins: in the UK agencies were the answer to insufficient managerial autonomy, while in the Netherlands agencies were the solution for too much managerial autonomy for ZBOs. This underlying difference in origin is reflected in significant differences in the timing and pace of agency creation. Obviously, extensiveness and depth of convergence are easily overstated (Pollitt, 2002).

Other examples are easily found. For example, the use of public–private partnerships in the UK and the Netherlands may sound alike in name, but in practice the authors of Chapter 5 found that the Dutch approach favours a much more consensual way of working between governments and private companies than in the UK, where there is a more cut-throat competitive flavour to public–private partnerships. In fact, in most cases where we have the UK as a comparator (for example, Chapters 4, 5, 8 and 9) it usually seems that the UK approach is somehow more hard-edged and directive – closer to the initial Anglo-American phrasing of NPM reforms – than the continental applications. The introduction of performance indicators in the health care sector is another clear example in this respect (see Chapter 9). This conclusion supports and deepens the interpretations offered in some of the standard comparative texts (Kickert, 1997; Pollitt and Bouckaert, 2004) to the effect that the most radical applications of NPM are to be found in the 'Anglo-Saxon' countries – Australia, New Zealand and the UK, with the US following close behind (cf. Kettl, 2005; Barzelay, 2001). Continental European countries seem to have adopted more of a neo-Weberian state (NWS) model, with two different variations: one emphasizing legitimacy and accountability (Nordic countries and the Netherlands) and one emphasizing flexibility and professionalism (France, Spain, Portugal and federal Germany).

Being a more radical adopter of NPM reforms is, however, only one of the possible explanations for differences between European countries. For example, in Chapter 6 it is not so much the state tradition, but rather the existing administrative (or bureaucratic) systems that helped to explain why in some countries performance-related pay and temporary tenure have been implemented more often than in others. The career-based system of tenure in countries such as France and Italy allows central policy-making when it comes to personnel policies, contrary to position-based systems in which more decentralized units like ministries can adopt, adapt or even resist reforms. Alternatively, Chapters 8 and 10 suggest that the instruments of the implementation of reforms, like ICT and evaluation, are not neutral and can/do in fact shape and mould reforms to fit – or reinforce or reproduce – existing structures and interests.

The variety of actual NPM implementations and their underlying antecedents renders any meaningful international comparison of trajectories difficult, if not hazardous, as the authors of the chapter on international benchmarking (Chapter 7) have shown. Although the concept of benchmarking is widespread in a number of countries, such as Denmark, the Netherlands, Austria, Sweden and the UK, there is little guarantee that its application occurs in the same way, or even that indicators measure the same activity in different countries. In other words, apparent and quantitatively expressed convergence might in fact be spurious or misleading.

To believe that one set of relatively uniform management technologies are being rolled out across continental Europe, let alone the world, just does not fit at all with the various theories, analyses, cases and stories unfolded in the preceding eleven chapters. There *is* no global model (except in the minds of some enthusiasts quoted in Chapter 2) and there is no distinct, homogeneous continental European model either. Even the two variants of the neo-Weberian state (NWS) set out in Chapter 2 – which are in any case quite loose general models – do not cover the whole range of reform practices in continental Europe. It is evident, for example from Chapter 3, that they do not fit Spain very well; moreover Italy, although dynamic in several directions, is hard to categorize. There is a rough pattern, but it is complex and approximate.

Apparently, governments in continental Europe have taken a 'shopping basket' approach to NPM. Although labels are similar in various countries, actual implementations of reform consist of various blends and flavours. If convergence exists, it occurs mainly through political language: symbolic use of concepts at a rhetorical level. Decisional and operational convergence, however, are less likely to occur in various national contexts. Politicians seem to prefer to pick and choose whatever seems appropriate (or is actually achievable given political capacity). A more thorough understanding, however, should include more than just selective shopping approaches. Until the present, a rigorous understanding has been lacking. Below, we identify candidate building blocks that might contribute to an improved explanation of observed differences.

Explanations

The previous chapters have offered various explanations for the differences in the implementation of NPM reforms in European countries. We distinguish three categories of explanations, relating to (i) the concept of NPM, (ii) the context in which it is implemented, and (iii) the implementation of reforms.

First, the contradictions and tensions within the NPM concept give room to adapt and change reforms' original form and intentions. Chapters 7 and 8 would seem to fit into such a line of reasoning; the reforms themselves – e-government and benchmarking respectively – are flexible enough to be applied to different ends (for example, more efficiency versus more responsiveness). Chapter 5 offers more corroboration; the two interpretations of public–private partnership are a testament to the ambiguity of the concept. In Chapter 1, ten trade-offs were identified that are inherent to NPM. Below we will reconsider these trade-offs in light of the evidence presented in this volume.

Second, the context in which reforms are implemented exerts pressure to fit with existing structures and traditions of politico-administrative systems and traditions, both at national and sectoral level. Such an explanation could be based on, for example, path dependency models or institutionalism. Chapters 2 (convergence) and 3 (Napoleonic systems) offer theoretical support to this type of explanation; the applications discussed in Chapters 4 (agencies), 5 (PPP), 6 (HRM) and 9 (hospital indicators) offer empirical illustrations.

Third, the implementation of NPM reforms takes place in a dynamic context in which simultaneous events and developments may influence the outcome in an unforeseen way. This last explanation was elaborated most upon in Chapter 11 on complexity theory, but there was also some reference to it in Chapters 10 (on evaluation) and 5 (on PPP).

The concept of NPM: inherent contradictions and trade-offs

NPM is like a chameleon: it constantly changes its appearance to blend in with the local context. Previous chapters in which the implementation of a specific type of reform is compared between different countries offer ample evidence to support this conclusion. Such adaptability is possible, because NPM is not a coherent set of ideas and tools. The labels may be the same, but the underlying story differs all the time. This is corroborated by the analysis in Chapter 2. Politicians quoted in this chapter mention very different motives and objectives for the same reforms. State modernizers, like the Nordic countries, emphasize the contribution of NPM reforms to a strong state and active citizenship, while marketizing governments like the UK refer to a retreat of the state, selling off all non-essential state tasks. Examples of this contradictory use of the same reform are found in, for example, Chapters 4 and 8; executive agencies are used in the UK to grant more managerial autonomy to those who implement policies, while in the Netherlands agencies are preferred because they have less autonomy than statutory bodies; e-government is meant to improve service delivery to clients (rather than citizens) in the UK, and to improve citizens' participation in government affairs in Denmark (empowerment).

The inherent contradictions of NPM create leeway to adapt reforms to specific circumstances. Politicians and bureaucrats can both use this leeway to make reforms fit with their own agenda, either in talk or in practice (Pollitt, 2001; James, 2003). Chapter 1 listed ten seemingly incompatible objectives of reforms to illustrate the inherent tensions of NPM. Most of these can be recovered in the chapters of this book.

For example, the use of performance indicators (see Chapters 7 and 9) is intended, on the one hand, to increase the effectiveness of public sector organizations, to help cut costs and achieve savings (efficiency), while on the other hand indicators are expected to improve the quality of, for example, customer service as well as improve performance overall. Moreover, performance indicators are expected to contribute to a reduction of administrative burdens while at the same time improving (horizontal) accountability, because governments can use a limited number of performance indicators to monitor executive organizations (cf. Chapter 4 on agencies and Chapter 10 on evaluation). However, none of these expectations seems to take into account that the implementation of performance indicators will lead to extra costs (so-called monitoring costs), nor that the introduction of performance measurement can lead to all kinds of perverse effects that obstruct insight into performance or even lead to a decline in performance (cf. Chapter 10; Van Thiel and Leeuw, 2002).

'Freeing managers to manage' is another important goal of NPM. To that end, managers are given more responsibility (accountability) and competencies. However, this is matched with a desire for more flexibility in personnel policy, which is translated in a weaker tenure system leading to less stability in civil servants' career patterns (cf. Chapter 6). Whether this will motivate staff, as expected in the NPM ideology, is not obvious; it might also undermine the willingness of civil servants to co-operate in the implementation of reforms. The slow pace of implementing performance-related pay schemes could be seen as an example of such reluctance.

A third example relates to public–private partnerships (PPP, see Chapter 5), which are in some countries seen as an opportunity to reduce government's tasks (and fiscal pressure) and administrative burdens. In other countries, however, PPPs are seen as an instrument to achieve a 'joined-up' government; that is, a government that works together with other organizations and citizens to achieve new solutions for existing problems (see also Chapter 11 for an illustration). Both objectives are expected to contribute to government's legitimacy, but through completely different mechanisms, respectively decentralization (less state interference) and co-ordination (more state control). The Dutch usage of PPPs shows this tension most clearly; official policy emphasizes the decentralization aspects (contractual relations), but in practice the co-ordination aspect is dominant (active partnerships).

The context of NPM: shaping and moulding by institutional frameworks

Institutional frameworks or contexts are probably the most frequently cited factor to explain differences in the implementation of NPM reforms in

European countries (see Chapters 3, 4, 5, 6, 8 and 9). In particular, the national politico-administrative system is expected to help or impede reforms. Chapter 3 is the clearest illustration in this respect, as it shows how the legal traditions in countries such as France, Spain and Italy have influenced the advent (or lack thereof) of NPM. Chapters 4, 5 and 9 offer a similar analysis when comparing the UK and Dutch experiences with agencies, PPPs and performance indicators respectively. A majoritarian centralized system, such as the UK, permits and, indeed, encourages types of policy response and implementation strategy, which are discouraged, or even impossible, in more decentralized and/or consensual systems. This may well account for the 'harder edge' to UK reforms, which has already been referred to. Similarly, there are big differences between the impacts of management reforms in a country like the Netherlands, which enjoys a non-partisan civil service with low levels of corruption, and a country like Italy, where measured corruption levels are considerably higher, and political patronage reaches far into public sector employment (cf. Chapter 6). Specific projects and innovations (performance-related pay, or contracting-out, or autonomization) can seldom escape these general influences, although there may be ways of ameliorating their effects. A problem here, however, is that while we may have very strong (and possibly somewhat stereotyped) images of the culture in particular countries, large-scale and comparative empirical research to underpin the images and cases is rather thin (but see for some good examples: Feigenbaum et al., 1999; Pollitt and Bouckaert, 2004; Pollitt et al., 2004; Smullen, forthcoming).

Certain chapters (5, 6, 7 and 9) also refer to sectoral factors. Performance indicators, for example, are less difficult to install in an organization that delivers a simple service (such as issuing driving licences or passports) than for highly complex and individualized services such as health care and education (cf. Chapter 7). Some parts of the public sector are dominated by powerful professional groups – doctors or lawyers – who may not take kindly to the rather mechanistic NPM approach, and who may well believe that they already have their own high standards of service and expertise (cf. Chapter 10 on the 'repertoires' of groups/individuals). Some countries have, for example, more powerful and entrenched public sector trade unions than others (France and Denmark, for example, compared with the UK) and that may influence the speed and penetration of NPM-style HRM reforms. In Chapter 5 it was noted that PPPs have tended to emerge in certain sectors, particularly urban development and physical infrastructure development, and that contractual forms are more likely to appear in the latter than the former.

Implementation of NPM: dynamic processes and co-evolution

Chapter 11 stressed the dynamic nature of the implementation process and showed how, in complex systems, unforeseen conjunctions of factors can shape turning points for new policies and projects. The implementation of a reform depends largely on the way in which it is connected to co-evolving developments, to the context in which the reform is implemented, and to the way in which this context is subject to change as well (evolution). As such, complexity perspectives add important insights to institutional perspectives and can help managers and researchers to develop a more dynamic, adaptive and process-oriented perspective on implementing NPM reforms. For example, the rise of executive agencies in the Netherlands can only be understood completely when taking into consideration that the political debate at the time evolved around problems with ministerial accountability for statutory bodies (see Chapter 4). Similarly, the rise of a new government in Italy was used as a leverage to change personnel policies, in particular the appointment procedures for top civil servants (Chapter 6). And in Chapter 5 it was argued that the arrival of a new government may lead to the addition of new actors and objectives to existing PPPs, which will create a more complex situation and possibly a reinterpretation of the function of PPPs.

Chapter 10 adds to this understanding of reform trajectories another theoretical perspective, namely that of the repertoire of actors; the interests, position, prior experience and resources of people and organizations determine to which extent they are interested or engaged in evaluations of reforms and in learning from these evaluations for future reforms. The examples in Chapter 7 on international benchmarking show, for example, that the most important lesson is that we cannot learn from the experiences in other countries unless we also understand how a particular reform was selected, presented and implemented.

The future research agenda

It is all very well to stress the importance of differences, and to indicate some broad factors (type of reform, institutional context, co-evolving developments) that are likely to influence public management reform. This is a valuable start. But the explanatory task arguably requires more than this.

First, in the analysis of notable differences or presumed convergence of NPM reforms in various contexts, more attention should be paid to differences in the starting points of reforms. The institutional breeding ground moulds, shapes and reinforces particular elements of NPM reforms, and therefore is an important candidate variable for meaningfully explaining how actual NPM reforms are shaped and crafted in various national settings.

Second, it would be useful to argue for the inclusion of variables indicating key contextual dimensions in explanatory theory. This could be useful both for theories that are notably functional in character as well as for social-constructivist theories of convergence/divergence. Functional theories – notably contingency theories (Donaldson, 1985; see also Pollitt, 2002) that emphasize adaptation of forms and practices to specific circumstances – might benefit from a deeper understanding and appreciation of differences in contexts. But also constructivists' accounts of spread of managerial reforms could be strengthened and improved by means of inclusion of localized practices, fashions and symbolism that might explain the selective appropriation and attribution of the NPM phenomenon. In some chapters our authors have started this task, but in none has the process yet gone very far. Thus, for example, in Chapter 9 it is suggested that the particular features of the Dutch acute health care sector (public regulation plus social insurance plus private not-for-profit provision) makes the development of performance indicators different from the UK (centralized public provision, free-access system based mainly on general taxation). However, one would need to go much deeper in order to see the specific mechanisms through which these factors exerted their pull – ideally to a series of detailed case studies which traced the perceptions and moves of key actors and related these to their institutional positions. Concepts like repertoires (Chapter 10) and the unpredictability of implementation dynamics (Chapter 11) are intriguing, but still remain very general and cannot be used very easily until more is said about how/when they occur and how they affect the reform process.

Thirdly, arguably the most challenging element of a future research agenda is the development of theories and empirical accounts that address the complex mixture of durable differences and striking similarities (Pollitt, 2002) between various countries and in specific sectors. An important starting point for such an approach is the distinction between rhetorical, decisional and operational convergence (Brunsson, 1989; Pollitt, 2002). In many of the chapters in this volume, it has been noted that if convergence exists, it is mainly rhetorical in nature, sometimes decisional and rarely operational. Continued research efforts addressing this distinction could reveal whether, and if so in what particular order, various forms of convergence are to be observed. Such an approach might even be useful to reconcile traditionally crude functionalist accounts of 'failure' of reforms and presumably less elegant, but possible more nuanced constructivist accounts of payoffs between (fallible) talk, decisions and applications.

In conclusion, therefore, we note that the academic study of the NPM continues to evolve, but is itself pluralistic, involving a range of ontologies, theories, methods and value standpoints. When these pluralistic approaches are brought to bear on the recent reform experiences of continental Europe, no single story emerges. The one thing we can say with certainty is that diversity exists – both in the theorist's world and in the practitioner's. In this situation dialogues which cross institutional and academic boundaries are likely to be more useful than those which simply deepen the debate within the confines of a single position. We trust that this book makes one such contribution.

Bibliography

4Ps, *Procurement Options* (London: Public Private Partnerships Programme, 2006) (www.4ps.gov.uk).

C. W. A. M. Aarts, R. E. Leenes and J. S. Svensson, *Kiezen op afstand Monitor* (Den Haag: Ministerie van Binnenlandse Zaken, 2001).

T. A. Abma, *Responsief evalueren: discourses, controversen en allianties in het postmoderne* (Rotterdam, 1996).

Accenture, *eGovernment Leadership – Realizing the Vision* (April 2002), 88 pp.

M. Adler and P. Henman, 'Computerizing the welfare state: an international comparison of computerization in social security', *Information, Communication and Society* 8 (3) (2005): 315–42.

C. R. Alba, 'L'administration publique Espagnol: réforme ou modernisation', *Revue Française d'Administration Publique*, 75 (July–August 1995): 387–400.

C. R. Alba Tercedor, 'Politique et administration en Espagne: continuité perspectives', *Revue Française d'Administration Publique*, 86 (April–June 1998): 229–42.

Algemene Bestuursdienst, *Jaarverslag Bureau ABD 2002* (The Hague: Ministerie van BZK, 2003).

Algemene Bestuursdienst, *Kenmerken ABD-populatie 2003* (The Hague: Ministerie van BZK, 2004).

Algemene Rekenkamer, *Verslag 1994; deel 3: Zelfstandige bestuursorganen en ministeriële verantwoordelijkheid*, Tweede Kamer, vergaderjaar 1994–95, 24 130, nr3 (Den Haag: Sdu, 1995)

N. J. Allen and J. P. Meyer, 'The measurement and antecedents of affective, continuance and normative commitment to the organization', *Journal of Occupational Psychology*, 63 (1990): 1–18.

M. Allix and S. van Thiel, 'Mapping the field of quasi-autonomous organizations in France and Italy', *International Journal of Public Management*, 8 (1) (2005): 39–55.

M. I. M. Allix, *Rapport sur les enquêtes aupres des établissements publics nationaux des autorités administratives indépendantes et des services à compétence nationale* [Report] (Rotterdam, 2005).

I. M. Alvarez de Cienfuegos, 'Spain: still the primacy of corporatism?', in E. C. Page and V. Wright (eds), *Bureaucratic Elites in Western European States* (Oxford: Oxford University Press, 1999), pp. 32–54.

F. Andreescu, 'Changing HR roles in commercializing public sector organizations: from personnel administration to strategic partnership?' Paper for the European Group of Public Administration Conference (Berne, 31 August–1 September 2005).

R. N. Anthony and D. W. Young, *Managerial Control in Nonprofit Organizations*, 6th edn (Boston: Irwin/McGraw-Hill, 1999).

A. Asbroek, O. Arah, J. Geelhoed, T. Custers, D. Delnoij and N. Klazonga, 'Developing a national performance indicator framework for the Dutch health system', *International Journal for Quality in Health Care*, 16, Supplement 1, (2004): 65–71.

K. Ascher, *The Politics of Privatisation: Contracting Out Public Services* (Basingstoke: Macmillan, 1987).

Audit Commission, *PFI in Schools* (London: Audit Commission, 2003).

M. Baena del Alcazar, 'On the nature of power: an examination of the governing elite and institutional power in Spain, 1939–92', *Public Administration*, 80 (2) (2002): 323–38.

S. R. Barley, 'Technology as an occcasion for structuring: evidence from observations of CT scanners and the social order of radiology departments', *Administrative Science Quarterly* 31 (1) (1986): 78–108.

J. Barlow, D. Farnham, S. Horton and F. F. Ridley, 'Comparing senior public officials', in D. Farnham, S. Horton, J. Barlow and A. Hondeghem (eds), *New Senior Public Officials in Europe: Public Servants in Transition* (Basingstoke: Macmillan, 1996), pp. 3–25.

S. Bartolini, A. Chiaramonte and R. d'Alimonte, 'The Italian party system between parties and coalition', *West European Politics*, 27 (1) (2004): 1–19.

M. Barzelay, *The New Public Management: Improving Research and Policy Dialogue* (USA: University of California Press, 2001).

F. Bassanini, 'La décentralisation et la réforme de l'état. L'expérience de l'Italie', lecture at ENA (Paris, 27 November 2002).

S. Battini, 'Administration et politique en Italie: des logiques contradictoires', *Revue Française d'Administration Publique*, 86 (1998): 205–17.

R. D. Behn, 'The new public management paradigm and the search for government accountability', *International Public Management Journal*, 1 (2) (1998): 131–64.

V. J. J. M. Bekkers, 'New forms of steering and the ambivalency of transparency', in I. T. M. Snellen and W. B. H. J. v. d. Donk (eds), *Public Administration in an Information Age: a Handbook* (Amsterdam: IOS Press, 1998), pp. 341–57.

V. J. J. M. Bekkers, *Grenzeloze overheid. Over informatisering en grensveranderingen in het openbaar bestuur* (Alphen aan den Rijn: Samsom, 1998).

V. J. J. M. Bekkers and V. M. F. Homburg (eds), *The Information Ecology of E-Government* (Amsterdam: IOS Press, 2005).

C. Bellamy and J. Taylor, *Governing in the Information Age* (Buckingham: Open University Press, 1998).

F. Belz, 'A transition towards sustainability in the Swiss agri-food chain (1970–2000): using und improving the multi-level perspective', in B. Elzen, F. W. Geels and K. Green (eds), *System Innovation and the Transition to Sustainability: Theory, Evidence and Policy* (Cheltenham: Edward Elgar, 2004), pp. 97–113.

A. Benz, *Der moderne Staat* (München: Oldenbourg Verlag, 2001).

Berenschot, *De evaluatie van het baten-lastendienstmodel: een bijdrage aan doelmatiger werken*, report (Utrecht, 2002).

M. Berg, Y. Meijerink, M. Gras, A. Eland, W. Schellekens, J. Haeck, M. Kallewaard and H. Kingma, 'Feasibility first: developing public performance indicators on patient safety and clinical effectiveness for Dutch hospitals', *Health Policy*, 75 (2005): 59–73.

P. Bezes, 'Defensive versus offensive approaches to administrative reform in France (1988–1997): the leadership dilemmas of French prime ministers', *Governance*, 14 (2001): 99–132.

P. Bezes, 'Aux origines des politiques de réforme administrative sous la V-ème République: la construction du "souci de soi de l'état" ', *Revue Française d'Administration Publique*, 102 (2002a): 307–25.

P. Bezes, *La construction historique des politiques de réforme de l'administration en France depuis les années 1960*, VII congrès de l'Association Française de Science Politique (Lille, 18–21 September 2002b).

T. Blackman, 'Complexity theory and the new public management', *Social Issues*, 1 (2) (2001), electronic journal: www.whb.co.uk/socialissues.

T. Blair, 'I have learned the limits of government', *Independent*, 20 May 2002, p. 15.

J. L. T. Blank, 'Benchmarking of de kunst van het vergelijken', *ESB*, 4154 (29 May 1998): 432–5.

206   *Bibliography*

R. Blank, and V. Burau, *Comparative Health Policy* (Basingstoke: Palgrave Macmillan, 2004).

V. Bogdanor (ed.), *Joined–Up Government* (Oxford: Oxford University Press/British Academy, 2005).

P. Bordewijk, and H. L. Klaassen, *Wij laten ons niet kennen; Een onderzoek naar het gebruik van kengetallen bij negen grotere gemeenten* (VNG Uitgeverij, 2000).

J. Boston, J. Martin, J. Pallot and P. Walsh, *Public Management: the New Zealand Model* (Auckland: Oxford University Press, 2004).

T. Bovaird and E. Löffler (eds), *Public Management and Governance* (London: Routledge, 2003).

R. C. Box, *Citizen Governance: Leading American Communities into the 21st Century* (Thousand Oaks: Sage, 1998).

G. A. Boyne, C. Farrell, J. Law, M. Powell and R. M. Walker, *Evaluating Public Management Reforms* (Buckingham/Philadelphia: Open University Press, 2003).

J. Broadbent and R. Laughlin, 'Evaluating the "new public management" reforms in the UK: a constitutional possibility', *Public Administration* 75 (1997): 487–507.

N. Brunsson, *The Organisation of Hypocrisy: Talk, Decisions and Actions in Organisations* (Chichester, UK: John Wiley, 1989).

J. R. N. Bullivant, *Benchmarking for Continuous Improvement in the Public Sector* (Essex: Longman, 1994).

R. C. Camp, *Benchmarking: the Search for Industry Best Practices that Lead to Superior Performance* (New York: ASQC-Quality Press, 1989).

R. C. Camp, *Benchmarking: Het zoeken naar de beste werkmethoden die leiden tot superieure prestaties* (Deventer: Kluwer, 1992).

M. Canoy, M. Janssen and B. Vollaard, *PPS: een uidagend huwelijk, publiek-private Samenwerking bij Combinatieprojecten* (Den Haag: CPB, 2001).

Cap Gemini Ernst and Young, *Online Availability of Public Services: How is Europe Progressing? Web Based Survey on Electronic Public Services*, Report of the Fourth Measurement (October 2003, January 2005).

G. Capano, 'Administrative traditions: Italian administrative reforms during the 1990s', *Public Administration* (2003): 781–801.

R. Carr, *Modern Spain 1875–1980* (Oxford: Oxford University Press, 1980).

S. Cassese, 'The higher civil service in Italy', in E. N. Suleiman (ed.), *Bureaucrats and Policy-making* (New York: Holmes, 1984).

S. Cassese, 'Hypotheses on the Italian administrative system', *West European Politics*, 16 (1993): 316–28.

S. Cassese, 'Les succès et les échecs de la modernisation de l'administration Italienne: L'expérience du gouvernement Ciampi', *Revue Française d'Administration Publique*, 75 (1995): 377–86.

S. Cassese, 'Italy's senior civil service: an ossified world', in C. E. Page and V. Wright (eds), *Bureaucratic Elites in Western European States* (Oxford and New York: Oxford University Press, 1999), pp. 55–64.

S. Cassese, 'Le nouveau régime de la haute function publique en Italie: une modification constituelle', *Revue Française d'Administration Publique*, 104 (2002): 677–88.

A. Chadwick and C. May, 'Interaction between states and citizens in the age of the Internet: "e-government" in the United States, Britain and the European Union', paper presented at the APSA, San Francisco (2001).

Chancellor of the Duchy of Lancaster, *Next Steps Agencies in Government: Review, 1996* (London: HMSO, 1997).

J. Charlton, R. Silver, R. Hartley and W. Holland, 'Geographical variations in mortality from conditions amenable to medical intervention in England and Wales', *Lancet* (26 March 1983), pp. 691–6.

J. Chevallier, 'La Réforme de l'Etat', *Administration Française* (Paris: ENA, 2004).

Chief Secretary to the Treasury, *Spending Review: Public Service Agreements*, Cm. 4808 (London: HMSO, 2000).

J. G. Christensen, 'Ministers and mandarins in a parliamentary system', *International Journal of Public Administration*, special issue (2005).

T. Christensen, and P. Lægreid, *New Public Management: the Transformation of Ideas and Practices* (Aldershot: Ashgate, 2003).

T. Christensen, P. Lægreid and L. R. Wise, 'Evaluating public management reforms in central government: Norway, Sweden and the United States of America', in H. Wollmann (ed.), *Evaluation in Public-sector Reform: Concepts and Practice in International Perspective* (Cheltenham, UK and Northampton, Mass: Edward Elgar, 2003), pp. 56–79.

M. Clark, *Modern Italy 1871–1982*, 6th edn (London: Longman, 1990).

J. Clarke and J. Newman, *The Managerial State* (London: Sage, 1997). Committee Dijkstal (2004) (http://www.minbzk.nl/contents/pages/8415/commissiedijkstal-rapport.pdf).

C. Cornforth (ed.), *The Governance of Public and Non-profit Organisations: What Do Boards Do?* (London: Routledge, 2003).

A. Coulson (ed.), *Trust and Contracts* (Bristol: Polity Press, 1998).

Country report – The Netherlands, *Benchmarking Study on Services Offered to People with Disabilities* (Copenhagen: Ramboll Management, April 2005).

Country report – Sweden, *Benchmarking Study on Services Offered to People with Disabilities* (Copenhagen: Ramboll Management, April 2005).

Country report – UK, *Benchmarking Study on Services Offered to People with Disabilities* (Copenhagen: Ramboll Management, April 2005).

Country report – USA, *Benchmarking Study on Services Offered to People with Disabilities* (Copenhagen: Ramboll Management, April 2005).

J. B. Cousins and L. M. Earl, 'The case for participatory evaluation', *Educational Evaluation and Policy Analysis*, 14 (4) (1992): 397–418.

J. Cowper and M. Samuels, 'Performance benchmarking in the public sector: the United Kingdom experience', in *OECD Working Papers, Vol. V, Benchmarking*, CPS (2005) (http://www.cps.org.uk/pdf/pub/402.pdf).

S. Dawson, *Analysing Organisations* (Basingstoke: Macmillan, 1996).

J. E. De Bettignies and T. W. Ross, 'The economics of public–private partnerships', *Canadian Public Policy – Analyse de Politiques*, 30 (2) (2004).

H. De Bruijn, E. Ten Heuvelhof and R. in 't Veld, *Procesmanagement: over procesontwerp en besluitvorming* (Schoonhoven: Acedimic Service, 1998).

L. De Sousa, 'Political parties and corruption in Portugal', *West European Politics*, 24 (1) (2001): 157–80.

G. Della Cannanea, 'L'expérience de la haute école d'administraion publique en Italie', *Revue Française d'Administration Publique*, 87 (1998): 433–42.

J. Dempsey, 'Schröder announces his resignation', *International Herald Tribune*, 13 October 2005, p. 3.

Department of Health and Social Security, *NHS to be asked to improve accountability: Norman Fowler announces new moves and regional allocations*, Press Release no. 82/14 (22 January 1982).

H. U. Derlien, *From Administrative Reform to Administrative Modernization* (Bamberg: Vewaltungswissenschaftlichte Beitrage 33, 1998).

H. U. Derlien, 'Mandarins or managers? The bureaucratic elite in Bonn, 1970 to 1987 and beyond', *Governance*, 16 (3) (2003): 401–28.

DETR, *Best Value – Circular 10/99* (London: HMSO, 1999).

DfES, *Building Schools for the Future: a New Approach to Capital Investment* (London: Department for Education and Skills, 2003).

208 *Bibliography*

Digital Taskforce, *Towards E-Government: Vision and Strategy for the Public Sector in Denmark* (Copenhagen: Digital Taskforce, 2002).

Digital Taskforce, *The Danish eGovernment Strategy – Realizing the Potential* (Copenhagen: Digital Taskforce, 2004).

P. DiMaggio and W. W. Powell, 'The iron cage revisited: institutional isomorphism and collective rationality in organizational fields', *American Sociological Review*, 52 (1983): 147–60.

DoH, *Public Private Partnerships in the NHS: NHS Local Improvement Finance Trust Prospectus* (London: Department of Health, 2001).

DoH, *LIFT Guidance: New Policy Requirements* (London: Department of Health, 2006).

S. Dorrell, 'Public sector change is a world-wide movement', speech by the Financial Secretary of the Treasury to the Chartered Institute of Public Finance and Accountancy (London, 25 September 1993).

G. Drewry and T. Butcher, *The Civil Service Today* (Oxford: Blackwell, 1988).

G. Dudkin and T. Välilä, *Transaction costs in PPPs ... a First Look at the Evidence* (European Investment Bank, 2005).

H. P. M. v. Duivenboden and A. M. B. Lips, 'Taking citizens seriously', paper presented at the EGPA, Vaasa (2001).

P. Dunleavy, *Democracy, Bureaucracy and Public Choice: Economic Explanations in Political Science* (New York: Harvester Wheatsheaf, 1991).

P. Dunleavy and H. Margetts, 'The advent of digital government: public bureaucracies and the state in the information age', paper presented at the Annual Conference of the American Political Science Association, Washington (2000).

Ecorys, *Evaluatie voortgang PPS in Nederland* (Rotterdam, May 2002).

J. Edelenbos, *Proces in vorm: procesbegeleiding van interactieve beleidsvorming over lokale ruimtelijke projecten* (Utrecht: Lemma, 2000).

Efficiency Unit, *Making the Most of Next Steps* (London: HMSO, 1991).

S. N. Eisenstadt and R. Lemarchand, *Political Clientelism, Patronage and Development* (London: Sage, 1981).

B. Elzen, F. W. Geels and K. Green, *System Innovation and the Transition to Sustainability: Theory, Evidence and Policy* (Cheltenham, UK: Edward Elgar, 2004).

European Commission, *Living and Working in the Information Society* (European Commisson, 1996).

European Commission, *Building the European Information Society for All of Us* (European Commission, 1997).

European Commission, *Government Online* (European Commission, 2000).

D. Farnham, A. Hondeghem and S. Horton (eds), *Staff Participation and Public Management Reform: Some International Comparisons* (Basingstoke: Palgrave Macmillan, 2005).

D. Farnham, S. Horton, J. Barlow and A. Hondeghem (eds), *New Senior Public Officials in Europe: Public Servants in Transition* (Basingstoke: Palgrave Macmillan, 1996).

H. Feigenbaum, J. Henig and C. Hamnett, *Shrinking the State: the Political Underpinnings of Privatization* (Cambridge: Cambridge University Press, 1999).

M. Ferrera and E. Gualmini, *Rescued by Europe? Social and Labour Market Reforms in Italy form Maastricht to Berlusconi* (Amsterdam, Amsterdam University Press, 2003).

H. Finer, *The Theory and Practice of Modern Government* (London: Methuen, 1954).

M. Forbes and L. E. Lynn Jr., 'How does public management affect government performance? Findings from international research', *Journal of Public Administration Research and Theory*, 15 (2005): 559–84.

J. Fountain, *Building the Virtual State* (Washington DC: Brookings Institution, 2001).

J. Fulk, C.W. Steinfield and J. Schmitz, 'A social information processing model of media use in organizations', *Communication Research*, 14 (1987): 529–52.

F. Gains, 'Understanding department–Next Steps agency relationships', PhD thesis (University of Sheffield: Department of Politics, 1999).

F. Gains, 'Adapting the agency concept: variations within "Next Steps" ', in C. Pollitt and C. Talbot (eds), *Unbundled Government* (London: Taylor & Francis, 2004), pp. 53–74.

R. Gallego, 'Public management policy-making in Spain, 1982–1996', *International Public Management Journal*, 6 (3) (2003): 283–307.

M. Gascó, 'New technologies and institutional change in public administration', *Social Science Computer Review* 21 (1) (2003): 6–14.

H. W. M. Gazendam, *Variety Controls Variety: On the Use of Organization Theories in Information Management* (Groningen: Wolters-Noordhoff, 1993).

M. Gell-Mann, 'What is complexity?', *Complexity*, 1 (1) (1995): 16–19.

J. Gibbons, *Spanish Politics Today* (Manchester: Manchester University Press, 1999).

P. Gibert, and J. C. Thoenig, 'La gestion publique: entre amnésie et apprentissage', *Revue Politiques et Management Public*, 11 (1) (1993).

P. Ginsbourg, *A History of Contemporary Italy. Society and Politics 1943–1988* (Harmondsworth: Penguin, 1990).

M. Granovetter, 'Economic action and social structure: the problem of embeddedness', *American Journal of Sociology*, 91(3) (1985): 481–510.

A. Gray and B. Jenkins, 'Evaluation and collaborative government: lessons and challenges', in A. Gray, B. Jenkins, F. Leeuw and J. Mayne (eds), *Collaboration in Public Services: the Challenge for Evaluation* (New Brunswick, NJ: Transaction Publishers, 2003), pp. 227–44.

A. Gray, B. Jenkins, F. Leeuw and J. Mayne, 'Collaborative government and evaluation: the implications of a new policy instrument', in A. Gray, B. Jenkins, F. Leeuw and J. Mayne (eds), *Collaboration in Public Services: the Challenge for Evaluation* (New Brunswick, NJ: Transaction Publishers, 2003), pp. 1–28.

J. C. Green, 'The inequality of performance measurements', *Evaluation* 5 (2) (1999): 160–72.

J. Greenaway, B. Salter and S. Hart, 'The evolution of a meta-policy: the case of PFI in the health sector', *British Journal of Politics and International Relations* (2004).

C. Greve, M. V. Flinders and S. van Thiel, 'Quangos: what's in a name? Defining quasi-autonomous bodies from a comparative perspective', *Governance*, 12 (1999): 129–46.

A. Grönlund, 'Emerging electronic infrastructures (exploring democratic components)', *Social Science Computer Review*, 21 (1) (2003): 55–72.

L. Groth, 'Future organizational design', in L. Groth (ed.), *Future Organizational Design* (Chicester: John Wiley & Sons, 1999), pp. 325–44.

G. Gruening, 'Origin and theoretical basis of New Public Management', *International Public Management Journal*, 4 (1) (2001): 1–25.

E. G. Guba and Y. S. Lincoln, *Fourth Generation Evaluation* (Newbury Park, London, New Delhi: Sage, 1989).

H. Guillaume, G. Dureau and F. Silvent, *Gestion Publique: l'etat et la performance* (Paris: Presse de Sciences Po et Dalloz, 2002).

A. Guyomarch, ' "Public service", "public management" and the modernization of French public administration', *Public Administration*, 77 (1) (1999): 171–93.

H.M. Treasury, *Breaking New Ground – Towards a New Partnership Between the Public and Private Sectors* (London: HMSO, 1993).

H.M. Treasury, *Private Opportunity, Public Benefit – Progressing the Private Finance Initiative* (London: H.M. Treasury, 1995).

H.M. Treasury, *News Release 69/97* (1997a).
H.M. Treasury, *Partnerships for Prosperity – a New Framework for PFI* (London: H.M. Treasury, 1997b).
H.M. Treasury, *Second Review of the Private Finance Initiative* (London: H.M. Treasury, 1999a).
H.M. Treasury, *Review of Civil Government Procurement* (London: HMSO, 1999b).
H.M. Treasury, *Public–Private Partnerships – the Government's Approach* (London: H.M. Treasury, 2000).
H.M. Treasury, *PFI: Meeting the Investment Challenge* (London: H.M. Treasury, 2003).
H.M. Treasury, *Value for Money Assessment Guidance* (London: H.M. Treasury, 2004).
H.M. Treasury, *PFI Signed Projects List* (London: H.M. Treasury, 2005).
M. S. Hacque, 'The diminishing publicness of public service under the current mode of governance', *Public Administration Review*, 61 (1) (2001): 65–83.
J. L. M. Hakvoort and H. L. Klaassen, 'Benchmarking in non-profit organizations', *Beleidsanalyse*, 3 (1999): 11–19.
J. L. M. Hakvoort and H. L. Klaassen, *Bedrijfsvoeringstechnieken voor overheid en non-profitorganizaties* (Den Haag: Sdu Uitgevers, 2004).
H. van der Ham and J. F. M. Koppenjan (eds), *Publiek-private samenwerking bij transportinfrastructuur: wenkend of wijkend perspectief* [Public–private partnerships in transport-infrastructure] (Utrecht: Lemma, 2002).
S. Harrison, *Managing the National Health Service in the 1980s: Policymaking on the Hoof?* (Aldershot: Avebury, 1994).
P. 't Hart et al., *Politiek-Ambtelijke verhoudingen in beweging* (Amsterdam: Boom, 2002).
F. Hartung, *Deutsche Verfassungsgeschichte* (Stuttgart: Köhler Verlag, 1950).
L. Haynes and N. Roden, 'Commercialising the management and maintenance of trunk roads in the United Kingdom', *Transportation*, 26 (1999).
P. Haynes and M. L. Rhodes, 'Social housing in Ireland: a study in complexity', paper presented at the ENHR Conference (Cambridge, UK, 2–6 July 2004).
Ph. Haynes, *Managing Complexity in the Public Services* (Milton Keynes: Open University Press (2003).
C. A. Hazeu, *Institutionele economie: een optiek op organisatie- en sturingsvraagstukken* (Bussum: Coutinho, 2000).
R. Heeks, *Reinventing Government in the Information Age: International Practice in IT-Enabled Public Sector Reform* (London: Routledge, 2001).
A. J. Heidenheimer, M. Johnston and V. T. LeVine (eds), *Political Corruption: a Handbook* (Oxford: Transaction Publishers, 1989).
C. J. Heinrich and L. E. Lynn, jr. (eds), *Governance and Performance: New Perspectives* (Washington DC: Georgetown University Press, 2000).
J. K. Helderman, F. Schut, T. Van der Grinten and W. van de Ven, 'Market-oriented health care reforms and policy learning in the Netherlands', *Journal of Health Politics, Policy and Law*, 30 (1–2) (2005): 189–210.
M. Heper (ed.), *The State and Public Bureaucracy: a Comparative Perspective* (New York: Greenwood Press, 1987).
P. Heywood, *The Politics and Government of Spain* (Basingstoke and New York: Palgrave Macmillan, 1995).
P. Heywood, 'Political corruption: problems and perspectives', *Political Studies*, 45 (1997): 417–35.
G. Hodge and C. Greve (eds), *The Challenge of Public–Private Partnerships: Learning from International Experience* (Cheltenham: Edward Elgar, 2005).
G. Hofstede, *Culture's Consequences: Comparing Values, Behaviors, Institutions and Organizations across Nations* (Thousand Oaks, CA: Sage, 2001).

J. Holland, *Hidden Order: How Adaptation Builds Complexity* (Reading, MA: Addison Wesley, 1995).

V. M. F. Homburg, *The Political Economy of Information Management* (Groningen: SOM, 1999a).

V. M. F. Homburg, *The Political Economy of Information Management: a Theoretical and Empirical Study on the Development and Use of Interorganizational Information Systems* (Groningen: SOM, 1999b).

V. M. F. Homburg, *The Political Economy of Information Management: a Theoretical and Empirical Analysis of Decision Making Regarding Interorganizational Information Systems* (Capelle aan den IJssel: Labyrinth, 1999c).

V. M. F. Homburg and S. van Thiel, 'Lessen en inzichten voor zbo-beleid', *Openbaar Bestuur*, 12 (2) (2002): 21–4.

C. Hood, 'A public management for all seasons?', *Public Administration*, 69 (1994): 3–19.

C. Hood, 'Exploring variations in public management reform of the 1980s', in H. Bekke, J. Perry and T. Toonen (eds), *Civil Service Systems in Comparative Perspective* (Bloomington, IN: Indiana University Press, 1996), pp. 268–317.

C. Hood, 'Paradoxes of public-sector managerialism, old public management and public service bargains', *International Public Management Journal*, 3 (1) (2000): 1–22.

C. Hood, O. James, B. G. Peters and C. Scott (eds), *Controlling Modern Government: Variety, Commonality and Change* (London: Edward Elgar, 2004).

J. Hopkin, 'A southern model of electoral mobilization: clientelism and electoral politics in Spain', *Western European Politics*, 24 (1) (2001): 115–36.

House of Commons, *Treasury Select Committee Sixth Report – The Private Finance Initiative* (London: HMSO, 1996).

House of Commons, *Fourth Report of the Public Accounts Committee – The Private Finance Initiative* (London: HMSO, 1999).

House of Commons, *The Private Finance Initiative – Research Paper 01/117* (London: House of Commons, 2001).

O. Hughes, *Public Management and Administration: an Introduction*, 3rd edn (Basingstoke: Palgrave Macmillan, 2003).

P. Hupe and F. B. v. d. Meer, *Doorwerking van emancipatie-effectrapportages in beleidsprocessen* (Den Haag: Ministerie van Sociale Zaken en Werkgelegenheid, 2002).

N. Hyndman and R. Anderson, 'Performance information, accountability and executive agencies', *Public Money and Management*, 18 (3) (1998): 23–30.

N. Hyndman and R. Eden, 'Executive agenices, performance targets and external reporting', *Public Money and Management*, 22 (3) (2002): 17–24.

P. W. Ingraham, P. G. Joyce and A. K. Donahue, *Government Performance: Why Management Matters* (Baltimore and London: Johns Hopkins University Press, 2003).

O. James, *The Executive Agency Revolution in Whitehall: Public Interest versus Bureau-Shaping Perspectives*, Transforming Government Series (Basingstoke: Palgrave Macmillan, 2003).

O. James, 'The UK government's use of public service agreements as a tool of governance', *Public Administration* 82 (2) (2004): 397–419.

K. Jenkins, K. Caines et al., *Improving Management in Government: the Next Steps*, (London: HMSO, 1998).

Johnson, 'State and society in Britain: some contrasts with German experience', in H. Wollmann and E. Schröter (eds), *Comparing public sector reform in Britain and Germany: Key Traditions and Trends of Modernisation* (Aldershot: Ashgate, 2000), pp. 27–46.

J. K. Kampen, D. Janssen, S. Rothier and K. Snijders (eds), *Spoor eGovernment. De praktijk van eGovernment in zeven landen van de OECD*, Steunount Beleidsrelevant Onderzoek (Louvain: Bestuurlijke Organisatie Vlaanderen, 2003).

R. S. Kaplan and D. P. Norton, *Balanced Scorecard* (Cambridge, MA: Harvard Business School Press, 1996).

R. S. Kaplan and D. P. Norton, *Op kop met balanced scorecard. Strategie vertaald naar actie* (Amsterdam: Uitgeverij Contact, 1999).

Kenniscentrum, Ministerie van Financiën, *Voortgangsrapportage 2002*, Progress report 2002 (Den Haag: Kenniscentrum PPS, May 2002).

Kenniscentrum PPS, Knowledge Centre, Ministry of Finance, Projectbureau PPS, *Eindrapport Meer Waarde door Samen Werken*, Final report on Added Value through Co-operation (Den Haag: Kenniscentrum PPS, 1998).

Kenniscentrum PPS, Knowledge Centre, *Ministerie van Financiën, Kenniscentrum Publiek-Private Samenwerking, Voortgangsrapportage PPS*, Ministry of Finance, Knowledge Centre Public–Private Partnership, PPP Progress Report (April 1999).

Kenniscentrum PPS, Knowledge centre PPP, Ministerie van Financiën, *Voortgangsrapportage 2001*, Progress report 2001 (Den Haag: Kenniscentrum PPS, 2001).

Kenniscentrum Publiek-Private Samenwerking, *Voortgangsreportage 'van incidenteel naar structureel'*, November 2004 (Den Haag: Ministerie van Financiën, 2004).

N. Kersting and A. Vetter (eds), *Reforming Local Government in Europe: Closing the Gap between Democracy and Efficiency* (Opladen, Leske and Budrich, 2003).

D. F. Kettl, *The Global Public Management Revolution* (Washington DC: Brookings Institution Press, 2nd edition, 2005).

D. F. Kettl, C. J. Pollitt and J. H. Svara, *Towards a Danish Concept of Public Governance: an International Perspective*, Report to the Danish forum for top executive management (August 2004).

W. Kickert (ed.), *Public Management and Administrative Reform in Western Europe* (Cheltenham: Edward Elgar, 1997).

W. Kickert, 'Public management in the United States and Europe', in W. Kickert (ed.), *Public Management and Administrative Reform in Western Europe* (Cheltenham: Edward Elgar, 1997).

W. Kickert, 'Public governance in Europe: a historical-institutional tour d'horizon', in O. van Heffen, W. Kickert and J. Thomassen (eds), *Governance in Modern Society* (Dordrecht: Kluwer Academic Publishers, 2000).

W. J. M. Kickert, 'Public management of hybrid organizations: governance of quasi-autonomous executive agencies', *International Public Management Journal*, 4 (2001): 135–50.

J. W. Kingdon, *Agendas, Alternatives and Public Policy* (Boston: Little, Brown and Company, 1984).

Kings Fund, *The Private Finance Initiative – Briefing Paper* (London: Kings Fund, 2005).

I. Kirkpatrick, 'The worst of both worlds? Public services without markets or bureaucracy', *Public Money and Management*, 19 (4) (1999): 7–14.

H. Kitschelt, P. Lange, G. Marks and J. D. Stephens, 'Convergence and divergence in advanced capitalist democracies', in H. Kitschelt, P. Lange, G. Marks and J. D. Stephens (eds), *Continuity and Change in Contemporary Capitalism* (Cambridge: Cambridge University Press, 1999).

E. H. Klijn, 'Governing networks in the hollow state; contracting out, process management or a combination of the two', *Public Management Review*, 4 (2002): 149–65.

E. H. Klijn and G. R. Teisman, 'Governing public–private partnerships: analysing and managing the processes and institutional characteristics of public–private partnerships', in S. P. Osborne (ed.), *Public–Private Partnerships: Theory and Practice in International Perspective* (London: Routledge, 2000).

E. H. Klijn and G. R. Teisman, 'Institutional and strategic barriers to public–private partnership: an analysis of Dutch cases', *Public Money and Management*, 23 (3) (2003): 137–46.

E. H. Klijn, J. Edelenbos, M. B. Kort and M. J. W. van Twist, *Management op het grensvlak van publieke en privaat* (preliminary title) (Utrecht: Lemma, forthcoming)

E. H. Klijn, J. F. M. Koppenjan and H. van der Ham, 'Slotbeschouwing: partnerships passing through the night?' [Conclusion: partnerships passing through the night] in H. van der Ham and J. F. M. Koppenjan (eds), *Publiek-private samen werking bij transport infrastructuur: wenkend of wijkend perspectief* (Utrecht: Lemma, 2002), pp. 457–82.

R. Kling, 'Learning about information technologies and social change: the contribution of social informatics', *The Information Society*, 16 (3) (2000): 217–32.

K. König and J. Beck, *Modernisierung von Staat und Verwaltung* (Baden-Baden: Nomos Verlagsgesellschaft, 1997).

J. F. M. Koppenjan and E. H. Klijn, *Managing Uncertainties in Networks: a Network Perspective on Problem Solving and Decision Making* (London: Routledge, 2004).

A. Kraak and R. van Oosteroom (eds), *Agentschappen: innovatie in bedrijfsvoering. Een resultaatgericht besturingsmodel bij uitvoeringsorganisaties van de rijksoverheid*, Public Controlling Reeks No. 1 (Den Haag: SDU, 2002).

P. Lægreid, 'Transforming top civil servant systems', in T. Christensen and P. Lægreid (eds), *New Public Management: the Transformation of Ideas and Practices* (Aldershot: Ashgate, 2003), pp. 145–72.

J. Lane, *New Public Management* (London: Routledge, 2000).

J. Le Grand and W. Bartlett (eds), *Quasi-Markets and Social Policy* (Basingstoke: Macmillan, 1993).

G. Learmont, *Review of Prison Service Security in England and Wales and the Escape from Parkhurst Prison on Tuesday 3rd January 1995* (London: HMSO, 1995).

D. Lewis, *Hidden Agendas: Politics, Law and Disorder* (London: Hamish Hamilton, 1997).

A. Lijphart, *Democracies: Patterns of Majoritarian and Consensus Government in Twenty-one Countries* (New Haven and London: Yale University Press, 1984).

A. Lijphart, *Patterns of Democracy: Governance Forms and Performance in Thirty-six Countries* (New Haven and London: Yale University Press, 1999).

E. Löffler and M. Vintar (eds), *Improving the Quality of East and West European Public Services* (Aldershot: Ashgate, 2004).

C. Low, D. Hulls and A. Rennison, *Public–Private Partnerships in Scotland – Evaluation of the Evidence* (Cambridge: Cambridge Economic Associates, 2005).

L. E. Lynn, 'A critical analysis of the new public management', *International Public Management Journal*, 1 (1) (1998): 107–23.

M. Maas, H.Witjes and I. Zaat, *Benchmarking bij overheid en non-profitorganizaties* (Den Haag: Elsevier, 1998).

D. MacKenzie and J. Wajcman (eds), *The Social Shaping of Technology: How the Refrigerator Got its Hum* (Milton Keynes: Open University Press, 1985).

J. M. Magone, *Contemporary Spanish Politics* (London: Routledge, 2004).

M. L. Markus, 'Power, politics and MIS implementation', *Communications of the ACM*, 26 (1983): 430–44.

M. McFadyen and D. Rowland, *PFI v Democracy?* (London: Menard Press, 2002).

W. Medd, 'Making (dis)connections: complexity and the policy process?' *Social Issues*, 1 (2) (2001), electronic journal: www.whb.co.uk/socialissues.

U. Merry, 'Organizational strategy on different landscapes: a new science approach', *Systemic Practice and Action Research*, 12 (3) (1999): 257–78.

M. W. Meyer and V. Gupta, 'The performance paradox', *Research in Organizational Behavior*, 16 (1994): 309–69.

J. Millard, J. S. Iversen, H. Kubicek, H. Westholm and R. Cimander, *Reorganisation of Government Back-offices for Better Electronic Public Services – European Good Practices (Back-office Reorganisation)* (Brussels: EU DG Information Society, 2004).

Minister for the Cabinet Office, *Modernising Government* (London: Minister for the Cabinet Office, 1999).

Minister for the Cabinet Office, *E-Government: a Strategic Framework for Public Services in the Information Age* (London: Minister for the Cabinet Office, 2000).

Ministerie van BZK, *Over dienen en verdienen. Adviescommissie beloning en rechtspositie ambtelijke topstructuur*, Report (Den Haag, 2004).

Ministeriet for Videnskab, T. o. U., *The Info-Society for All – the Danish Model* (1996) accessed January 2006, from http://www.fsk.dk/fsk/publ/1996/it96-uk/inde0002.htm.

Ministeriet for Videnskab Teknologi og Udvikling, *Statement to Parliament on 'Infosociety 2000'* (1995). Retrieved 19 April 2006, from http://www.videnskabsministeriet.dk/fsk/publ/it95-uk/inde0002.htm.

Ministry of Economic Affairs, *The Digital Delta* (The Hague: Ministry of Economic Affairs, 1999).

Ministry of Finance, *Verder bouwen aan beheer: rapport van de heroverwegingsgroep beheersregels* (Den Haag, 1991).

Ministry of the Interior and Kingdom Relationships, *Action Programme for Electronic Government* (The Hague: Ministry of the Interior and Kingdom Relationships, 1999).

Ministry of the Interior and Kingdom Relationships, *Contract with the Future* (The Hague: Ministry of the Interior and Kingdom Relationships, 2000).

Ministry of Research and Information Technology, *From Vision to Action: Info-Society 2000* (Copenhagen: Ministry of Research and Information Technology, 1995).

M. Minogue, C. Polidano and D. Hulme (eds), *Beyond the New Public Management: Changing Ideas and Practices in Governance* (London: Edward Elgar, 1998).

E. Mittleton-Kelly, 'Ten principles of complexity and enabling structures', in E. Mittleton-Kelly (ed.), *Complex Systems and Evolutionary Perspectives of Organisations: the Application of Complexity Theory to Organisations* (Amsterdam: Elsevier, 2003).

M. J. Moon, 'The evolution of e-government among municipalities: rhetoric or reality?', *Public Administration Review*, 62 (4) (2002): 424–33.

L. Morlino and M. Tarchi, 'The dissatisfied society: the roots of political change in Italy', *European Journal of Political Research*, 30 (1) (1996): 41–63.

P. Mouritzen and J. Svara, *Leadership at the Apex: Politicians and Administrators in Western Local Governments* (Pittsburg: University of Pittsburgh Press, 2002).

P. Muller, 'Le modèle français d'administration', in P. Muller (ed.), *Administration Française. Est elle en Crise?* (Paris: L'Harmattan, 1992).

National Audit Office, *The Meteorological Office Executive Agency*, HC693 (London: HMSO, 1995).

National Audit Office, *Benefits Agency: Performance Measurement*, HC952 (London: HMSO, 1998).

National Audit Office, *Good Practice in Performance Reporting in Executive Agencies and Non-departmental Public Bodies*, HC272 (London: HMSO, 2000).

National Audit Office, *Better Public Service through E-government* (London: National Audit office, 2002a).

National Audit Office, *Managing the Relationship to Secure a Successful Partnership in PFI Projects* (London: NAO, 2002b).

National Audit Office, *PFI Construction Performance* (London: National Audit Office, 2003).

National Performance Review, *Conversations with America* (National Performance Review, 2000).

N. J. M. Nelissen, M. P. C. Bressers and S. J. F. Engelen, *De opkomst van een nieuwe over-heidsmanager: een onderzoek naar significante topambtenaren* (Bussum: Coutinho, 1996).

G. Nicolis and I. Prigogine, *Exploring Complexity* (San Fransisco: W. H. Freeman, 1989).

N. Nohria and J. D. Berkley, 'The virtual organization (bureaucracy, technology and the implosion of control)', in C. Heckscher and A. Dennelon (eds), *The Post-bureaucratic Organization* (Thousand Oaks: Sage, 1994), pp. 108–28.

M. Noordegraaf, *Attention! Work and Behaviour of Senior Public Officials amidst Ambiguity* (Delft: Eburon, 2001).

ODPM, *Best Value and Performance Improvement – Circular 2002–03* (London: Office of the Deputy Prime Minister, 2002).

ODPM, *Strategic Partnering Task Force – Final Report* (London: ODPM, 2004a).

ODPM, *Making the Partnership a Success – Rethinking Service Delivery Volume 5* (London: Office of the Deputy Prime Minister, Strategic Partnering Taskforce, 2004b).

OECD, *Information Technology as an Instrument of Public Management Reform* (Paris: OECD, 1998).

OECD, *Implementing the Vision: Addressing Challenges to Results-Focused Management and Budgeting* (2002a) (http://www.oecd.org/dataoecd/54/46/2487821.pdf).

OECD (2002b) *Distributed Public Governance: Agencies, Authorities and Other Government Bodies*, CCNM/GOV/PUBG 2, 2002 (Paris: OECD Public Management Service, 20 November 2002).

OECD, *Public Sector Modernization: Changing Organizations*, GOV/PUMA 19 (Paris, 28 October 2003).

OECD, *The e-Government Imperative* (Paris: OECD, 2003).

OECD, *Modernising Government: the Way Forward* (Paris, 2005).

Office of Public Service Reform and H.M. Treasury, *Better Government Services – Executive Agencies in the 21st Century* (London: Cabinet Office, 2002) (www.civilservice.gov.uk/agencies).

W. J. Orlikowski and S. R. Barley, 'Technology and institutions: what can research on information technology and research on organizations learn from each other?', *MIS Quarterly*, 25 (2) (2001): 145–65.

D. Osborne and T. Gaebler, *Reinventing Government: How the Entrepreneurial Spirit is Transforming the Public Sector* (Reading, MA: Addison Wesley, 1992).

S. P. Osborne (ed.), *Public–Private Partnerships: Theory and Practice in International Perspective* (London: Routledge, 2000).

C. E. Page and V. Wright, *Bureaucratic Elites in Western European States* (Oxford and New York: Oxford University Press, 1999).

E. Page, *Political Authority and Bureaucratic Power* (New York: Harvester Wheatsheaf, 1992).

F. Panozzo, 'Management by decree: paradoxes in the reform of Italian public sector', *Scandinavian Journal of Management*, 16 (2000): 357–73.

Partnerships for Schools, *Building Schools for the Future: the Local Educational Partnership Model* (London: Partnerships for Schools, 2004).

M. Q. Patton, *Utilization-Focused Evaluation* (Thousand Oaks, London, New Delhi: Sage, 1997).

B. G. Peters, *The Future of Governing: Four Emerging Models* (Kansas: Kansas University Press, 1996).

B. G. Peters, *The Politics of Bureaucracy: an Introduction to Comparative Public Administration*, 6th edn (London: Routledge, 2004).

P. Pierson, *Politics in Time: History, Institutions and Social Analysis* (Princeton: Princeton University Press, 2004).

C. Pollitt, *Manipulating the Machine: Changing the Pattern of Ministerial Departments, 1960–83* (London: Allen & Unwin, 1984).

C. Pollitt, 'Measuring performance: a new system for the National Health Service', *Policy and Politics*, January (1985): 1–15.

C. Pollitt, *Managerialism and the Public Services* (Oxford: Blackwell, 1990).

C. Pollitt, 'Justification by works or by faith? Evaluating the new public management', *Evaluation*, 1 (2) (1995): 133–54.

C. Pollitt, 'Convergence: the useful myth?', *Public Administration*, 79 (4) (2001): 933–47.

C. Pollitt, 'Clarifying convergence: striking similarities and durable differences in public management reform', *Public Management Review*, 4 (1) (2002): 471–92.

C. Pollitt, *The Essential Public Manager* (Maidenhead and Philadelphia: Open University Press/McGraw-Hill, 2003).

C. Pollitt, 'Performance management in practice: a comparative study of executive agencies', *Journal of Public Administration Theory and Research* (2006, forthcoming).

C. Pollitt and G. Bouckaert, 'Evaluation in public sector reforms: an international perspective', in H. Wollmann (ed.), *Evaluation in Public Sector Reform* (Cheltenham: Edward Elgar, 2003), pp. 12–35.

C. Pollitt and G. Bouckaert, *Public Management Reform: a Comparative Analysis*, 2nd edn (Oxford: Oxford University Press, 2004).

C. Pollitt and C. Talbot (eds), *Unbundled Government: a Critical Analysis of the Global Trend to Agencies, Quangos and Contractualisation* (London: Routledge, 2004).

C. Pollitt, J. Birchall and K. Putman, *Decentralising Public Service Management: the British Experience* (Basingstoke: Palgrave Macmillan, 1998).

C. Pollitt, C. Talbot, J. Caulfield and A. Smullen, *Agencies: How Governments Do Things through Semi-autonomous Organizations* (Basingstoke: Palgrave Macmillan, 2004).

C. Pollitt, X. Girre, J. Lonsdale, R. Mul, H. Summa and M. Waerness, *Performance or Compliance? Performance Audit and Public Management in Five Countries* (Oxford: Oxford University Press, 1999).

M. Power, *The Audit Explosion* (London: Demos, 1994).

J. W. Pratt and R. J. Zeckhauser, *Principals and Agents* (Boston, MA: Harvard Business School Press, 1991).

R. Premfors, 'Reshaping the democratic state: Swedish experiences in a comparative perspective', *Public Administration*, 76 (1) (1998): 141–59.

H. Preskill and R. T. Torres, *Evaluative Inquiry for Learning in Organizations* (Thousand Oaks, London, New Delhi: Sage, 1999).

Pricewaterhouse Coopers en Berenschot B. V., *Benchmarkonderzoek Thuiszorg biedt aanknopingspunten voor instellingen en overheid* (Utrecht, March 1999).

S. J. Prins, *Zoek, rapporteer, vergelijk en verbeter! Een verkennend onderzoek naar de zin en mogelijkheden van het gebruik van benchmarks binnen het prestatiemeetsysteem* (Rotterdam: Stichting Moret Fonds, 1997).

I. Proeller and K. Schedler, 'Change and continuity in the continental tradition of public management', in E. Ferlie, L. E. Lynn and C. Pollitt (eds), *The Oxford Handbook of Public Management* (Oxford: Oxford University Press, 2005).

PUMA, *Highlights of Public Sector Pay and Employment Trends: 2002 Update*, Human Resources Management (HRM) Working Party Meeting, PUMA/HRM (2002) 7 (Paris: OECD, 2002) (www.oecd.org).

PUMA, *Managing Senior Management: Senior Civil Service Reform in OECD Member Countries*, Background note GOV/PUMA (2003) 17 (Paris: OECD, 2003) (www.oecd.org).

R. D. Putnam, R. Leonardi and R. Y. Nanetti, *Making Democracy Work: Civic Traditions in Modern Italy* (Princeton: Princeton University Press, 1993).

P. M. Regan, 'Old issues, new context: privacy, information collection, and homeland security', *Government Information Quarterly*, 21 (4) (2004): 481–97.

Report, *Dansk handicappoltik i et internationalt perspektiv* (Aalborg: Ramboll Management, May 2005).

M. L. Rhodes and G. MacKechnie, 'Understanding public service systems: is there a role for complex adaptive systems?', *Emergence*, 5 (4) (2003): 57–85.

R. Rhodes, 'Reinventing Whitehall, 1979–1995', in W. J. M. Kickert (ed.), *Public Management and Administrative Reform in Western Europe* (Cheltenham: Edward Elgar, 1997), pp. 43–60.

H. Roberts, 'Performance and outcome measures in the Health Service', in M. Cave, M. Kogan and R. Smith (eds), *Output and Performance Measurement in Government: the State of the Art* (London: Jessica Kingsley, 1990), pp. 86–105.

P. Rosenau (ed.), *Public–Private Policy Partnerships* (Westwood, MA: Massachusetts Institute of Technology, 2000).

L. Rouban, 'France: political argument and institutional change', in C. Hood and G. Peters (eds), *Rewards at the Top* (London: Sage, 1994), pp. 90–105.

L. Rouban, 'The administrative modernisation policy in France', in W. J. M. Kickert (ed.), *Public Management and Administrative Reform in Western Europe* (Cheltenham: Edgar Elgar, 1997), pp. 141–56.

L. Rouban, *The French Civil Service* (Paris: La Documentation Française, 1998).

L. Rouban, 'Réformer ou recomposer l'Etat ? Les enjeux sociopolitiques d'une mutation annoncée', *Revue Française d'Administration Publique*, 105–106 (2003): 153–66.

K. Ryan and L. DeStefano, 'Dialogue as a democratizing evaluation method', *Evaluation*, 7 (2) (2001): 188–203.

Sahlin-Andersson, 'National, international and transnational constructions of New Public Management', in T. Christensen and P. Laegreid (eds), *New Public Management: the Transformation of Ideas and Practice* (Aldershot: Ashgate, 2001), pp. 43–72.

D. Saint-Martin, *Building the New Managerialist State: Consultants and the Politics of Public Sector Reform in Comparative Perspective* (Oxford: Oxford University Press, 2000).

I. Sanderson, 'Evaluation in complex policy systems', *Evaluation*, 6 (4) (2000): 433–54.

I. Sanderson, 'Performance management, evaluation and learning in "modern" local government', *Public Administration*, 79 (2) (2001): 297–313.

E. Schein, 'Drie managementculturen: de sleutel tot bedrijfsleerprocessen', *Holland/Belgium Management Review*, 51 (1996): 25–35.

J. Shaoul, 'The private finance initiative or the public funding of private profit?', in G. Hodge and C. Greve (eds), *The Challenge of Public–Private Partnerships: Learning from International Experience* (Cheltenham: Edward Elgar, 2005), pp. 190–206.

J. L. Siciliani, *La remuneration au merite des directeurs d'administration centrale: mobiliser les directeurs pour conduire le changement*, Rapport au Premier Ministre (Paris: La documentation française 45, 2004).

D. M. Smith, *Modern Italy: a Political History* (New Haven: Yale University Press, 1997).

A. Smullen, 'Lost in translation? Shifting interpretations of the concept of "agency": the Dutch case', in C. Pollitt and C. Talbot (eds), *Unbundled Government* (London and New York: Routledge/Taylor & Francis, 2004), pp. 184–202.

A. Smullen, A. 'Translating agency reform: rhetoric and culture in comparative perspective', PhD thesis (Rotterdam, forthcoming).

A. Smullen, S. van Thiel and C. Pollitt, 'Agentschappen en de verzelfstandigingspara-dox', *Beleid & Maatschappij*, 28 (4) (2001): 190–201.

I. T. M. Snellen (ed.), *Public Administration in an Information Age* (Amsterdam: IOS Press, 1998).

D. A. Sotiropoulos, 'Souther European public bureaucracies in comparative perspec-tive', *West European Politics*, 27 (3) (2004): 405–22.

M. Spackman, 'Public–private partnerships: lessons from the British approach', *Economic Systems*, 26 (2002): 283–301.

C. Spanou, 'Penelope's suitors: administrative modernisation and party competition in Greece', *West European Politics*, 19 (1) (1996): 97–124.

R. E. Stake, 'Program evaluation, particularly responsive evaluation', in G. F. Madaus, M. Scriven and D. L. Stufflebeam (eds), *Evaluation Models* (Boston: Kluwer-Nijhoff, 1983), pp. 287–310.

A. J. Steijn, 'Human resource management and job satisfaction in the Dutch public sector', *Review of Public Personnel Administration*, 24 (4) (2004): 291–303.

A. Stevens, 'The Mitterrand government and the French civil service', in J. Howorth and G. Ross (eds), *Comtemporary France* (London: Pinter, 1988).

R. J. Stillman, 'The formal structure: the concept of bureaucracy', in R. J. Stillman, *Public Administration: Concepts and Cases*, 5th edition (Boston: Houghton Mifflin, 1992).

J. Subirats, *Modernising the Spanish Public Administration or Reform in Disguise*, Working paper no. 20/90 (Barcelona: Autonomous University Barcelona, 1990).

N. E. Suleiman, *Les ressorts caches de la reussite française* (Paris: Editions du Seuil, 1995).

H. Sullivan and C. Skelcher, *Working across Boundaries: Collaboration in Public Services* (Basingstoke: Palgrave Macmillan, 2002).

M. Symonds, 'The next revolution', *The Economist*, 355 (8176) (2000).

A. Taket and L. White, 'Working with heterogeneity: a pluralist strategy for evalua-tion', *Systems Research and Behavioral Science*, 14 (2) (1997): 101–11.

C. Talbot, *Ministers and Agencies: Control, Performance and Accountability* (London: Chartered Institute of Public Finance and Accountancy, 1996).

C. Talbot, 'UK civil service personnel reforms: devolution, decentralisation and delu-sion', *Public Policy and Administration*, 12 (4) (1997): 14–34.

C. Talbot, 'Executive agencies: have they improved management in government?' *Public Money and Management*, 24 (1) (2004): 104–11.

C. Talbot, 'The agency idea: sometimes old, sometimes new, sometimes borrowed, sometimes untrue', in C. Pollitt and C. Talbot (eds), *Unbundled Government: a Critical Analyis of the Global Trend to Agencies, Quangos and Contractualization*, Routledge Studies in Public Management (London: Routledge, 2004), pp. 3–21.

G. R. Teisman, 'Procesmanagement: de basis voor partnerschap?', *ESB*, 83 (4170) (1998): 21–6.

G. R. Teisman, *Public Management on the Edge of Chaos and Order* (in Dutch) (The Hague: Academic Services, 2005).

G. R. Teisman and E. H. Klijn, 'Public–private partnerships in the European Union: officially suspect, embraced in daily practice', in S. P. Osborne (ed.), *Public–Private Partnerships: Theory and Practice in International Perspective* (London: Routledge, 2000), pp. 165–86.

G. R. Teisman and E. H. Klijn, 'Partnership arrangements: governmental rhetoric or governance scheme?', *Public Administration Review*, 62 (2) (2002): 197–205.

G. R. Teisman and F. B. van der Meer, *Evalueren om te leren: naar een evaluatiearrange-ment voor de Vijfde Nota RO* (Rotterdam: Erasmus University, 2002).

Bibliography 219

G. R. Teisman and T. J. M. Verheij, 'Draagvlakvorming bij technisch-complexe projecten', in J. A. d. Bruijn, P. d. Jong, A. F. A. Korsten and W. P. C. van Zanten, *Grote
projecten* (Alphen aan den Rijn: Samson H.D. Tjeenk Willink, 1996), pp. 174–92.

G. R. Teisman and R. J. in 't Veld, *Innovatief investeren in infrastructuur*, Studie voor
GWWO (Den Haag, 1992).

C. Thain and M. Wright, *Treasury and Whitehall: the Planning and Control of Public
Expenditure, 1976–1993* (Oxford: Clarendon Press, 1996).

K. Thelen, 'How institutions evolve: insights from comparative historical analysis', in
J. Mahoney and D. Rueschemeyer (eds), *Comparative Historical Analysis in the Social
Sciences* (Cambridge: Cambridge University Press, 2003).

J. C. Thoenig, 'Learning from evaluation practice: the case of public-sector reforms', in
H. Wollmann (ed.), *Evaluation in Public-Sector Reform: Concepts and Practice in
International Perspective* (Cheltenham: Edward Elgar, 2003), pp. 209–30.

G. Thuiller and J. Tulard, *Histoire de l'Administration Française* (Paris: Presses
Universitaires de France, 1984).

P. W. Tops and R. Weterings, 'Gemeentelijk beleid en co-productie', in A. F. A. Korsten
and P. W. Tops (eds), *Lokaal bestuur in Nederland, inleiding in de gemeentekunde*
(Alphen aan den Rijn: Samsom, 1998), pp. 518–28.

L. Torres and V. Pina, 'Reshaping public administration: the Spanish experience compared to the UK', *Public Administration*, 82 (2) (2004): 445–64.

Transparency International, *Transparency International Corruption Perceptions Index
2005* (2005) (http://www.transparency.org, accessed 17 October 2005).

Treasury and Civil Service Committee, *Eighth Report: Civil Service Management Reform:
the Next Steps, vols 1 and 2*, HC494 (London: HMSO, 1990).

United Nations, *Global E-Government Readiness Report 2004: Towards Access for
Opportunity* (New York, 2004).

M. W. van Buuren and J. Edelenbos, 'Innovation in the polder: communities of practice and the challenge of co-evolution', *Emergence*, 8 (1) (2006): 41–8.

M. W. van Buuren and L. Gerrits, 'Complexity', in M. Bevir (ed.), *Encyclopedia of
Governance* (Sage Publications, forthcoming 2006).

J. C. J. M. van den Bergh and J. M. Gowdy, 'Evolutionary theories in environmental
and resource economics: approaches and applications', *Environmental and Resource
Economics*, 17 (2000): 37–57.

F. B. van der Meer, 'Evaluation and the social construction of impacts', *Evaluation* 5 (4)
(1999): 387–406.

F. B. van der Meer, G. J. D. de Vries and G. A. N. Vissers, 'Evaluatie en leerprocessen bij de
overheid: de rol van institutionele condities', *Beleidswetenschappen* 14 (3) (2000): 253–77.

F. B. van der Meer and J. Edelenbos, 'Evaluation in multi-actor policy processes:
accountability, learning and cooperation', *Evaluation*, 12 (2) (2006): 201–18.

R. van Oosteroom and S. van Thiel, 'Agentschappen: kruiwagen voor modernisering?',
Bestuurskunde, 14 (7) (2004): 292–300.

S. van Thiel, *Quangos: Trends, Causes and Consequences* (Aldershot: Ashgate Publishing
Ltd., 2001).

S. van Thiel, 'Sturen op afstand: over de aansturing van verzelfstandigde organisaties
door kerndepartementen', *Management in Overheidsorganisaties*, 39 (mei) A5215
(2003): 1–25.

S. van Thiel (ed.), *Governance van uitvoeringsorganisaties* (Apeldoorn: Kadaster, 2004).

S. van Thiel and M.W. van Buuren, 'Ontwikkeling van het aantal zelfstandige bestuursorganen tussen 1993 en 2000: zijn zbo's 'uit' de mode?', *Bestuurswetenschappen*, 55
(5) (2001): 386–404.

S. van Thiel and F. Leeuw, 'The performance paradox in the public sector', *Public Performance and Management Review*, 25 (3) (2002): 267–81.

S. van Thiel, M. Allix and J. Dwarswaard, *Respondentenrapport onderzoek directies agentschappen* (Rotterdam: Erasmus University Rotterdam, internal report, 2004a).

S. van Thiel, A. Jansen, R. Timmerman and P. Plug, 'Competenties voor relatie-management: tussen ministerie en uitvoeringsorganisatie in', *Bestuurswetenschappen*, 58 (6) (2004b): 495–514.

S. van Thiel, M. Allix and J. Dwarswaard, *Respondentenrapport onderzoek directies verzelf-standigde organisaties* (Rotterdam, 29 April 2004).

M. J. W. van Twist and P. J. Plug, 'Een moeizame verbinding: over de vormgeving van interfaces bij kerndepartementen', *Beleidsanalyse*, 98 (3) (1998): 15–22.

E. Vigoda and R. T. Golembiewski, 'Citizenship behavior and the spirit of new managerialism: a theoretical framework and challenge for governance', *American Review of Public Administration*, 31 (3) (2001): 273–95.

M. M. Waldrop, *Complexity: the Emerging Science at the Edge of Order and Chaos* (Washington: Washington Square Press, 1994).

G. H. Watson, *Strategisch benchmarken: Hoe vergelijkt u de prestatie van uw bedrijf met die van de beste ter wereld?* (Schiedam: Scriptum, 1998).

M. Weber, *Wirtschaft und Gesellschaft. Grundriss der verstehenden Soziologie*, 5th edn (Tübingen: Mohr, 1972).

K. E. Weick, *Social Psychology of Organizing* (Reading, MA: Addison-Wesley, 1979).

K. E. Weick, *Sensemaking in Organizations* (London: Sage, 1995).

C. H. Weiss, 'Evaluation for decisions: is anybody there? Does anybody care?', in M. C. Alkin (ed.), *Debates on Evaluation* (Newbury Park, London, New Delhi: Sage, 1990), pp. 171–84.

L. White, ' "Effective governance" through complexity thinking and management science', *Systems Research and Behavioural Science*, 18 (2001): 241–57.

R. Williams (ed.), *Explaining Corruption* (Cheltenham: Edward Elgar, 2000).

R. Williams and D. Edge, 'The social shaping of technology', *Research Policy*, 25 (1996): 865–99.

R. Williams, J. Moran and R. Flanary (eds), *Corruption in the Developed World* (Cheltenham: Edward Elgar, 2000).

O. E. Williamson, *The Economic Institutions of Capitalism* (New York: Free Press, 1985).

O. E. Williamson, *The Mechanisms of Governance* (London: Oxford University Press, 1996).

J. Q. Wilson, *Bureaucracy: What Government Agencies Do and Why they Do It* (New York: Basic Books, 1989).

W. Wilson, 'The study of administration', *Political Science Quarterly*, 2 (2) (1987): 206.

D. Wolfson, *Publieke sector en economische orde* (Groningen: Wolters-Noordhoff, 1988).

H. Wollmann (ed.), *Evaluation in Public-sector Reform: Concepts and Practice in International Perspective* (Cheltenham: Edward Elgar, 2003).

World Summit on the Information Society, *WSIS Activity: E-governance for Efficiency and Effectiveness Programme*, Retrieved 13 April 2006, from http://www.itu.int/wsis/stocktaking/scripts/documents.asp?project=1103088763andlang=en.

V. Wright, *Government and Politics in France*, 3rd edn (London: Routledge, 1989).

V. Wright, 'The administrative machine: old problems and new dilemmas', in P. A. Hall, J. Hayward and H. Machin (eds), *Developments in French Politics* (Basingstoke: Macmillan, 1990).

B. Wunder (ed.), *The Influences of the Napoleonic 'Model' of Administration on the Administrative Organization of Other Countries* (Brussels: IIAS-cahier, 1995).

E. Zapico-Goni, 'La modernisation de l'administration publique Espagnol: un éclatement des réformes', *Revue Française d'Administration Publique*, 66 (1993): 309–17.

M. Zbaracki, 'The rhetoric and reality of Total Quality Management', *Administrative Science Quarterly*, 43 (1998): 602–36.

J. Ziller, 'The continental system of administrative legality', in B. Guy Peters and J. Pierre (eds), *Handbook of Public Administration* (London: Sage, 2003), pp. 260–8.

S. Zouridis, *Digitale disciplinering: over ICT, organisatie, wetgeving en het automatiseren van beschikkingen* (Tilburg: Katholieke Universiteit Brabant, 2000).

Name Index

Note: page numbers in bold refer to figures and tables

Subject Index

Note: page numbers in bold refer to figures and tables